Delta Lake: Up and Running
Modern Data Lakehouse Architectures
with Delta Lake

Bennie Haelen and Dan Davis

Beijing · Boston · Farnham · Sebastopol · Tokyo

Delta Lake: Up and Running

by Bennie Haelen and Dan Davis

Published by O'Reilly Media, Inc., 1005 Gravenstein Highway North, Sebastopol, CA 95472.

O'Reilly books may be purchased for educational, business, or sales promotional use. Online editions are also available for most titles (*http://oreilly.com*). For more information, contact our corporate/institutional sales department: 800-998-9938 or *corporate@oreilly.com*.

Acquisitions Editor: Aaron Black	**Indexer:** nSight, Inc.
Development Editor: Gary O'Brien	**Interior Designer:** David Futato
Production Editor: Ashley Stussy	**Cover Designer:** Karen Montgomery
Copyeditor: Charles Roumeliotis	**Illustrator:** Kate Dullea
Proofreader: Sonia Saruba	

October 2023:   First Edition

Revision History for the First Edition

2023-10-16:   First Release

See *http://oreilly.com/catalog/errata.csp?isbn=9781098139728* for release details.

978-1-098-13972-8

[LSI]

Table of Contents

Preface

The goal of this book is to provide data practitioners with practical instructions on how to set up Delta Lake and start using its unique features. This book is designed for an audience that fits any of the following profiles:

- Data practitioners with a Spark background
- Data practitioners unfamiliar with or new to Delta Lake needing an introduction to the technology, the problems it solves, its main features and terminology, as well as how to get started using it
- Data practitioners looking to learn about the features and benefits of modern lakehouse architectures

It is important to note that this book and the features discussed apply to the Delta Lake open source framework (*https://oreil.ly/NMohm*) (Delta Lake OSS). Proprietary features and optimizations that some companies offer around Delta Lake are considered out of the scope of this book.

First, we discuss why Delta Lake is an important tool for building modern enterprise data platforms and data science and AI solutions, followed by instructions on how to set up Delta Lake with Spark. Each of the subsequent chapters will walk you through the fundamental functions and operations of Delta Lake using step-by-step instructions and real-world examples.

The code examples in the book range from snippets that can be used in a PySpark shell to those designed to be run with a complete end-to-end notebook. In this book, all code snippets will be in Python, SQL, and, where necessary, shell commands.

A GitHub repository (*https://github.com/benniehaelen/delta-lake-up-and-running*) is provided to aid readers in following along throughout the book. Datasets, files, and code samples are provided in the repo and referred to throughout the book. Below are some important things to note about using the GitHub repo:

Code samples

Code samples are organized in the repo by chapter, and for most chapters a *chapter initialization* script is intended to be executed before executing any of the related code for that particular chapter. This *chapter initialization* code is required before executing code in order to set up the appropriate Delta tables and datasets to best demonstrate the topics being discussed. These *chapter initialization* scripts are explicitly called out in the text of the book before executing the first set of sample code for a given chapter.

Code sample data files

Data files required to execute the provided code samples live in the GitHub repository. The data files in the GitHub repo come from the popular NYC Yellow and Green taxi trip records (*https://oreil.ly/8KC4J*). These files were downloaded and curated for effective demonstration throughout this book.

Method for running Delta Lake for this book

The method for running Delta Lake for the purposes of this book and the code in the provided GitHub repo is Databricks Community Edition (*https://oreil.ly/0psx4*). Databricks Community Edition was chosen to develop and run the code samples because it is free, simplifies setup of Spark and Delta Lake, and does not require your own cloud account or for you to supply cloud compute or storage resources. The Delta tables, datasets, and code samples used in this book and the GitHub repo were developed and tested on Databricks Community Edition hosted on Azure, using Azure Data Lake Storage Gen2 as the underlying storage layer and Databricks Runtime 12.2 LTS. Please note that if you are running the code samples on Spark and Delta Lake outside of Databricks (e.g., on your local machine), then there will be additional setup, configuration, and potential editor syntax options to be accounted for by the reader.

Notebooks

You will also see the term *notebook*. A notebook refers to a Databricks notebook (*https://oreil.ly/dDDKr*), the primary tool for developing code and presenting results throughout the book.

Code languages

Delta Lake supports multiple languages (Scala, Java, Python, and SQL) for a variety of functionality. This book will focus primarily on Python and SQL. Code samples will provide code in the language deemed most appropriate to the topic being discussed. Alternatives for similar functionality in other languages will not always be provided. Please refer to the Delta Lake documentation (*https://oreil.ly/nAECc*) to view similar functionality in alternative languages.

For code snippets used throughout this book, the default language is Python. To indicate use of a language other than Python in a code snippet, you will see language magic commands (*https://oreil.ly/5sdMF*), that is, %<language> (e.g.,

`%sql`). You can assume that code snippets without a language magic command are using Python.

How to Contact Us

Please address comments and questions concerning this book to the publisher:

O'Reilly Media, Inc.
1005 Gravenstein Highway North
Sebastopol, CA 95472
800-889-8969 (in the United States or Canada)
707-829-7019 (international or local)
707-829-0104 (fax)
support@oreilly.com
https://www.oreilly.com/about/contact.html

We have a web page for this book, where we list errata, examples, and any additional information. You can access this page at *https://oreil.ly/delta-lake-up-and-running-1e*.

For news and information about our books and courses, visit *https://oreilly.com*.

Find us on LinkedIn: *https://linkedin.com/company/oreilly-media*.

Follow us on Twitter: *https://twitter.com/oreillymedia*.

Watch us on YouTube: *https://youtube.com/oreillymedia*.

Conventions Used in This Book

The following typographical conventions are used in this book:

Italic
:   Indicates new terms, URLs, email addresses, filenames, and file extensions.

`Constant width`
:   Used for program listings, as well as within paragraphs to refer to program elements such as variable or function names, databases, data types, environment variables, statements, and keywords.

`Constant width bold`
:   Shows commands or other text that should be typed literally by the user.

`Constant width italic`
:   Shows text that should be replaced with user-supplied values or by values determined by context.

This element signifies a tip or suggestion.

This element signifies a general note.

This element indicates a warning or caution.

Using Code Examples

Supplemental material (code examples, exercises, etc.) is available for download at *https://github.com/benniehaelen/delta-lake-up-and-running*.

If you have a technical question or a problem using the code examples, please send email to *support@oreilly.com*.

This book is here to help you get your job done. In general, if example code is offered with this book, you may use it in your programs and documentation. You do not need to contact us for permission unless you're reproducing a significant portion of the code. For example, writing a program that uses several chunks of code from this book does not require permission. Selling or distributing examples from O'Reilly books does require permission. Answering a question by citing this book and quoting example code does not require permission. Incorporating a significant amount of example code from this book into your product's documentation does require permission.

We appreciate, but generally do not require, attribution. An attribution usually includes the title, author, publisher, and ISBN. For example: "*Delta Lake: Up and Running* by Bennie Haelen and Dan Davis (O'Reilly). Copyright 2024 O'Reilly Media, Inc., 978-1-098-13972-8."

If you feel your use of code examples falls outside fair use or the permission given above, feel free to contact us at *permissions@oreilly.com*.

O'Reilly Online Learning

O'REILLY® For more than 40 years, *O'Reilly Media* has provided technology and business training, knowledge, and insight to help companies succeed.

Our unique network of experts and innovators share their knowledge and expertise through books, articles, and our online learning platform. O'Reilly's online learning platform gives you on-demand access to live training courses, in-depth learning paths, interactive coding environments, and a vast collection of text and video from O'Reilly and 200+ other publishers. For more information, visit *https://oreilly.com*.

Acknowledgment

We would like to thank our technical reviewers: Adam Breindel, Andrei Ionescu, and Jobenish Purushothaman. Their attention to detail, feedback, and thoughtful suggestions played a pivotal role in helping shape the content of this book while ensuring its accuracy. Their input undoubtedly helped make this book a better quality product that will be a valuable resource to readers.

Aside from the technical reviewers, we also received valuable feedback throughout the process of writing the book from other contributors. We would like to extend our thanks to the following: Alex Ott, Anthony Krinsky, Artem Sheiko, Bilal Obeidat, Carlos Morillo, Eli Swanson, Guillermo G. Schiava D'Albano, Jitesh Soni, Joe Widen, Kyle Hale, Marco Scagliola, Nick Karpov, Nouran Younis, Ori Zohar, Sirui Sun, Susan Pierce, and Youssef Mrini. Without your input, this book would not be the valuable resource it is.

Finally, we would like to thank the open source community. Without the community's contributions and collective efforts, Delta Lake would not have the remarkable capabilities it has today. The community's commitment to innovation helps drive Delta Lake's evolution and impact, and we, along with others, cannot express our thanks and appreciation enough.

Bennie Haelen

I would like to thank my wonderful wife Jenny. You have always been there to encourage and motivate me throughout the writing of this book; you are the great inspiration of my life. Thanks to my co-author Dan for being there through difficult periods in my life. Dan, you have a great career ahead of you. Thanks to my friends and colleagues that I can always reach out to with challenging questions no matter what time of the day.

Dan Davis

I would like to thank my family. Your continued encouragement and support have provided the foundation of my journey to where I am today and in writing this book. Thank you for always being a constant source of motivation. I would also like to thank all of my friends and colleagues that I have learned from and who have continually provided support to me along the way. I cannot thank my co-author, Bennie, enough. Thank you for being the mentor that you are, providing me with support, and presenting me with great opportunities. And last but not least, I would like to thank my beloved companion, who is always by my side whether he enjoys it or not, my dog River.

## CHAPTER 1

The Evolution of Data Architectures

As a data engineer, you want to build large-scale data, machine learning, data science, and AI solutions that offer state-of-the-art performance. You build these solutions by ingesting large amounts of source data, then cleansing, normalizing, and combining the data, and ultimately presenting this data to the downstream applications through an easy-to-consume data model.

As the amount of data you need to ingest and process is ever increasing, you need the ability to scale your storage horizontally. Additionally, you need the ability to dynamically scale your compute resources to address processing and consumption spikes. Since you are combining your data sources into one data model, you not only need to append data to tables, but you often need to insert, update, or delete (i.e., MERGE or UPSERT) records based upon complex business logic. You want to be able to perform these operations with transactional guarantees, and without having to constantly rewrite large data files.

In the past, the preceding set of requirements was addressed by two distinct toolsets. The horizontal scalability and decoupling of storage and compute were offered by cloud-based data lakes, while relational data warehouses offered transactional guarantees. However, traditional data warehouses tightly coupled storage and compute into an on-premises appliance and did not have the degree of horizontal scalability associated with data lakes.

Delta Lake brings capabilities such as transactional reliability and support for UPSERTs and MERGEs to data lakes while maintaining the dynamic horizontal scalability and separation of storage and compute of data lakes. Delta Lake is one solution for building *data lakehouses*, an open data architecture combining the best of data warehouses and data lakes.

In this introduction, we will take a brief look at relational databases and how they evolved into data warehouses. Next, we will look at the key drivers behind the emergence of data lakes. We will address the benefits and drawbacks of each architecture, and finally show how the Delta Lake storage layer combines the benefits of each architecture, enabling the creation of data lakehouse solutions.

A Brief History of Relational Databases

In his historic 1970 paper,[1] E.F. Codd introduced the concept of looking at data as logical *relations*, independent of physical data storage. This logical relation between data entities became known as a *database model* or *schema*. Codd's writings led to the birth of the relational database. The first relational database systems were introduced in the mid-1970s by IBM and UBC.

Relational databases and their underlying SQL language became the standard storage technology for enterprise applications throughout the 1980s and 1990s. One of the main reasons behind this popularity was that relational databases offered a concept called transactions. A database transaction is a sequence of operations on a database that satisfies four properties: atomicity, consistency, isolation, and durability, commonly referred to by their acronym *ACID*.

Atomicity ensures that all changes made to the database are executed as a single operation. This means that the transaction succeeds only when all changes have been performed successfully. For example, when the online banking system is used to transfer money from savings to checking, the atomicity property will guarantee that the operation will only succeed when the money is deducted from my savings account and added to my checking account. The complete operation will either succeed or fail as a complete unit.

The *consistency* property guarantees that the database transitions from one consistent state at the beginning of the transaction to another consistent state at the end of the transaction. In our earlier example, the transfer of the money would only happen if the savings account had sufficient funds. If not, the transaction would fail, and the balances would stay in their original, consistent state.

Isolation ensures that concurrent operations happening within the database are not affecting each other. This property ensures that when multiple transactions are executed concurrently, their operations do not interfere with each other.

---

1 Codd, E.F. (1970). *Relational Database: A Practical Foundation for Productivity*. San Jose: San Jose Research Laboratory.

Durability refers to the persistence of committed transactions. It guarantees that once a transaction is completed successfully, it will result in a permanent state even in the event of a system failure. In our money transfer example, durability will ensure that updates made to both my savings and checking account are persistent and can survive a potential system failure.

Database systems continued to mature throughout the 1990s, and the advent of the internet in the mid-1990s led to an explosive growth of data and the need to store this data. Enterprise applications were using relational database management system (RDBMS) technology very effectively. Flagship products such as SAP and Salesforce would collect and maintain massive amounts of data.

However, this development was not without its drawbacks. Enterprise applications would store the data in their own, proprietary formats, leading to the rise of *data silos*. These data silos were owned and controlled by one department or business unit. Over time, organizations recognized the need to develop an enterprise view across these different data silos, leading to the rise of *data warehouses*.

Data Warehouses

While each enterprise application has some type of reporting built in, business opportunities were missed because of the lack of a comprehensive view across the organization. At the same time, organizations recognized the value of analyzing data over longer periods of time. Additionally, they wanted to be able to slice and dice the data over several cross-cutting subject matters, such as customers, products, and other business entities.

This led to the introduction of the data warehouse, a central relational repository of integrated, historical data from multiple data sources that presents a single integrated, historical view of the business with a unified schema, covering all perspectives of the enterprise.

Data Warehouse Architecture

A simple representation of a typical data warehouse architecture is shown in Figure 1-1.

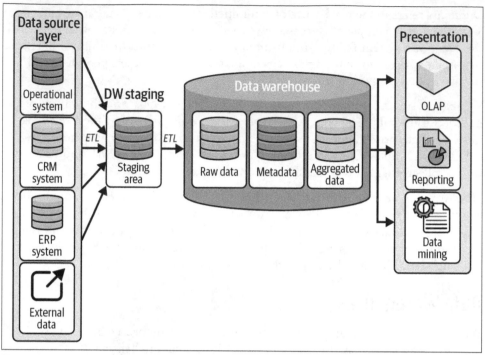

Figure 1-1. Data warehouse architecture

When we look at the diagram in Figure 1-1, we start with the data source layer on the left. Organizations need to ingest data from a set of heterogeneous data sources. While the data from the organization's enterprise resource planning (ERP) system(s) forms the backbone of the organizational model, we need to augment this data with the data from the operational systems running the day-to-day operations, such as human resources (HR) systems and workflow management software. Additionally, organizations might want to leverage the customer interaction data covered by their customer relationship management (CRM) and point of sale (POS) systems. In addition to the core data sources listed here, there is a need to ingest data from a wide array of external data sources, in a variety of formats, such as spreadsheets, CSV files, etc.

These different source systems each might have their own data format. Therefore, the data warehouse contains a *staging area* where the data from the different sources can be combined into one common format. To do this the system must ingest the data from the original data sources. The actual ingestion process varies by data source type. Some systems allow direct database access, and others allow data to be ingested through an API, while many data sources still rely on file extracts.

Next, the data warehouse needs to transform the data into a standardized format, allowing the downstream processes to access the data easily. Finally, the transformed data is loaded into the staging area. In relational data warehouses, this staging area is typically a set of flat relational staging tables without any primary or foreign keys or simple data types.

This process of extracting data, transforming it to a standard format, and loading it into the data warehouse is commonly referred to as extract, transform, and load (ETL). ETL tools can perform several other tasks on the ingested data before finally loading the data into the data warehouse. These tasks include the elimination of duplicate records. Since a data warehouse will be the one source of truth, we do not want it to contain multiple copies of the same data. Additionally, duplicate records prevent the generation of a unique key for each record.

ETL tools also allow us to combine data from multiple data sources. For example, one view of our customers might be captured in CRM systems, while other attributes are found in an ERP system. The organization needs to combine these different aspects into one comprehensive view of a customer. This is where we start to introduce a schema to the data warehouse. In our example of a customer, the schema will define the different columns for the customer table, which columns are required, the data type and constraints of each column, and so on.

Having canonical, standardized representations of columns, such as date and time, is important. ETL tools can ensure that all temporal columns are formatted using the same standard throughout the data warehouse.

Finally, organizations want to perform quality checks on the data in keeping with their data governance standards. This might include dropping low-quality data rows that do not meet this minimal standard.

Data warehouses are physically implemented on a monolithic physical architecture, made up of a single large node, combining memory, compute, and storage. This monolithic architecture forces organizations to scale their infrastructure vertically, resulting in expensive, often overdimensioned infrastructure, which was provisioned for peak user load, while being near idle at other times.

A data warehouse typically contains data that can be classified as follows:

Metadata
Contextual information about the data. This data is often stored in a data catalog. It enables the data analysts to describe, classify, and easily locate the data stored in the data warehouse.

Raw data
Maintained in its original format without any processing. Having access to the raw data enables the data warehouse system to reprocess data in case of load failures.

Summary data

Automatically created by the underlying data management system. The summary data will automatically be updated as new data is loaded into the warehouse. It contains aggregations across several conformed dimensions. The main purpose of the summary data is to accelerate query performance.

The data in the warehouse is consumed in the *presentation layer*. This is where the consumers can interact with the data stored in the warehouse. We can broadly identify two large groups of consumers:

Human consumers

These are the people within the organization who have a need to consume the data in the warehouse. These consumers can vary from knowledge workers, who need access to the data as an essential part of their job, to executives who typically consume highly summarized data, often in the form of dashboards and key performance indicators (KPIs).

Internal or external systems

The data in a data warehouse can be consumed by a variety of internal or external systems. This can include machine learning and AI toolsets, or internal applications that need to consume warehouse data. Some systems might directly access the data, others might work with data extracts, while still others might directly consume the data in a pub-sub model.

Human consumers will leverage various analytical tools and technologies to create actionable insights into the data, including:

Reporting tools

These tools enable the user to develop insights into the data through visualizations such as tabular reports and a wide array of graphical representations.

Online analytical processing (OLAP) tools

Consumers need to slice and dice the data in a variety of ways. OLAP tools present the data in a multidimensional format, allowing it to be queried from multiple perspectives. They leverage pre-stored aggregations, often stored in memory, to serve up the data with fast performance.

Data mining

These tools allow a data analyst to find patterns in the data through mathematical correlations and classifications. They assist the analysts in recognizing previously hidden relationships between different data sources. In a way, data mining tools can be seen as a precursor to modern data science tools.

Dimensional Modeling

Data warehouses introduced the need for a comprehensive data model that spans the different subject areas in a corporate enterprise. The technique used to create these models became known as *dimensional modeling*.

Driven by the writings and ideas of visionaries such as Bill Inmon and Ralph Kimball, dimensional modeling was first introduced in Kimball's seminal book *The Data Warehouse Toolkit: The Complete Guide to Dimensional Modeling*.[2] Kimball defines a methodology that focuses on a bottom-up approach, ensuring that the team delivers real value with the data warehouse as soon as possible.

A dimensional model is described by a *star schema*. A star schema organizes data for a given business process (e.g., sales) into a structure that facilitates easy analytics. It consists of two types of tables:

- A *fact table*, which is the primary, or central table for the schema. The fact table captures the primary measurements, metrics, or "facts" of the business process. Staying with our sales business process example, a sales fact table would include units sold and sales amount.
  - Fact tables have a well-defined grain. Grain is determined by the combination of dimensions (columns) represented in the table. A sales fact table can be of low granularity if it is just an annual rollup of sales, or high granularity if it includes sales by date, store, and customer identifier.
- Multiple *dimension* tables that are related to the fact table. A dimension provides the context surrounding the selected business process. In a sales scenario example, the list of dimensions could include product, customer, salesperson, and store.

The dimension tables "surround" the fact table, which is why these types of schemas are referred to as "star schemas." A star schema consists of fact tables, linked to their associated dimensional tables through primary and foreign key relationships. A star schema for our sales subject area is shown in Figure 1-2.

---

2 Kimball, R. (1996). *The Data Warehouse Toolkit: The Complete Guide to Dimensional Modeling*. The Kimball Group.

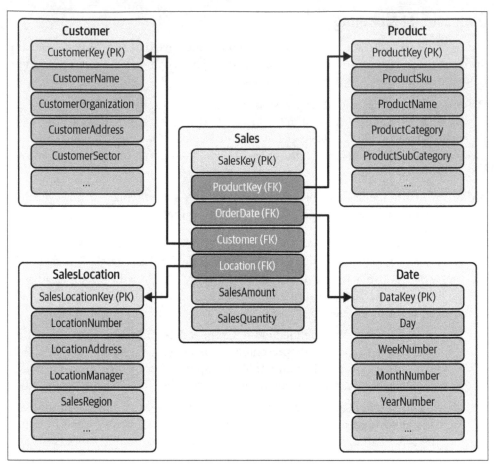

Figure 1-2. Sales dimensional model

Data Warehouse Benefits and Challenges

Data warehouses have inherent strengths that have served the business community well. They serve up high-quality, cleansed, and normalized data from different data sources in a common format. Since data from the different departments is presented in a common format, each department will review results in line with the other departments. Having timely, accurate data is the basis for strong business decisions.

- Since they store large amounts of historical data, they enable historical insights, allowing users to analyze different periods and trends.
- Data warehouses tend to be very reliable, based on the underlying relational database technology, which executes ACID transactions.

- Warehouses are modeled with standard star-schema modeling techniques, creating fact tables and dimensions. More and more prebuilt template models became available for various subject areas, such as sales and CRM, further accelerating the development of such models.

- Data warehouses are ideally suited for business intelligence and reporting, basically addressing the "What happened?" question of the data maturity curve. A data warehouse combined with business intelligence (BI) tools can generate actionable insights for marketing, finance, operations, and sales.

The fast rise of the internet and social media and the availability of multimedia devices such as smartphones disrupted the traditional data landscape, giving rise to the term *big data*. Big data is defined as data that arrives in ever higher *volumes*, with more *velocity*, in a greater *variety* of formats with higher *veracity*. These are known as the four Vs of data:

Volume

The volume of data created, captured, copied, and consumed globally is increasing rapidly. As described in Statista (*https://oreil.ly/DWUrE*), over the next two years, global data creation is projected to grow to more than 200 zettabytes (a zettabyte is a 2 to the power 70 number of bytes).

Velocity

In today's modern business climate, timely decisions are critical. To make these decisions, organizations need their information to flow quickly, ideally as close to real time as possible. For example, stock trading applications need to have access to near-real-time data so advanced trading algorithms can make millisecond decisions, and need to communicate these decisions to their stakeholders. Access to timely data can give organizations a competitive advantage.

Variety

Variety refers to the number of different "types" of data that are now available. The traditional data types were all structured and typically offered as relational databases, or extracts thereof. With the rise of big data, data now arrives in new unstructured types. Unstructured and semi-structured data types, such as Internet of Things (IoT) device messages, text, audio, and video, require additional preprocessing to derive business meaning. Variety is also expressed through the different types of ingestion. Some data sources are best ingested in batch mode, while others lend themselves to incremental ingestion, or real-time, event-based ingestion such as IoT data streams.

Veracity

Veracity defines the trustworthiness of the data. Here, we want to make sure that the data is accurate and of high quality. Data can be ingested from several sources; it is important to understand the chain of custody of the data, ensure we have rich metadata, and understand the context under which the data was collected. Additionally, we want to ensure that our view of the data is complete, with no missing components or late-arriving facts.

Data warehouses have a hard time addressing these four Vs.

Traditional data warehouse architectures struggle to facilitate exponentially increasing data *volumes*. They suffer from both storage and scalability issues. With volumes reaching petabytes, it becomes challenging to scale storage capabilities without spending large amounts of money. Traditional data warehouse architectures do not use in-memory and parallel processing techniques, preventing them from scaling the data warehouse vertically.

Data warehouse architectures are also not a good fit to address the *velocity* of big data. Data warehouses do not support the types of streaming architecture required to support near-real-time data. ETL data load windows can only be shortened so much until the infrastructure starts to buckle.

While data warehouses are very good at storing structured data, they are not well suited to store and query the *variety* of semi-structured or unstructured data.

Data warehouses have no built-in support for tracking the trustworthiness of the data. Data warehouse metadata is mainly focused on schema, and less on lineage, data quality, and other *veracity* variables.

Further, data warehouses are based upon a closed, proprietary format and typically only support SQL-based query tools. Because of their proprietary format, data warehouses do not offer good support for data science and machine learning tools.

Because of these limitations, data warehouses are expensive to build. As a result, projects often fail before going live, and those that do go live have a hard time keeping up with the ever-changing requirements of the modern business climate and the four Vs.

The limitations of the traditional data warehouse architecture gave rise to a more modern architecture, based upon the concept of a *data lake*.

Introducing Data Lakes

A data lake is a cost-effective central repository to store structured, semi-structured, or unstructured data at any scale, in the form of files and blobs. The term "data lake" came from the analogy of a real river or lake, holding the water, or in this case data, with several tributaries that are flowing the water (aka "data") into the lake in real time. A canonical representation of a typical data lake is shown in Figure 1-3.

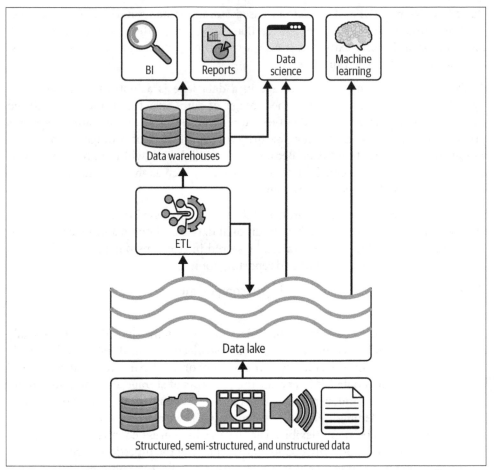

Figure 1-3. Canonical data lake

The initial data lakes and big data solutions were built with on-premises clusters, based upon the Apache Hadoop open source set of frameworks. Hadoop was used to efficiently store and process large datasets ranging in size from gigabytes to petabytes of data. Instead of using one large computer to store and process the data, Hadoop leveraged the clustering of multiple commodity compute nodes to analyze large volumes of datasets in parallel more quickly.

Hadoop would leverage the MapReduce framework to parallelize compute tasks over multiple compute nodes. The Hadoop Distributed File System (HDFS) was a file system that was designed to run on standard or low-end hardware. HDFS was very fault-tolerant and supported large datasets.

Starting in 2015, cloud data lakes, such as Amazon Simple Storage Service (Amazon S3), Azure Data Lake Storage Gen 2 (ADLS), and Google Cloud Storage (GCS), started replacing HDFS. These cloud-based storage systems have superior service-level agreements (SLAs) (often greater than 10 nines), offer geo-replication, and, most importantly, offer extremely low cost with the option to utilize even lower-cost cold storage for archival purposes.

At the lowest level, the unit of storage in a data lake is a blob of data. Blobs are by nature unstructured, enabling the storage of semi-structured and unstructured data, such as large audio and video files. At a higher level, the cloud storage systems provide file semantics and file-level security on top of the blob storage, enabling the storage of highly structured data. Because of their high bandwidth ingress and egress channels, data lakes also enable streaming use cases, such as the continuous ingestion of large volumes of IoT data or streaming media.

Compute engines enable large volumes of data to be processed in an ETL-like fashion and delivered to consumers, such as traditional data warehouses and machine learning and AI toolsets. Streaming data can be stored in real-time databases, and reports can be created with traditional BI and reporting tools.

Data lakes are enabled through a variety of components:

Storage
> Data lakes require very large, scalable storage systems, like the ones typically offered in cloud environments. The storage needs to be durable and scalable and should offer interoperability with a variety of third-party tools, libraries, and drivers. Note that data lakes separate the concepts of storage and compute, allowing both to scale independently. Independent scaling of storage and compute allows for on-demand, elastic fine-tuning of resources, allowing our solution architectures to be more flexible. The ingress and egress channels to the storage systems should support high bandwidths, enabling the ingestion or consumption of large batch volumes, or the continuous flow of large volumes of streaming data, such as IoT and streaming media.

Compute
> High amounts of compute power are required to process the large amounts of data stored in the storage layer. Several compute engines are available on the different cloud platforms. The go-to compute engine for data lakes is *Apache Spark*. Spark is an open source unified analytics engine, which can be deployed through various solutions such as Databricks or other cloud providers' developed solutions. Big data compute engines will leverage compute clusters. Compute clusters pool compute nodes to tackle complete data collection and processing tasks.

Formats

The shape of the data on disk defines the formats. A wide array of storage formats are available. Data lakes use mostly standardized, open source formats, such as Parquet, Avro JSON, or CSV.

Metadata

Modern, cloud-based storage systems maintain metadata (i.e., contextual information about the data). This includes various timestamps that describe when data was written or accessed, data schemas, and a variety of tags which contain information about the usage and owner of the data.

Data lakes have some very strong benefits. A data lake architecture enables the consolidation of an organization's data assets into one central location. Data lakes are format agnostic and rely on open source formats, such as Parquet and Avro. These formats are well understood by a variety of tools, drivers, and libraries, enabling smooth interoperability.

Data lakes are deployed on mature cloud storage subsystems, allowing them to benefit from the scalability, monitoring, ease of deployment, and low storage costs associated with these systems. Automated DevOps tools, such as Terraform, have well-established drivers, enabling automated deployments and maintenance.

Unlike data warehouses, data lakes support all data types, including semi-structured and unstructured data, enabling workloads such as media processing. Because of their high throughput ingress channels, they are very well suited for streaming use cases, such as ingesting IoT sensor data, media streaming, or web clickstreams.

However, as data lakes become more popular and widely used, organizations started recognizing some challenges with traditional data lakes. While the underlying cloud storage is relatively inexpensive, building and maintaining an effective data lake requires expert skills, resulting in high-end staffing or increased consulting services costs.

While it is easy to ingest data in its raw form, transforming the data into a form that can deliver business values can be very expensive. Traditional data lakes have poor latency query performance, so they cannot be used for interactive queries. As a result, the organization's data teams must still transform and load the data into something like a data warehouse, resulting in an extended time to value. This resulted in a data lake + warehouse architecture. This architecture continued to dominate the industry for quite a while (we have personally implemented dozens of those types of these systems), but is now declining because of the rise of lakehouses.

Data lakes typically use a "schema on read" strategy, where data can be ingested in any format without schema enforcement. Only when the data is read can some type of schema be applied. This lack of schema enforcement can result in data quality issues, allowing the pristine data lake to become a "data swamp."

Data lakes do not offer any kind of transactional guarantees. Data files can only be appended to, leading to expensive rewrites of previously written data to make a simple update. This leads to an issue called the "small file problem," where multiple small files are created for a single entity. If this issue is not managed well, these small files slow the read performance of the overall data lake, leading to stale data and wasted storage. Data lake administrators need to run repeated operations to consolidate these smaller files into larger files optimized for efficient read operations.

Now that we have discussed the strengths and weaknesses of both data warehouses and data lakes, we will introduce the data lakehouse, which combines the strengths and addresses the weaknesses of both technologies.

Data Lakehouse

Armbrust, Ghodsi, Xin, and Zaharia first introduced the concept of the data lakehouse in 2021 (*https://oreil.ly/jIRtm*). The authors define a lakehouse as "a data management system based upon low-cost and directly accessible storage that also provides analytics DBMS management and performance features such as ACID transactions, data versioning, auditing, indexing, caching and query optimization."

When we unpack this statement, we can define a lakehouse as a system that merges the flexibility, low cost, and scale of a data lake with the data management and ACID transactions of data warehouses, addressing the limitations of both. Like data lakes, the lakehouse architecture leverages low-cost cloud storage systems with the inherent flexibility and horizontal scalability of those systems. The goal of a lakehouse is to use existing high-performance data formats, such as Parquet, while also enabling ACID transactions (and other features). To add these capabilities, lakehouses use an *open-table format*, which adds features like ACID transactions, record-level operations, indexing, and key metadata to those existing data formats. This enables data assets stored on low-cost storage systems to have the same reliability that used to be exclusive to the domain of an RDBMS. Delta Lake is an example of an open-table format that supports these types of capabilities.

Lakehouses are an especially good match for most, if not all, cloud environments with separate compute and storage resources. Different computing applications can run on demand on completely separate computing nodes, such as a Spark cluster, while directly accessing the same storage data. It is, however, conceivable that one could implement a lakehouse over an on-premises storage system such as the aforementioned HDFS.

Data Lakehouse Benefits

An overview of the lakehouse architecture is shown in Figure 1-4.

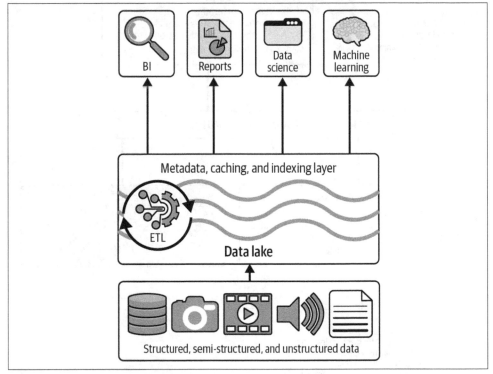

Figure 1-4. Lakehouse architecture overview

With the lakehouse architecture, we no longer need to have a copy of our data in the data lake, and another copy in some type of data warehouse storage. Indeed, we can source our data from the data lake through the Delta Lake storage format and protocol with comparable performance to a traditional data warehouse.

Since we can continue to leverage the low-cost cloud-based storage technologies and no longer need to copy data from the data lake to a data warehouse, we can realize significant cost savings, both in infrastructure and in staff and consulting overhead.

Since less data movement takes place and our ETL is simplified, opportunities for data quality issues are significantly reduced, and finally, because the lakehouse combines the ability to store large data volumes and refined dimensional models, development cycles are reduced, and the time to value is significantly reduced.

The evolution from data warehouses to data lakes to a lakehouse architecture is shown in Figure 1-5.

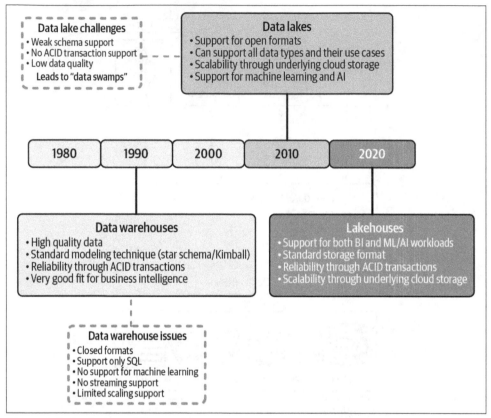

Figure 1-5. Evolution of data architectures

Implementing a Lakehouse

As we mentioned earlier, lakehouses leverage low-cost object stores, like Amazon S3, ADLS, or GCS, storing the data in an open source table format, such as Apache Parquet. However, since lakehouse implementations run ACID transactions against this data, we need a transactional metadata layer on top of the cloud storage, defining which objects are part of the table version.

This will allow a lakehouse to implement features such as ACID transactions and versioning within that metadata layer, while keeping the bulk of the data in the low-cost object storage. The lakehouse client is able to keep using data in an open source format that they are already familiar with.

Next, we need to address system performance. As we mentioned earlier, lakehouse implementations need to achieve great SQL performance to be effective. Data warehouses were very good at optimizing performance because they worked with a closed storage format and a well-known schema. This allowed them to maintain statistics, build clustered indexes, move hot data on fast SSD devices, etc.

In a lakehouse, which is based upon open source standard formats, we do not have that luxury, since we cannot change the storage format. However, lakehouses can leverage a plethora of other optimizations which leave the data files unchanged. This includes caching, auxiliary data structures such as indexes and statistics, and data layout optimizations.

The final tool that can speed up analytic workloads is the development of a standard DataFrame API. Most of the popular ML tools out there, such as TensorFlow and Spark MLlib, have support for DataFrames. DataFrames were first introduced by R and pandas and provide a simple table abstraction of the data with a multitude of transformation operations, most of which originate from relational algebra.

In Spark, the DataFrame API is declarative, and lazy evaluation is used to build an execution DAG (directed acyclic graph). This graph can then be optimized before any action consumes the underlying data in the DataFrame. This gives the lakehouse several new optimization features, such as caching and auxiliary data. Figure 1-6 shows how these requirements fit into an overall lakehouse system design.

Since Delta Lake is the focus of this book, we will illustrate how Delta Lake facilitates the requirements for implementing a lakehouse.

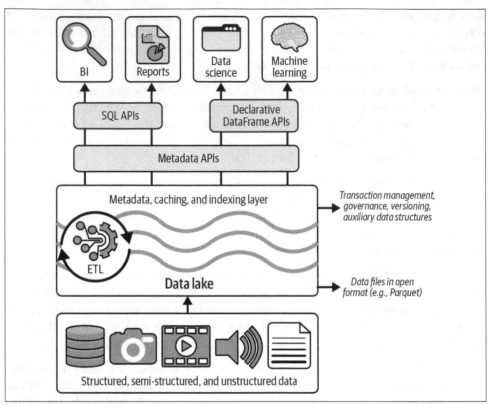

Figure 1-6. Lakehouse implementation

Delta Lake

As mentioned in the previous section, a possible lakehouse solution can be built on top of *Delta Lake* (*https://oreil.ly/iuNdo*). Delta Lake is an open-table format that combines metadata, caching, and indexing with a data lake storage format. Together these provide an abstraction level to serve ACID transactions and other management features.

The Delta Lake open-table format, open source metadata layer ultimately enables lakehouse implementations. Delta Lake provides ACID transactions, scalable metadata handling, a unified process model that spans batch and streaming, full audit history, and support for SQL data manipulation language (DML) statements. It can run on existing data lakes and is fully compatible with several processing engines, including Apache Spark.

Delta Lake is an open source framework, the specification of which can be found at *https://delta.io*. The work of Armbrust et al. (*https://oreil.ly/LOPyp*) offers a detailed description of how Delta Lake provides ACID transactions.

Delta Lake provides the following features:

Transactional ACID guarantees
Delta Lake will make sure that all data lake transactions using Spark, or any other processing engine, are committed for durability and exposed to other readers in an atomic fashion. This is made possible through the Delta transaction log. In Chapter 2, we will cover the transaction log in detail.

Full DML support
Traditional data lakes do not support transactional, atomic updates to the data. Delta Lake fully supports all DML operations, including deletes and updates, and complex data merge or upsert scenarios. This support greatly simplifies the creation of dimensions and fact tables when building a modern data warehouse (MDW).

Audit history
The Delta Lake transaction log records every change made to the data, in the order that these changes were made. Therefore, the transaction log becomes the full audit trail of any changes made to the data. This enables admins and developers to roll back to earlier versions of data after accidental deletions and edits. This feature is called time travel and is covered in detail in Chapter 6.

Unification of batch and streaming into one processing model
Delta Lake can work with batch and streaming sinks or sources. It can perform MERGEs on a data stream, which is a common requirement when merging IoT data with device reference data. It also enables use cases where we receive CDC data from external data sources. We will cover streaming in detail in Chapter 8.

Schema enforcement and evolution
Delta Lake enforces a schema when writing or reading data from the lake. However, when explicitly enabled for a data entity, it allows for a safe schema evolution, enabling use cases where the data needs to evolve. Schema enforcement and evolution are covered in Chapter 7.

Rich metadata support and scaling
Having the ability to support large volumes of data is great, but if the metadata cannot scale accordingly, the solution will fall short. Delta Lake scales out all metadata processing operations by leveraging Spark or other compute engines, allowing it to efficiently process the metadata for petabytes of data.

A lakehouse architecture is made up of three layers, as shown in Figure 1-7. The lakehouse storage layer is built on standard cloud-storage technology, such as ADLS, GCS, or Amazon S3 storage. This provides the lakehouse with a highly scalable, low-cost storage layer.

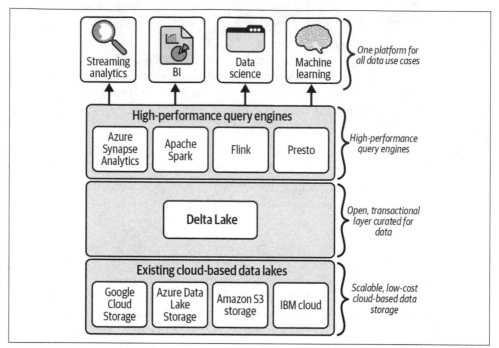

Figure 1-7. Lakehouse layered architecture

The transactional layer of the lakehouse is provided by Delta Lake. This brings ACID guarantees to the lakehouse, enabling an efficient transformation of raw data into curated, actionable data. Besides the ACID support, Delta Lake offers a rich set of additional features, such as DML support, scalable metadata processing, streaming support, and a rich audit log. The top layer of the lakehouse stack is made up of high-performance query and processing engines, which leverage underlying cloud compute resources. Supported query engines include:

- Apache Spark
- Apache Hive
- Presto
- Trino

Please consult the Delta Lake website (*https://delta.io*) for a complete list of supported compute engines.

The Medallion Architecture

An example of a Delta Lake-based lakehouse architecture is provided in Figure 1-8. This architectural pattern with Bronze, Silver, and Gold layers is often referred to as the *medallion architecture*. While it is only one of many lakehouse architecture patterns, it is a great fit for modern data warehouses, data marts, and other analytical solutions.

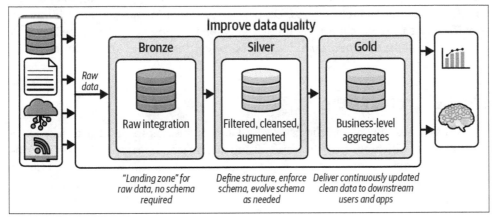

Figure 1-8. Data lakehouse solution architecture

At the highest level, we have three components in this solution. To the left we have the different data sources. A data source can take on many forms; some examples are provided here:

- A set of CSV or TXT files on an external data lake
- An on-premises database, such as Oracle or SQL Server
- Streaming data sources, such as Kafka or Azure Event Hubs
- REST APIs from a SAS service, such as Salesforce or ADP

The central component implements the medallion architecture. A medallion architecture is a data design pattern used to logically organize data in a lakehouse, through Bronze, Silver, and Gold layers. The Bronze layer is where we land the data ingested from our source systems on the left. Data in the Bronze zone is typically landed "as is," but can be augmented with additional metadata, such as the loading date and time, processing identifiers, etc.

In the Silver layer, the data from the Bronze layer is cleansed, normalized, merged, and conformed. This is where the enterprise view of the data across the different subject areas is gradually coming together.

The data in the Gold layer is "consumption-ready" data. This data can be in the format of a classic star schema, containing dimensions and fact tables, or it could be in any data model that is befitting to the consuming use case.

The goal of the medallion architecture is to improve the structure and quality of the data incrementally and progressively as it flows through each layer of the architecture, with each layer having an inherent purpose. This data design pattern will be covered in much greater depth in Chapter 10, but it is important to understand how a lakehouse, together with Delta Lake, can support reliable, performant data design patterns, or multihop architectures. Design patterns, like the medallion architecture, provide some of the architectural foundations for unifying your data pipelines in a lakehouse in order to support multiple use cases (e.g., batch data, streaming data, and machine learning).

The Delta Ecosystem

As we have laid out in this chapter, Delta Lake enables us to build data lakehouse architectures, which enable data warehousing and machine learning/AI applications to be hosted directly on a data lake. Today, Delta Lake is the most widely utilized lakehouse format, currently used by over 7,000 organizations, processing exabytes of data per day.

However, data warehouses and machine learning applications are not the only application target of Delta Lake. Beyond its core transactional ACID support, which brings reliability to data lakes, Delta Lake enables us to seamlessly ingest and consume both streaming and batch data with one solution architecture.

Another important component of Delta Lake is Delta Sharing, which enables companies to share data sets in a secure manner. Delta Lake 3.0 now supports standalone readers and writers, enabling any client (Python, Ruby, or Rust) to write data directly to Delta Lake without requiring any big data engine, such as Spark or Flink. Delta Lake ships with an extended set of open source connectors, including Presto, Flink, and Trino. The Delta Lake storage layer is now used extensively on many platforms, including ADLS, Amazon S3, and GCS. All components of Delta Lake 2.0 have been open sourced by Databricks.

The success of Delta Lake and lakehouses has spawned a completely new ecosystem, built around the Delta technology. This ecosystem is made up of a variety of individual components, including the Delta Lake storage format, Delta Sharing, and Delta Connectors.

Delta Lake Storage

The *Delta Lake storage format* is an open source storage layer that runs on top of cloud-based data lakes. It adds transactional capabilities to data lake files and tables, bringing data warehouse-like features to a standard data lake. Delta Lake storage is the core component of the ecosystem because all other components depend on this layer.

Delta Sharing

Data sharing is a common use case in business. For example, a mining company might want to securely share IoT information from its massive mining truck engines with the manufacturer for preventative maintenance and diagnostic purposes. A thermostat manufacturer might want to securely share HVAC data with a public utility to optimize the power grid load on high-usage days. However, in the past, implementing a secure, reliable data sharing solution was very challenging, and required expensive, custom development.

Delta Sharing is an open source protocol for securely sharing large datasets of Delta Lake data. It allows users to securely share data stored in Amazon S3, ADLS, or GCS. With Delta Sharing, users can directly connect to the shared data, using their favorite toolsets like Spark, Rust, Power BI, etc., without having to deploy any additional components. Notice that the data can be shared across cloud providers, without any custom development.

Delta Sharing enables use cases such as:

- Data stored in ADLS can be processed by a Spark Engine on AWS.
- Data stored in Amazon S3 can be processed by Rust on GCP.

Please refer to Chapter 9 for a detailed discussion of Delta Sharing.

Delta Connectors

The main goal of *Delta Connectors*[3,4] is to bring Delta Lake to other big data engines outside of Apache Spark. Delta Connectors are open source connectors that directly connect to Delta Lake. The framework includes *Delta Standalone*, a Java native library that allows direct reading and writing of the Delta Lake tables without requiring an Apache Spark cluster. Consuming applications can use Delta Standalone to directly connect to Delta tables written by their big data infrastructure. This eliminates the need for data duplication into another format before it can be consumed.

---

3 Delta Lake Integrations (*https://oreil.ly/a2uaa*)

4 Delta Lake Connectors (*https://oreil.ly/b92Fy*)

Other native libraries are available for:

Hive
> The Hive Connector reads Delta tables directly from Apache Hive.

Flink
> The Flink/Delta Connector reads and writes Delta tables from the Apache Flink application. The connector includes a sink for writing to Delta tables from Apache Flink, and a source for reading Delta tables using Flink.

sql-delta-import
> This connector allows for importing data from a JDBC data source directly into a Delta table.

Power BI
> The Power BI connector is a custom Power Query function that allows Power BI to read a Delta table from any file-based data source supported by Microsoft Power BI.

Delta Connectors is a fast-growing ecosystem, with more connectors becoming available regularly. In fact, included in the recently announced Delta Lake 3.0 release is Delta Kernel (*https://oreil.ly/yEg5o*). Delta Kernel and its simplified libraries remove the need to understand Delta protocol details, thus making it much easier to build and maintain connectors.

Conclusion

Given the volume, velocity, variety, and veracity of data, the limitations and challenges of both data warehouses and data lakes have driven a new paradigm of data architectures. The lakehouse architecture, set forth by advancements in open-table formats such as Delta Lake, provides a modern data architecture that harnesses the best elements of its predecessors to bring a unified approach to a data platform.

As mentioned in the Preface, this book will do more than just scratch the surface; it will dive into some of the core features of Delta Lake already touched on in this chapter. You will learn how to best set up Delta Lake, identify use cases for different features, learn about best practices and different things to consider, and much more. It will continually provide data practitioners with context and evidence of how this open-table format supports a modern data platform in the form of a lakehouse architecture. By the end of this book you will feel confident in getting up and running with Delta Lake and building a modern data lakehouse architecture.

## CHAPTER 2

Getting Started with Delta Lake

In the previous chapter we introduced Delta Lake and saw how it adds transactional guarantees, DML support, auditing, a unified streaming and batch model, schema enforcement, and a scalable metadata model to traditional data lakes.

In this chapter, we will go hands-on with Delta Lake. We will first set up Delta Lake on a local machine with Spark installed. We will run Delta Lake samples in two interactive shells:

1. First, we will run the *PySpark interactive* shell with the Delta Lake packages. This will allow us to type in and run a simple two-line Python program that creates a Delta table.

2. Next, we will run a similar program with the *Spark Scala shell*. Although we do not cover the Scala language extensively in this book, we want to demonstrate that both the Spark shell and Scala are options with Delta Lake.

Next, we will create a *helloDeltaLake* starter program in Python inside your favorite editor and run the program interactively in the PySpark shell. The environment we set up in this chapter, and the *helloDeltaLake* program, will be the basis for most other programs we create in this book.

Once the environment is up and running, we are ready to look deeper into the Delta table format. Since Delta Lake uses Parquet as the underlying storage medium, we first take a brief look at the Parquet format. Since partitions and partition files play an important role when we study the transaction log later, we will study the mechanism of both automatic and manual partitioning. Next, we move on to Delta tables and investigate how a Delta table adds a transaction log in the *_delta_log* directory.

The remainder of this chapter is dedicated to the *transaction log*. We will create and run several Python programs to investigate the details of transaction log entries, what kind of actions are recorded, and what Parquet data files are written when and how they relate to the transaction log entries. We will look at more complex update examples and their impact on the transaction log. Finally, we will introduce the concept of checkpoint files and how they help Delta Lake implement a scalable metadata system.

Getting a Standard Spark Image

Setting up Spark on a local machine can be daunting. You have to adjust many different settings, update packages, and so on. Therefore, we chose to use a Docker container. If you do not have Docker installed, you can download it free from their website (*https://www.docker.com*). The specific container that we used was the standard Apache Spark image (*https://oreil.ly/VE2Ny*). To download the image, you can use the following command:

```
docker pull apache/spark
```

Once you have pulled down the image, you can start the container with the following command:

```
docker run -it apache/spark /bin/sh
```

The Spark installation is in the *opt/spark* directory. PySpark, spark-sql, and all other tools are in the *opt/spark/bin* directory. We have included several instructions on how to work with the container in the readme of the book's GitHub repository (*https://github.com/benniehaelen/delta-lake-up-and-running*).

Using Delta Lake with PySpark

As mentioned before, Delta Lake runs on top of your existing storage and is fully compatible with the existing Apache Spark APIs. This means it is easy to start with Delta Lake if you already have Spark installed or a container as specified in the previous section.

With Spark in place, you can install the *delta-spark 2.4.0* package. You can find the delta-spark package in its PySpark directory (*https://oreil.ly/w67kM*). Enter the following command in a command shell:

```
pip install delta-spark
```

Once you have delta-spark installed, you can run the Python shell interactively like this:

```
pyspark --packages io.delta:<delta_version>
  --conf "spark.sql.extensions=io.delta.sql.DeltaSparkSessionExtension"
  --conf "spark.sql.catalog.spark_catalog=
   org.apache.spark.sql.delta.catalog.DeltaCatalog"
```

This will give you a PySpark shell from which you can interactively run commands:

```
Welcome to

      ____              __
     / __/__  ___ _____/ /__
    _\ \/ _ \/ _ `/ __/  '_/
   /__ / .__/\_,_/_/ /_/\_\   version 3.2.2
      /_/

Using Python version 3.9.13 (tags/v3.9.13:6de2ca5, May 17 2022 16:36:42)
Spark context Web UI available at http://host.docker.internal:4040
Spark context available as 'sc' (master - local[*],
 app id = local-1665944381326).
SparkSession available as 'spark'.
```

Inside the shell, you can now run interactive PySpark commands. We always do a quick test by creating a `range()` with Spark, resulting in a DataFrame that we can then save in Delta Lake format (more details on this in "Creating and Running a Spark Program: helloDeltaLake" on page 29).

The full code is provided here:

```
data = spark.range(0, 10)
data.write.format("delta").mode("overwrite").save("/book/testShell")
```

The following is a full run:

```
>>> data = spark.range(0, 10)
>>> data.write.format("delta").mode("overwrite").save("/book/testShell")
>>>
```

Here we see the statement to create the `range()`, followed by the `write` statement. We see that the Spark Executors do run. When you open up the output directory, you will find the generated Delta table (more details on the Delta table format in the next section).

Running Delta Lake in the Spark Scala Shell

You can also run Delta Lake in the interactive Spark Scala shell. As specified in the Delta Lake Quickstart (*https://oreil.ly/EcHRO*), you can start the Scala shell with the Delta Lake packages as follows:

```
spark-shell --packages io.delta:<delta_version>
  --conf "spark.sql.extensions=io.delta.sql.DeltaSparkSessionExtension"
  --conf "spark.sql.catalog.spark_catalog=
  org.apache.spark.sql.delta.catalog.DeltaCatalog"
```

This will start up the interactive Scala shell:

```
Spark context Web UI available at http://host.docker.internal:4040
Spark context available as 'sc' (master = local[*],
 app id = local-1665950762666).
```

```
Spark session available as 'spark'.
Welcome to

      ____              __
     / __/__  ___ _____/ /__
    _\ \/ _ \/ _ `/ __/  '_/
   /___/ .__/\_,_/_/ /_/\_\   version 3.2.2
      /_/

Using Scala version 2.12.15 (Java HotSpot(TM) 64-Bit Server VM, Java 1.8.0_311)
Type in expressions to have them evaluated.
Type :help for more information.

scala>
```

Inside the shell, you can now run interactive Scala commands. Let's do a similar test on Scala as you did for the PySpark shell:

```
val data = spark.range(0, 10)
data.write.format("delta").mode("overwrite").save("/book/testShell")
```

Here is a full run:

```
cala> val data = spark.range(0, 10)
data: org.apache.spark.sql.Dataset[Long] = [id: bigint]

scala> data.write.format("delta").mode("overwrite").save("/book/testShell")
```

Again, when you check your output, you can find the generated Delta table.

Running Delta Lake on Databricks

For the examples later on in this book, the Databricks Community Edition (*https://oreil.ly/mPls9*) was chosen to run Delta Lake. This was chosen to develop and run the code samples because it is free, simplifies setup of Spark and Delta Lake, and does not require your own cloud account or for you to supply cloud compute or storage resources. With the Databricks Community Edition, users can access a cluster with a complete notebook environment and an up-to-date runtime with Delta Lake installed on this platform.

If you do not want to run Spark and Delta Lake on your local machine, you can also run Delta Lake on Databricks on a cloud platform, like Azure, AWS, or Google Cloud. These environments make it easy to get started with Delta Lake, since their installed runtimes already have a version of Delta Lake installed.

The additional benefit of the cloud is that you can create real Spark clusters of arbitrary size, potentially up to thousands of cores spanning hundreds of nodes to process terabytes or petabytes of data.

When using Databricks in the cloud, you have two options. You can use its popular notebooks or you can connect your favorite development environment to a cloud-based Databricks cluster with dbx (*https://oreil.ly/8abOG*). dbx by Databricks labs is an open source tool that allows you to connect to a Databricks cluster from an editing environment.

Creating and Running a Spark Program: helloDeltaLake

Once you have the delta-spark package installed, creating your first PySpark program is very straightforward. Follow these steps to create the PySpark program.

Create a new file (we named ours *helloDeltaLake.py*). Add the necessary imports. At a minimum you need to import PySpark and Delta Lake:

```
import pyspark
from delta import *
```

Next, create a SparkSession builder, which loads up the Delta Lake extensions, as follows:

```
# Create a builder with the Delta extensions
builder = pyspark.sql.SparkSession.builder.appName("MyApp")        \
   .config("spark.sql.extensions",                                 \
               "io.delta.sql.DeltaSparkSessionExtension")          \
   .config("spark.sql.catalog.spark_catalog",                      \
               "org.apache.spark.sql.delta.catalog.DeltaCatalog")
```

Next, we can create the SparkSession object itself. We will create the SparkSession object and print out its version to ensure that the object is valid:

```
# Create a Spark instance with the builder
# As a result, you now can read and write Delta tables
spark = configure_spark_with_delta_pip(builder).getOrCreate()
print(f"Hello, Spark version: {spark.version}")
```

To verify that our Delta Lake extensions are working correctly, we create a range and write it out in Delta Lake format:

```
# Create a range, and save it in Delta Lake format to ensure
# that your Delta Lake extensions are indeed working
df = spark.range(0, 10)
df.write                                   \
   .format("delta")                        \
   .mode("overwrite")                      \
   .save("/book/chapter02/helloDeltaLake")
```

That completes the code for your starter program. You can find the full code file in the */chapter02/helloDeltaLake.py* location of the book's code repository. This code is a good place to start if you want to write your own code.

To run the program, we can simply start a command prompt on Windows, or a terminal on MacOS, and navigate to the folder with our code. We simply start PySpark with the program as input:

```
pyspark < helloDeltaLake.py
```

When we run the program, we get our Spark version output (the displayed version will depend on the version of Spark the reader has installed):

```
Hello, Spark version: 3.4.1
```

And when we look at the output, we can see that we have written a valid Delta table. The details of the Delta Lake format are covered in the next section.

At this point, we have PySpark and Delta Lake installed successfully, and we were able to code and run a full-fledged PySpark program with Delta Lake extensions. Now that you can run your own programs, we are ready to explore the Delta Lake format in detail in the next section.

The Delta Lake Format

In this section we will dive deeper into the Delta Lake open-table format. When we save a file using this format, we are just writing a standard Parquet file with additional metadata. This additional metadata is the foundation for enabling the core features of Delta Lake, and even just performing DML operations typically seen in traditional RDBMSs such as INSERT, UPDATE, and DELETE, among a vast array of other operations.

Since Delta Lake writes out data as a Parquet file, we will take a more in-depth look at the Parquet file format. We first write out a simple Parquet file and take a detailed look at the artifacts written by Spark. This will give us a good understanding of files we will leverage throughout this book.

Next, we will write out a file in Delta Lake format, noticing how it triggers the creation of the _delta_log directory, containing the transaction log. We will take a detailed look at this transaction log and how it is used to *generate a single source of truth*. We will see how the transaction log implements the ACID *atomicity* property mentioned in Chapter 1.

We will see how Delta Lake breaks down a transaction into individual, atomic commit actions, and how it records these actions in the transaction log as ordered, atomic units. Finally, we will look at several use cases and investigate what Parquet data files and transaction log entries are written, and what is stored in these entries.

Since a transaction log entry is written for every transaction, we might end up with multiple small files. To ensure that this approach remains scalable, Delta Lake will create a checkpoint file every 10 transactions (at the time of writing) with the full transactional state. This way, a Delta Lake reader can simply process the checkpoint file and the few transaction entries written afterward. This results in a fast, scalable metadata system.

Parquet Files

The Apache Parquet file format has been one of the most popular big data formats for the last 20 years. Parquet is open source, so it is free to use under the Apache Hadoop license and is compatible with most Hadoop data processing frameworks.

Unlike row-based formats such as CSV or Avro, Parquet is a column-oriented format, meaning that the values of each column/field are stored next to each other, rather than in each record. Figure 2-1 shows the differences between a row-based layout and a column-oriented layout and how that is represented in a logical table.

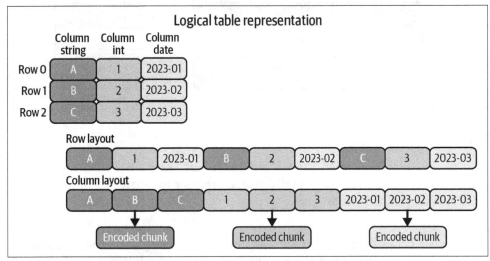

Figure 2-1. Difference between row-based and column-oriented layouts

Figure 2-1 demonstrates that instead of sequentially storing row values, as in the row layout, the column layout sequentially stores column values. This columnar format helps with compression on a column-by-column basis. This format is also built to support flexible compression options and extendable encoding schemas for each data type, meaning a different encoding can be used for compressing integer versus string data types.

Parquet files are also comprised of row groups and metadata. Row groups contain data from the same column, and thus each column is stored together in a row group. The metadata in a Parquet file not only contains information about these row groups, but also information about columns (e.g., min/max values, number of values) and the data schema, which makes Parquet a self-describing file with additional metadata to enable better data skipping.

Figure 2-2 shows how Parquet files are comprised of row groups and metadata. Each row group consists of a column chunk for each column in the dataset, and each column chunk consists of one or more pages with the column data. To explore more documentation and dive deeper into the Parquet file formats, you can look at the Apache Parquet website and documentation (*https://oreil.ly/DBjw_*).

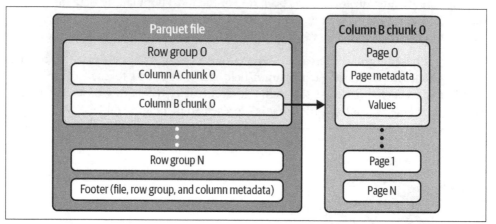

Figure 2-2. Parquet file composition

Advantages of Parquet files

Due to the column-oriented format, storage layout, metadata, and long-standing popularity, Parquet files have several strong advantages for analytical workloads and when working with big data:

High performance

Because Parquet files are a column-oriented format, they enable better compression and encoding since these algorithms can take advantage of the similar values and data types stored in each column. For I/O-intensive operations, this compressed data can improve performance significantly.

When column values are stored together in the case of Parquet files, queries only need to read the columns required for that query, as opposed to requiring all columns be read in the case of row-based formats. This means that the columnar format can reduce the amount of data that needs to be read for operations, resulting in better performance.

The metadata contained in Parquet files describes some of the features of the data. It contains information about row groups, data schemas, and, most importantly, columns. Column metadata includes information such as min/max values and the number of values. Together, this metadata reduces the amount of data that needs to be read for each operation (i.e., data skipping) and enables far better query performance.

Cost-effective

Since Parquet files are able to leverage better compression and encoding, this inherently makes the data more cost-effective to store. By nature, compressed data consumes less space on disk when storing files, which inevitably results in reduced storage space and reduced storage costs.

Interoperability

Since Parquet files have been very popular for the past 20 years, especially for legacy big data processing frameworks and tools (e.g., Hadoop), they are very widely supported across different tools and engines, and offer great interoperability.

Writing a Parquet file

In the book repository, the */chapter02/writeParquetFile* Python program creates a Spark DataFrame in memory, and writes it in Parquet format to the */parquetData* folder using the standard PySpark API:

```
data = spark.range(0, 100)
data.write.format("parquet")      \
          .mode("overwrite")      \
          .save('/book/chapter02/parquetData')
```

In our case, when we look at what is written to disk, we see the following (you may see a different result, depending on your local machine):

```
 Directory of C:\book\chapter02\parquetData
10/17/2022
10/17/2022  511 part-00000-a3885270-...-c000.snappy.parquet
10/17/2022  513 part-00001-a3885270-...-c000.snappy.parquet
10/17/2022  517 part-00002-a3885270-...-c000.snappy.parquet
10/17/2022  513 part-00003-a3885270-...-c000.snappy.parquet
10/17/2022  513 part-00004-a3885270-...-c000.snappy.parquet
10/17/2022  517 part-00005-a3885270-...-c000.snappy.parquet
10/17/2022  513 part-00006-a3885270-...-c000.snappy.parquet
10/17/2022  513 part-00007-a3885270-...-c000.snappy.parquet
10/17/2022  517 part-00008-a3885270-...-c000.snappy.parquet
10/17/2022  513 part-00009-a3885270-...-c000.snappy.parquet
10/17/2022  513 part-00010-a3885270-...-c000.snappy.parquet
10/17/2022  517 part-00011-a3885270-...-c000.snappy.parquet
```

A developer new to the big data world might be a bit shocked at this point. We only did a single write of 100 numbers, so how did we end up with 12 Parquet files? A bit of elaboration might be in order.

First, the filename we specified in the write is really the name of a *directory*, not a file. As you can see, the directory */parquetData* contains 12 Parquet files.

When we look at the *.parquet* files, we may see that we have 12 files. Spark is a highly parallel computational environment, where the system is attempting to keep each CPU core in your Spark cluster busy. In our case, we are running on a local machine, which means there is one machine in our cluster. When we look at the information for our system, we see that we have 12 cores.

When we look at the number of *.parquet* files that were written, we see that we have 12 files, which is equal to the number of cores on our cluster. And that is Spark's default behavior in this scenario. The number of files will be equal to the number of available cores. Assume we add the following statement to our code:

```
data = spark.range(0, 100)
data.write.format("parquet")      \
            .mode("overwrite")    \
            .save('/book/chapter02/parquetData')
print(f"The number of partitions is: {data.rdd.getNumPartitions()}")
```

We can see in the output that we indeed have 12 files:

```
The number of partitions is: 12
```

While this might look like overkill for a scenario where you are only writing 100 numbers, one can imagine a scenario where you are reading or writing very large files. Having the ability to split the files and process them in parallel can dramatically increase performance.

The *.crc* files you see in the output are *cyclic redundancy check* files. Spark uses them to ensure that data hasn't been corrupted. These files are always very small, so their overhead is very minimal compared to the utility that they provide. While there is a way to turn off the generation of these files, we would not recommend doing so since their benefit far outweighs their overhead.

The final files in your output are the *_SUCCESS* and *_SUCCESS.crc* files. Spark uses these files to provide a method to confirm that all partitions have been written correctly.

Writing a Delta Table

So far, we have been working with Parquet files. Now, let's take the first example from the previous section and save it in Delta Lake format instead of Parquet (code: */chapter02/writeDeltaFile.py*). All we need to do is replace the Parquet format with Delta format, as shown in the code:

```
data = spark.range(0, 100)
data.write                      \
    .format("delta")           \
    .mode("overwrite")         \
    .save('/book/chapter02/deltaData')
print(f"The number of filesis: {data.rdd.getNumPartitions()}")
```

We get the same number of partitions:

```
The number of files is: 12
```

And when we look at the output, we see the addition of the *_delta_log* file:

```
Directory of C:\book\chapter02\deltaData
10/17/2022   16 .part-00000-....-c000.snappy.parquet.crc
10/17/2022   16 .part-00001-....-c000.snappy.parquet.crc
10/17/2022   16 .part-00002-....-c000.snappy.parquet.crc
10/17/2022   16 .part-00003-....-c000.snappy.parquet.crc
10/17/2022   16 .part-00004-....-c000.snappy.parquet.crc
10/17/2022   16 .part-00005-....-c000.snappy.parquet.crc
10/17/2022   16 .part-00006-....-c000.snappy.parquet.crc
10/17/2022   16 .part-00007-....-c000.snappy.parquet.crc
10/17/2022   16 .part-00008-....-c000.snappy.parquet.crc
10/17/2022   16 .part-00009-....-c000.snappy.parquet.crc
10/17/2022   16 .part-00010-....-c000.snappy.parquet.crc
10/17/2022   16 .part-00011-....-c000.snappy.parquet.crc
10/17/2022  524 part-00000-....-c000.snappy.parquet
10/17/2022  519 part-00001-....-c000.snappy.parquet
10/17/2022  523 part-00002-....-c000.snappy.parquet
10/17/2022  519 part-00003-....-c000.snappy.parquet
10/17/2022  519 part-00004-....-c000.snappy.parquet
10/17/2022  522 part-00005-....-c000.snappy.parquet
10/17/2022  519 part-00006-....-c000.snappy.parquet
10/17/2022  519 part-00007-....-c000.snappy.parquet
10/17/2022  523 part-00008-....-c000.snappy.parquet
10/17/2022  519 part-00009-....-c000.snappy.parquet
10/17/2022  519 part-00010-....-c000.snappy.parquet
10/17/2022  523 part-00011-....-c000.snappy.parquet
10/17/2022 <DIR>          _delta_log
             24 File(s)          6,440 bytes
```

The *_delta_log* file contains a transaction log with every single operation performed on your data.

> Delta Lake 3.0 includes UniForm (short for "Universal Format"). With UniForm enabled, Delta tables can be read as if they were other open-table formats, such as Iceberg. This enables you to use a broader range of tools without worrying about table format compatibility.
>
> ```sql
> %sql
> CREATE TABLE T
> TBLPROPERTIES(
>   'delta.columnMapping.mode' = 'name',
>   'delta.universalFormat.enabledFormats' = 'iceberg')
> AS
>   SELECT * FROM source_table;
> ```
>
> UniForm automatically generates Apache Iceberg metadata alongside Delta metadata, atop one copy of the underlying Parquet data. The metadata for Iceberg is automatically generated on table creation and is updated whenever the table is updated.

The Delta Lake Transaction Log

The Delta Lake transaction log (also known as DeltaLog) is a sequential record of every transaction performed on a Delta Lake table since its creation. It is central to Delta Lake functionality because it is at the core of its important features, including ACID transactions, scalable metadata handling, and time travel.

The main goal of the transaction log is to enable multiple readers and writers to operate on a given version of a dataset file simultaneously and to provide additional information, like data skipping indexes to the execution engine for more performant operations. The Delta Lake transaction log always shows the user a consistent view of the data and serves as a *single source of truth*. It is the central repository that tracks all changes the user makes to a Delta table.

When a Delta table reader reads a Delta table for the first time or runs a new query on an open file that has been modified since the last time it was read, Delta Lake looks at the transaction log to get the latest version of the table. This ensures that a user's version of a file is always synchronized with the master record as of the most recent query and that users cannot make divergent, conflicting changes to a file.

How the Transaction Log Implements Atomicity

In Chapter 1, we learned that atomicity guarantees that all operations (e.g., INSERT, UPDATE, DELETE, or MERGE) performed on your file will either succeed as a whole or not succeed at all. Without atomicity, any hardware failure or software bug can cause a data file to be written partially, resulting in corrupted or, at a minimum, invalid data.

The transaction log is the mechanism through which Delta Lake can offer the atomicity guarantee. The transaction log is also responsible for metadata, time travel, and significantly faster metadata operations for large tabular datasets.

The transaction log is an ordered record of every transaction made against a Delta table since it was created. It acts as a single source of truth and tracks all changes made to the table. The transaction log allows users to reason about their data and trust its completeness and quality. The simple rule is if an operation is not recorded in the transaction log, it never happened. In the following sections, we will illustrate these principles with several examples.

Breaking Down Transactions into Atomic Commits

Whenever you perform a set of operations to modify a table or storage file (such as INSERTs, UPDATEs, DELETEs, or MERGEs), Delta Lake will break down that operation into a series of atomic, discrete steps composed of one or more of the actions shown in Table 2-1.

Table 2-1. List of possible actions in a transaction log entry

Action	Description
Add file	Adds a file.
Remove file	Removes a file.
Update metadata	Updates the table's metadata (e.g., changing the table or file's name, schema, or partitioning). A table or file's first transaction log entry will always contain an update metadata action with the schema, the partition columns, and other information.
Set transaction	Records that a structured streaming job has committed a micro-batch with the given stream ID. For more information, see Chapter 8.
Change protocol	Enables new features by switching the Delta Lake transaction log to the newest software protocol.
Commit info	Contains information about the commit, which operation was made, from where, and at what time. Every transaction log entry will contain a commit info action.

These actions are recorded in the transaction log entries *(*.json)* as ordered, atomic units known as commits. This is similar to how the Git source control system tracks changes as atomic commits. This also implies that you can replay each of the commits in the transaction log to get to the current state of the file.

For example, if a user creates a transaction to add a new column to a table and then adds data to it, Delta Lake would break this transaction down into its component action parts, and once the transaction completes, add them to the transaction log as the following commits:

1. *Update metadata*: change the schema to include the new column
2. *Add file*: for each new file added

The Transaction Log at the File Level

When you write a Delta table, that file's transaction log is automatically created in the *_delta_log* subdirectory. As you continue to make changes to the Delta table, these changes will be automatically recorded as ordered atomic commits in the transaction log. Each commit is written as a JSON file, starting with *000000000000000000.json*. If you make additional changes to the file, Delta Lake will generate additional JSON files in ascending numerical order, so the next commit is written as *000000000000000001.json*, the following one as *000000000000000002.json*, and so on.

In the remainder of this chapter, we will use an abbreviated form for the transaction log entries for readability purposes. Instead of showing up to 19 digits, we will use an abbreviated form with up to 5 digits (so you will use *00001.json* instead of the longer notation).

Additionally, we will be shortening the name of the Parquet files. These names typically look as follows:

part-00007-71c70d7f-c7a8-4a8c-8c29-57300cfd929b-c000.snappy.parquet

For demonstration and explanation, we will abbreviate a name like this to *part-00007.parquet*, leaving off the GUID and the *snappy.parquet* portion.

In our example visualizations, we will visualize each transaction entry with the action name and the data filename affected; for example, in Figure 2-3, we have a *remove* (file) action and another *add* (file) action in a single transaction file.

Action	Part name
Remove	*part-00001*
Add	*part-00004*

00002.json

Figure 2-3. Notation for a transaction log entry

Write multiple writes to the same file

Throughout this section, we will use a set of figures that describe each code step in detail. We show the following information for each step:

- The actual code snippet is shown in the second column.
- Next to the code snippet we show the Parquet data files written as a result of the code snippet execution.
- In the last column we show the transaction log entry's JSON files. We show the action and the affected Parquet data filename for each transaction log entry.

For this first example you will use *chapter02/MultipleWriteOperations.py* from the book's repository to show multiple writes to the same file.

Here is a step-by-step description of the different steps in Figure 2-4:

1. First, a new Delta table is written to the path. One Parquet file was written to the output path (*part-00000.parquet*). The first transaction log entry (*00000.json*) has been created in the *_delta_log* directory. Since this is the first transaction log entry for the file, a *metadata* action and an *add file* action are recorded, indicating a single partition file was added.

2. Next we append data to the table. We can see a new Parquet file (*part-00001.parquet*) has been written, and we created an additional entry (*00001.json*) in the

transaction log. Like the first step, the entry contains an *add file* action, because we added a new file.

3. We append more data. Again, a new data file is written (*part-00002.parquet*), and a new transaction log file (*00002.json*) is added to the transaction log with an *add file* action.

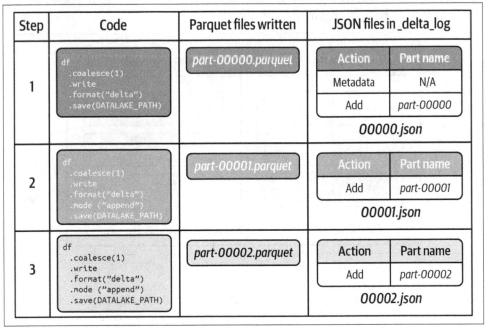

Figure 2-4. Multiple writes to the same file

Note that each transaction log entry will also have a *commit info* action, which contains the audit information for the transaction. We omitted the *commit info* log entries on the figures for readability purposes.

The sequence of operations for writes is very important. For each write operation, the data file is always written first, and only when that operation succeeds, a transaction log file is added to the *_delta_log* folder. *The transaction is only considered complete when the transaction log entry is written successfully.*

Reading the latest version of a Delta table

When the system reads a Delta table, it will iterate through the transaction log to "compile" the current state of the table. The sequence of events when reading a file is as follows:

1. The transaction log files are read first.

2. The data files are read based on the log files.

Next, we will describe that sequence for the Delta table written by the previous example (*multipleWriteOperations.py*). Delta will read all the log files (*00000.json*, *00001.json*, and *00002.json*). It will read the three data files based upon the log information, as shown in Figure 2-5.

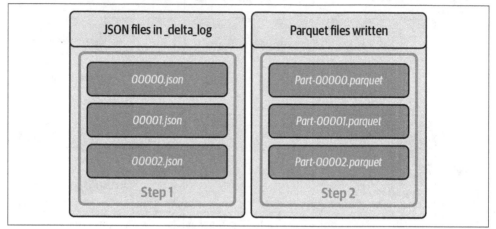

Figure 2-5. Read operations

Note that the sequence of operations also implies that there could be data files that are no longer referenced in the transaction log. Indeed, this is a common occurrence in UPDATE or DELETE scenarios. Delta Lake does not delete these data files since they might be required again if the user uses the time travel feature of Delta Lake (covered in Chapter 6). You can remove old, obsolete data files with the VACUUM command (also covered in Chapter 6).

Failure scenario with a write operation

Next, let's see what happens if a write operation fails. In the previous write scenario, let's assume the write operation in step 3 of Figure 2-4 fails halfway through. Part of the Parquet file might have been written, but the transaction log entry *00002.json* was not. We would have the scenario shown in Figure 2-6.

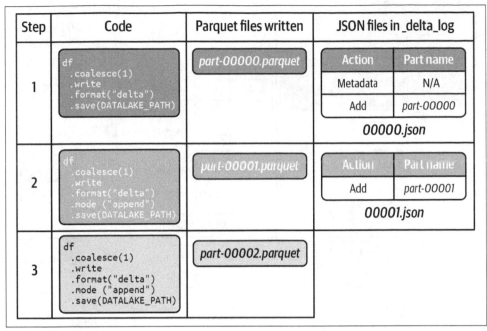

Step	Code	Parquet files written	JSON files in _delta_log	

1	`df`
	`.coalesce(1)`
	`.write`
	`.format("delta")`
	`.save(DATALAKE_PATH)`
		part-00000.parquet	**Action**	**Part name**

			Metadata	N/A
			Add	*part-00000*
			00000.json	

2	`df`
	`.coalesce(1)`
	`.write`
	`.format("delta")`
	`.mode ("append")`
	`.save(DATALAKE_PATH)`
		part-00001.parquet	**Action**	**Part name**

			Add	*part-00001*
			00001.json	

3	`df`
	`.coalesce(1)`
	`.write`
	`.format("delta")`
	`.mode ("append")`
	`.save(DATALAKE_PATH)`
		part-00002.parquet		

Figure 2-6. Failure during the last write operation.

As you can see in Figure 2-6, the last transaction file is missing. According to the read sequence specified earlier, Delta Lake will read the first and second JSON transaction files, and the corresponding *part-00000* and *part-00001* Parquet files. The Delta Lake reader will not read inconsistent data; it will read a consistent view through the first two transaction log files.

Update scenario

The last scenario is contained in the *chapter02/UpdateOperation.py* code repo. To keep things simple, we have a small Delta table with patient information. We are only tracking the `patientId` and the `PatientName` of each patient. In this use case, we create a Delta table with four patients, two in each file. Next, we add data from two more patients. Finally, we update the name of the first patient. As you will see, this update has a bigger impact than expected. The full update scenario is shown in Figure 2-7.

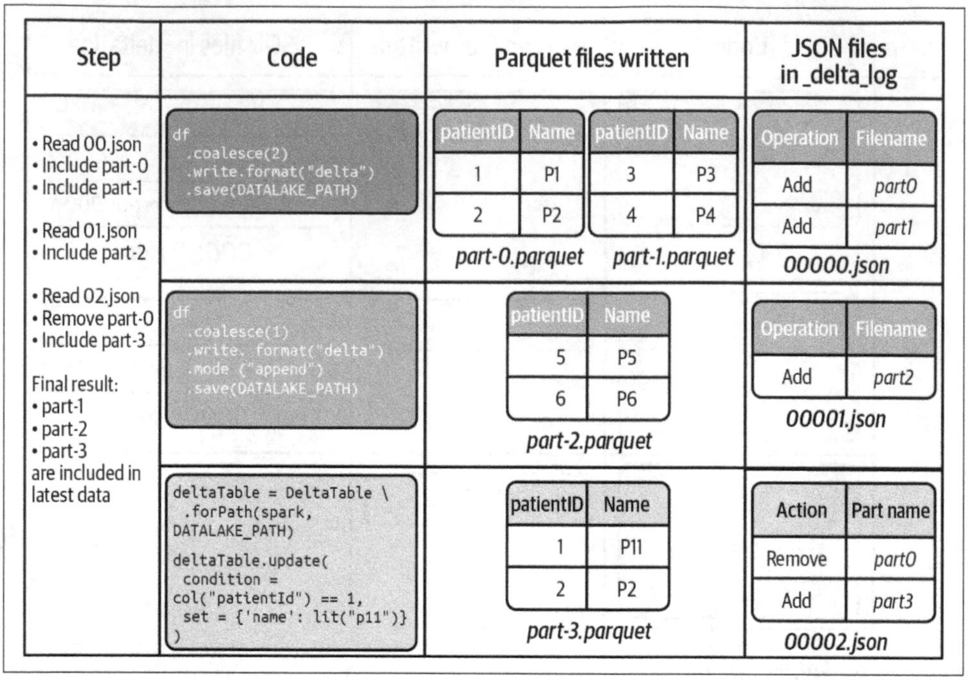

Step	Code	Parquet files written				JSON files in _delta_log	
• Read 00.json • Include part-0 • Include part-1 • Read 01.json • Include part-2	```df .coalesce(2) .write.format("delta") .save(DATALAKE_PATH)```	**patientID**	**Name**	**patientID**	**Name**	**Operation**	**Filename**
		1	P1	3	P3	Add	part0
		2	P2	4	P4	Add	part1
		part-0.parquet		*part-1.parquet*		*00000.json*	
• Read 02.json • Remove part-0 • Include part-3 Final result: • part-1 • part-2 • part-3 are included in latest data	```df .coalesce(1) .write. format("delta") .mode ("append") .save(DATALAKE_PATH)```	**patientID**	**Name**			**Operation**	**Filename**
		5	P5			Add	part2
		6	P6				
		part-2.parquet				*00001.json*	
	```deltaTable = DeltaTable \ .forPath(spark, DATALAKE_PATH) deltaTable.update(condition = col("patientId") == 1, set = {'name': lit("p11")})```	**patientID**	**Name**			**Action**	**Part name**
		1	P11			Remove	part0
		2	P2			Add	part3
		part-3.parquet				*00002.json*	

Figure 2-7. Updates and the transaction log

In this example, we execute the following steps:

1. The first code snippet creates a Spark DataFrame, with the `patientId` and `Name` of four patients. We write the DataFrame to a Delta table, forcing the data into two files with `.coalesce(2)`. As a result, we write two files. A transaction log entry is created (*00000.json*) once the *part-00000.parquet* and *part-00001.parquet* files are written. Note the transaction log entry contains two *add file* actions indicating the *part-00000.parquet* and the *part-00001.parquet* files were added.

2. The next code snippet appends the data for two more patients (P5 and P6). This results in the creation of the *part-00002.parquet* file. Again, once the file is written, the transaction log entry is written (*00001.json*), and the transaction is complete. Again, the transaction log file has one *add file* action, indicating that a file (*part-00002.parquet*) was added.

3. The code performs an update. In this case, we want to update the patient's name with `patientId` 1 from P1 to P11. Currently, the record for `patientId` 1 is present in part-0. To perform an update, part-0 is read and a map operator is used to update any record matching the `patientId` of 1 from P1 to P11. A new file is written as part-3. Finally, Delta Lake writes the transaction log entry (*00002.json*). Notice it writes a *remove file* action, saying that the part-0 file is removed, and an *add* action, saying that the part-3 file has been added. This is because the data from part-0 was rewritten into part-3, and all modified rows (along with the unmodified rows) have been added to part-3, rendering the part-0 file obsolete.

Notice that Delta Lake does not delete the part-0 file, since a user might want to go back in time with time travel, in which case the file is required. The VACUUM command can clean up unused files like this (Chapter 6 covers time travel and cleaning up unused files in detail).

Now that we have seen how the data is written during an update, let's look at how a read would determine what to read, as illustrated in Figure 2-8.

Final data read:

patientID	Name
3	P3
4	P4
5	P5
6	P6
1	P11
2	P2

Figure 2-8. Reading after an update

The read would proceed as follows:

1. The first transaction log entry is read (*00000.json*). This entry tells Delta Lake to include the part-0 and part-1 files.

2. The next entry (*00001.json*) is read telling Delta Lake to include the part-2 file.

3. The last entry (*00002.json*) is read, which informs the reader to remove the part-0 file and include part-3.

As a result, the reader ends up reading part-1, part-2, and part-3, resulting in the correct data shown in Figure 2-8.

Scaling Massive Metadata

Now that we have seen how the transaction log records each operation, we can have many very large files with thousands of transaction log entries for a single Parquet file. How does Delta Lake scale its metadata handling without needing to read thousands of small files, which would negatively impact Spark's reading performance? Spark tends to be most effective when reading large files, so how do we resolve this?

Once the Delta Lake writer has made the commits to the transaction log, it will save a *checkpoint file* in Parquet format in the *_delta_log* folder. The Delta Lake writer will continue to generate a new checkpoint every 10 commits.

A checkpoint file saves the entire state of the table at a given point in time. Note that "state" refers to the different actions, not the file's actual content. So, it will contain the *add file*, *remove file*, *update metadata*, *commit info*, etc., actions, with all the context information. It will save this list in native Parquet format. This will allow Spark to read the checkpoint quickly. This gives the Spark reader a "shortcut" to fully reproduce a table's state and avoid reprocessing thousands of small JSON files, which could be inefficient.

Checkpoint file example

Following is an example (illustrated in Figure 2-9) where we execute multiple commits, and a checkpoint file is generated as a result. This example uses the code file *chap02/ TransactionLogCheckPointExample.py* from the book's repository.

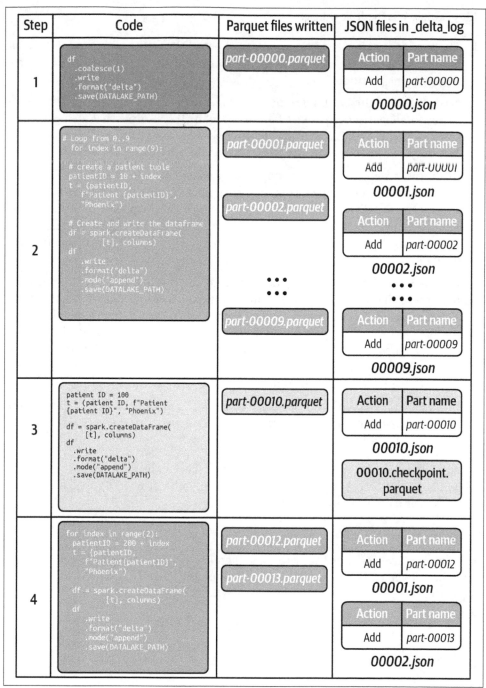

Step	Code	Parquet files written	JSON files in _delta_log
1	```df\n .coalesce(1)\n .write\n .format("delta")\n .save(DATALAKE_PATH)```	part-00000.parquet	**Action / Part name** Add / part-00000 *00000.json*
2	```# Loop from 0..9\nfor index in range(9):\n\n # create a patient tuple\n patientID = 10 + index\n t = (patientID,\n f"Patient {patientID}",\n "Phoenix")\n\n # Create and write the dataframe\n df = spark.createDataFrame(\n [t], columns)\n df\n .write\n .format("delta")\n .mode("append")\n .save(DATALAKE_PATH)```	part-00001.parquet part-00002.parquet · · · · · · part-00009.parquet	**Action / Part name** Add / part-00001 *00001.json* **Action / Part name** Add / part-00002 *00002.json* · · · · · · **Action / Part name** Add / part-00009 *00009.json*
3	```patient ID = 100\nt = (patient ID, f"Patient\n{patient ID}", "Phoenix")\n\ndf = spark.createDataFrame(\n [t], columns)\ndf\n .write\n .format("delta")\n .mode("append")\n .save(DATALAKE_PATH)```	part-00010.parquet	**Action / Part name** Add / part-00010 *00010.json* 00010.checkpoint.parquet
4	```for index in range(2):\n patientID = 200 + index\n t = (patientID,\n f"Patient{patientID}",\n "Phoenix")\n\n df = spark.createDataFrame(\n [t], columns)\n df\n .write\n .format("delta")\n .mode("append")\n .save(DATALAKE_PATH)```	part-00012.parquet part-00013.parquet	**Action / Part name** Add / part-00012 *00001.json* **Action / Part name** Add / part-00013 *00002.json*

Figure 2-9. Checkpoint file example

This example has the following steps:

1. The first code snippet creates a standard Spark DataFrame with several patients. Note that we apply a `coalesce(1)` transaction to the DataFrame, forcing that data into one partition.

   Next, we write the DataFrame in Delta Lake format to a storage file. We verify that a single *part-0001.parquet* file was written. We also see that a single transaction log entry (*00000.json*) has been created in the *_delta_log* directory. This directory entry contains an *add file* action for the *part-00001.parquet* file.

2. In the next step, we set up a loop over a `range(0, 9)`, which will loop nine times, creating a new patient row, then creating a DataFrame from that tuple, and writing the DataFrame to your storage file. Since you loop nine times, we create nine additional Parquet files, from *part-00001.parquet* through *part-00009.parquet*. We also see nine additional transaction log entries, from *00001.json* through *00009.json*.

3. In step 3, we create one more patient tuple, convert it to a DataFrame, and write it to the Delta table. This creates one additional data file *(part-00010.parquet)*. The transaction log has a standard log entry (*00010.json*) with the *add file* action for the *part-00010.parquet* file. But the interesting fact is that it also creates a *000010.checkpoint.parquet* file. This is the checkpoint mentioned earlier. A checkpoint is generated every 10 commits. This Parquet file contains the entire state of your table at the time of the commit in native Parquet format.

4. In the last step, the code generates two more commits, creating the *part-00011.parquet* and *part-00012.parquet*, and two new log entries with *add file* entries pointing to these files.

If Delta Lake needs to re-create the state of the table, it will simply read the checkpoint file *(000010.checkpoint.parquet)*, and reapply the two additional log entries (*00011.json* and *00012.json*).

Displaying the checkpoint file

Now that we have generated the *checkpoint.parquet* file, let's take a look at its content using the */chapter02/readCheckPointFile.py* Python file:

```
# Set your output path for your Delta table
DATALAKE_PATH = "/book/chapter02/transactionLogCheckPointExample"
CHECKPOINT_PATH = "/_delta_log/00000000000000000010.checkpoint.parquet"
# Read the checkpoint.parquet file
checkpoint_df =                                    \
    spark                                          \
    .read                                          \
    .format("parquet")                             \
    .load(f"{DATALAKE_PATH}{CHECKPOINT_PATH}")

# Display the checkpoint dataframe
checkpoint_df.show()
```

Notice how we do a Parquet format read here, because the checkpoint file is indeed stored in Parquet format, not Delta format.

The content of the checkpoint_df DataFrame is shown here:

```
+----+--------------------+------+--------------------+--------+
| txn|                 add|remove|            metaData|protocol|
+----+--------------------+------+--------------------+--------+
|null|{part-00000-f7d9f...|  null|                null|    null|
|null|{part-00000-a65e0...|  null|                null|    null|
|null|{part-00000-4c3ea...|  null|                null|    null|
|null|{part-00000-8eb1f...|  null|                null|    null|
|null|{part-00000-2e143...|  null|                null|    null|
|null|{part-00000-d1d13...|  null|                null|    null|
|null|{part-00000-650bf...|  null|                null|    null|
|null|{part-00000-ea06e...|  null|                null|    null|
|null|{part-00000-79258...|  null|                null|    null|
|null|{part-00000-23558...|  null|                null|    null|
|null|                null|  null|                null|  {1, 2}|
|null|                null|  null|{376ce2d6-11b1-46...|    null|
|null|{part-00000-eb29a...|  null|                null|    null|
+----+--------------------+------+--------------------+--------+
```

As you can see, the checkpoint file contains columns for the different actions (add, remove, metadata, and protocol). We see *add file* actions for the different Parquet data files, an *update metadata* action from when we created the Delta table, and a *change protocol* action resulting from the initial Delta table write.

Note that DataFrame.show() will not show the DataFrame records in order. The *change protocol* and *update metadata* records are always the first records in the checkpoint file, followed by the different *add file* actions.

Conclusion

As we begin the journey into Delta Lake, it all starts with the initial setup. This chapter walked through how to set up Delta Lake with PySpark and the Spark Scala shell on your local machine, while covering necessary libraries and packages to enable you to run a PySpark program with Delta Lake extensions. You can also simplify this setup process using a cloud-based tool like Databricks to develop, run, and share Spark-based applications like Delta Lake.

After reading about getting Delta Lake up and running, we began to learn about the foundational components of Delta Lake that inevitably enable most of the core features we will discuss throughout this book. By adding checkpoint files to enable scalable metadata and a transaction log to standard Parquet files to support ACID transactions, Delta Lake has the key elements to support reliability and scalability. And now that we have established these foundational components, you will learn more about basic operations on a Delta table in the next chapter.

## CHAPTER 3

Basic Operations on Delta Tables

Delta tables can be created in a variety of ways. How you create your tables largely depends on your familiarity with the toolset. If you are primarily a SQL developer, you can use SQL's `CREATE TABLE` to create a Delta table, while Python users may prefer the `DataFrameWriter` API or the fine-grained and easy to use `DeltaTableBuilder` API.

When creating tables you can define `GENERATED` columns, the values of which are automatically generated based on a user-specified function over other columns in the Delta table. While some restrictions apply, generated columns are a powerful way to enrich your Delta table schemas.

Delta tables can be read by standard ANSI SQL or using the popular PySpark `DataFrameReader` API. You can write to a Delta table by using the classic SQL `INSERT` statement, or you can append a DataFrame to the table. Finally, leveraging the SQL `COPY INTO` option is a great way to append large amounts of data quickly.

Partitioning a Delta table based upon your frequently used query pattern can dramatically improve your query and DML performance. The individual files that make up your Delta table will be organized in subdirectories that align to the values of your partitioning columns.

Delta Lake allows you to associate custom metadata with the commit entries in your transaction log. This can be leveraged to tag sensitive commits for auditing purposes. You can also store custom tags in your table properties, so just like you can have tags for your cloud resources, you can now associate those tags with your Delta tables. You can also modify certain Delta capabilities. For example, you can associate the `delta.appendonly` property to a table to prevent deletes and updates.

Creating a Delta Table

Delta Lake enables us to create tables in three different ways:

SQL Data Definition Language (DDL) commands
> SQL developers are already very familiar with the classic `CREATE TABLE` command, and you will be able to use it to create a Delta table by adding just a few attributes.

PySpark `DataFrameWriter` *API*
> Big data Python (and Scala) developers will very likely already be very familiar with this API, and you will be able to continue to use it with Delta tables.

`DeltaTableBuilder` *API*
> This is a new API specifically designed for Delta tables. It uses the popular *Builder* pattern, and it gives very fine-grained control over every Delta table and column attribute.

In the following sections we get hands-on with each of these table creation methods.

Creating a Delta Table with SQL DDL

The version of SQL used in Spark compute environments is called Spark SQL (*https://oreil.ly/NQ9UE*), which is a variant of ANSI SQL supported by Spark. Spark SQL is generally compatible with ANSI standard SQL. Refer to the Spark documentation (*https://oreil.ly/LWjZA*) for additional details on the Spark SQL variant.

As mentioned earlier, you can use the standard SQL DDL commands in Spark SQL to create a Delta table:[1]

```
%sql
-- Create a Delta table by specifying the delta format, followed
-- by the path in quotes
CREATE TABLE IF NOT EXISTS delta.`/mnt/datalake/book/chapter03/rateCard`
(
    rateCodeId   INT,
    rateCodeDesc STRING
)
USING DELTA
```

The notation that you are using for the table name is the `file_format` | `` `path_to_table` `` notation, where the `file_format` is delta, and `path_to_table` is the path to the Delta table.

---

1 GitHub repo location: */Chapter03/02 - CreateDeltaTableWithSql*

Using this format can get tedious, since filepaths can get rather long in the real world. This is where *catalogs* come in. A catalog allows you to register a table with a `database.table_name` notation, where database is a logical grouping of tables, and `table_name` is a shorthand for the table. For example, if you first created a database named `taxidb` as follows:

```
%sql
CREATE DATABASE IF NOT EXISTS taxidb;
```

Then you could create the above table as follows:

```
%sql
-- Create the table using the taxidb catalog
CREATE TABLE IF NOT EXISTS taxidb.rateCard
(
    rateCodeId    INT,
    rateCodeDesc  STRING
)
USING DELTA
LOCATION '/mnt/datalake/book/chapter03/rateCard'
```

From this point forward, you can refer to this Delta table as `taxidb.rateCard`, which is easier to remember and type than `delta./mnt/datalake/book/chapter03/rateCard`, or possibly an even longer pathname. The most widely used catalog in the Spark ecosystem is the *Hive* catalog.

When running a directory listing on the data lake location where the table was created, you can see that our directory is empty (since you have not loaded any data), except for the *_delta_log* directory, which contains the table's transaction log:

```
%sh
ls -al /dbfs/mnt/datalake/book/chapter03/rateCard
total 12
drwxrwxrwx 2 root root 4096 Dec  2 19:02 .
drwxrwxrwx 2 root root 4096 Dec  2 19:02 ..
drwxrwxrwx 2 root root 4096 Dec  2 16:40 _delta_log
```

Please note that since you are running this as a shell command in the Databricks Community Edition environment, you have to prefix our path for the `ls` command with `/dbfs`.

When you open the *_delta_log* directory, you see our first transaction log entry:

```
%sh
ls -al /dbfs/mnt/datalake/book/chapter03/rateCard/_delta_log
total 15
drwxrwxrwx 2 root root 4096 Dec  2 19:02 .
drwxrwxrwx 2 root root 4096 Dec  2 19:02 ..
-rwxrwxrwx 1 root root 1886 Dec  2 19:02 00000000000000000000.crc
-rwxrwxrwx 1 root root  939 Dec  2 19:02 00000000000000000000.json
```

In the transaction log discussion in Chapter 2, you read about the different *actions* that can be written to your transaction log entry. One of those actions is the *metadata* action, which describes the schema of the table, the partitioning columns (if applicable), and other information. This *metadata* action is always written to the first transaction log entry created for our new table.

To find this *metadata* action, you can do a search for the string *metadata* in the transaction entry:

```
%sh
grep metadata /dbfs/mnt/datalake/book/chapter03/rateCard
  /_delta_log/00000.json > /tmp/metadata.json
python -m json.tool /tmp/metadata.json
```

This produces the following output:

```
{
    "metaData": {
        "id": "f79c4c11-a807-49bc-93f4-2bbe778e2a04",
        "format": {
            "provider": "parquet",
            "options": {}
        },
        "schemaString": "{\"type\":\"struct\",
        \"fields\":[{\"name\":\"rateCodeId\",
        \"type\":\"integer\",\"nullable\":true,
        \"metadata\":{}},{\"name\":\"rateCodeDesc\",
        \"type\":\"string\",\"nullable\":true,
        \"metadata\":{}}]}",
        "partitionColumns": [],
        "configuration": {},
        "createdTime": 1670007736533
    }
}
```

Here, you see that Delta Lake has written the schema of the table to the transaction log entry, together with some auditing and partitioning information.

In the preceding command, we first perform a `grep` command, which searches for the string *metadata* in the transaction log entry. We then write the output of that to a temp file. The next line uses `python -m json.tool` with the temp file as input. The `json.tool` Python module will "pretty print" the content of a JSON file, which can be very handy for readability.

The DESCRIBE Statement

The SQL `DESCRIBE` command can be used to return the basic metadata for a Parquet file or Delta table. The metadata returned for a table includes one line for each column with the following information:

- The column name
- The column data type
- Any comments that were applied to the column

Following is an example of the `DESCRIBE` command at the table level:

```
%sql
DESCRIBE TABLE taxidb.rateCard;


+--------------+-----------+---------+
| col_name     | data_type | comment |
+--------------+-----------+---------+
| rateCodeId   | int       | <null>  |
| rateCodeDesc | string    | <null>  |
+--------------+-----------+---------+
```

When you want to find the Delta Lake-specific attributes, you can also use the `DESCRIBE TABLE EXTENDED` command, which provides more detailed metadata information, including the following generic attributes:

- The catalog name for the database in which the table was created (in this case the Hive metastore)
- The Hive database
- The table name
- The location of the underlying files
- The owner of the table
- The table properties

The following Delta Lake-specific attributes are also included:

delta.minReaderVersion

The minimum required protocol reader version for a reader that can read from this Delta table.

delta.minWriterVersion

The minimum required protocol writer version for a writer that can write to this Delta table. Please refer to the Delta Lake documentation (*https://oreil.ly/R-Q9M*) for a full listing of all available table properties.

Following is an example of the DESCRIBE TABLE EXTENDED command:

```
%sql
DESCRIBE TABLE EXTENDED taxidb.rateCard;
```

The generates the following output:

```
+-----------------------------+-------------------------------+---------+
| col_name                    | data_type                     | comment |
+-----------------------------+-------------------------------+---------+
| rateCodeId                  | int                           | <null>  |
| rateCodeDesc                | string                        | <null>  |
|                             |                               |         |
| # Detailed Table Information|                               |         |
| Catalog                     | hive_metastore                |         |
| Database                    | taxidb                        |         |
| Table                       | ratecard                      |         |
| Type                        | EXTERNAL                      |         |
| Location                    | dbfs:/.../chapter03/rateCard  |         |
| Provider                    | delta                         |         |
| Owner                       | root                          |         |
| Table Properties            | [delta.minReaderVersion=1,    |         |
|                             |   delta.minWriterVersion=2]   |         |
+-----------------------------+-------------------------------+---------+
```

So far, we have covered the creation of Delta tables with the SQL DDL. In the next section, we will switch back to Python, and look at how you can use the familiar PySpark DataFrames to create new Delta tables.

Creating Delta Tables with the DataFrameWriter API

Spark DataFrames resemble relational database tables or Excel spreadsheets with headers. The data resides in rows and columns of different data types. The collection of functions that lets us read, write, and manipulate DataFrames is collectively known as the Spark DataFrameWriter API.

Creating a managed table

When you read the Spark and/or Delta documentation, you will hear the terms *managed* and *unmanaged* table. A Delta table that is created *with a location* is known as an *unmanaged table*. For these tables, Spark only manages the metadata, and requires the user to specify the exact location where you wish to save the underlying data for the table, or alternatively, the source directory from which data will be pulled to create the table (if you are using the `DataFrameWriter` API).

A Delta table that is created *without a location* is referred to as a *managed table*. Spark manages both the metadata and the actual data for managed tables. The data is stored under the */spark-warehouse* subfolder (in the Apache Spark scenario) or the */user/hive/warehouse* folder (when running on Databricks), which is the default for managed tables.

One of the benefits of the `DataFrameWriter` API is that you can simultaneously create a table and insert data into it from a Spark DataFrame, as shown in the following code snippet:[2]

```
INPUT_PATH = '/databricks-datasets/nyctaxi/taxizone/taxi_rate_code.csv'
DELTALAKE_PATH = \
    'dbfs:/mnt/datalake/book/chapter03/createDeltaTableWithDataFrameWriter'

# Read the DataFrame from the input path
df_rate_codes = spark                                               \
                .read                                               \
                .format("csv")                                      \
                .option("inferSchema", True)                        \
                .option("header", True)                             \
                .load(INPUT_PATH)

# Save our DataFrame as a managed Hive table
df_rate_codes.write.format("delta").saveAsTable('taxidb.rateCard')
```

Here, we first populate the DataFrame from the *taxi_rate_code.csv* file, and then save the DataFrame as a Delta table by specifying the `.format("delta")` option. The schema of the table will be the schema of our DataFrame. Notice that this will be a managed table since we did not specify a location for our data file. You can verify this by running the SQL `DESCRIBE TABLE EXTENDED` command:

---

2 GitHub repo location: */chapter03/04 - The DataFrameWriter API*

```
%sql
DESCRIBE TABLE EXTENDED taxidb.rateCard;
+------------------------------+------------------------------------------------+
| col_name                     | data_type                                      |
+------------------------------+------------------------------------------------+
| RateCodeID                   | int                                            |
| RateCodeDesc                 | string                                         |
|                              |                                                |
| # Detailed Table Information |                                                |
| Catalog                      | hive_metastore                                 |
| Database                     | taxidb                                         |
| Table                        | ratecard                                       |
| Type                         | MANAGED                                        |
| Location                     | dbfs:/user/hive/warehouse/taxidb.db/ratecard   |
| Provider                     | delta                                          |
| Owner                        | root                                           |
| Is_managed_location          | true                                           |
| Table Properties             | [delta.minReaderVersion=1,                     |
|                              |   delta.minWriterVersion=2]                    |
+------------------------------+------------------------------------------------+
```

We see that the data for the table lives in the */user/hive/warehouse* location, and that the type of the table is set to MANAGED.

If you run a SELECT on the table, you can see the data was indeed loaded successfully from the CSV file:

```
%sql
SELECT * FROM taxidb.rateCard
+------------+----------------------+
| RateCodeID | RateCodeDesc         |
+------------+----------------------+
| 1          | Standard Rate        |
| 2          | JFK                  |
| 3          | Newark               |
| 4          | Nassau or Westchester|
| 5          | Negotiated fare      |
| 6          | Group ride           |
+------------+----------------------+
```

Creating an unmanaged table

You can create an unmanaged table by specifying both the path and the name of the Delta table. In the following code, we execute both steps in sequence. First, drop the existing table:

```
%sql
-- Drop the existing table
DROP TABLE IF EXISTS taxidb.rateCard;
```

Next, write out and create the table:

```
# Next, create our Delta table, specifying both
# the path and the Delta table N=name
df_rate_codes                            \
        .write                           \
        .format("delta")                 \
        .mode("overwrite")               \
        .option('path', DELTALAKE_PATH)  \
        .saveAsTable('taxidb.rateCard')
```

Again by performing a simple SELECT we can verify that the data of the DataFrame has been loaded:

```
%sql
SELECT * FROM taxidb.rateCard
```

```
+------------+-----------------------+
| RateCodeID | RateCodeDesc          |
+------------+-----------------------+
| 1          | Standard Rate         |
| 2          | JFK                   |
| 3          | Newark                |
| 4          | Nassau or Westchester |
| 5          | Negotiated fare       |
| 6          | Group ride            |
+------------+-----------------------+
```

Creating a Delta Table with the DeltaTableBuilder API

The last way to create a Delta table is by using the DeltaTableBuilder API. Since it is designed to work with Delta tables, it offers a higher degree of fine-grained control versus the traditional DataFrameWriter API. It is easier for a user to specify additional information such as column comments, table properties, and generated columns.

The *Builder* design pattern is popular in software languages. The Builder pattern aims to "separate the construction of a complex object from its representation so that the same construction process can create different representations." It is used to construct a complex object step-by-step, where the final step will return the object.

The complex object we are building in this case is a Delta table. Delta tables support so many options that it is challenging to design a standard API with many arguments for a single function. Instead, the DeltaTableBuilder has a number of small methods, such as addColumn(), which all return a reference to the Builder object. That way we can keep adding other calls to addColumn(), or other methods of the Builder. The final method we call is execute(), which gathers up all the attributes received, creates the Delta table, and returns a reference to the table to the caller. To use the DeltaTableBuilder, we will need the following import:

```
from delta.tables import *
```

This example creates a managed table:[3]

```
# In this Create Table, you do NOT specify a location, so you are
# creating a MANAGED table
DeltaTable.createIfNotExists(spark)                                   \
    .tableName("taxidb.greenTaxis")                                   \
    .addColumn("RideId", "INT", comment = "Primary Key")              \
    .addColumn("VendorId", "INT", comment = "Ride Vendor")            \
    .addColumn("EventType", "STRING")                                 \
    .addColumn("PickupTime", "TIMESTAMP")                             \
    .addColumn("PickupLocationId", "INT")                             \
    .addColumn("CabLicense", "STRING")                                \
    .addColumn("DriversLicense", "STRING")                            \
    .addColumn("PassengerCount", "INT")                               \
    .addColumn("DropTime", "TIMESTAMP")                               \
    .addColumn("DropLocationId", "INT")                               \
    .addColumn("RateCodeId", "INT", comment = "Ref to RateCard")      \
    .addColumn("PaymentType", "INT")                                  \
    .addColumn("TripDistance", "DOUBLE")                              \
    .addColumn("TotalAmount", "DOUBLE")                               \
    .execute()
```

Since each method returns a reference to the `Builder` object, we can keep calling `.addColumn()` to add each column. Finally, we call `.execute()` to create the Delta table.

Generated Columns

Delta Lake supports *generated columns*, which are a special type of column, the values of which are automatically generated based on a user-specified function over other columns in the Delta table. When you write to a Delta table with generated columns and don't explicitly provide values for them, Delta Lake automatically computes the values.

Let's create an example next. To stay with our taxi theme, we will create a simple version of a yellow taxi table:

```
%sql
CREATE TABLE taxidb.YellowTaxis
(
    RideId          INT        COMMENT 'This is our primary Key column',
    VendorId        INT,
    PickupTime      TIMESTAMP,
    PickupYear      INT        GENERATED ALWAYS AS(YEAR  (PickupTime)),
    PickupMonth     INT        GENERATED ALWAYS AS(MONTH (PickupTime)),
    PickupDay       INT        GENERATED ALWAYS AS(DAY   (PickupTime)),
    DropTime        TIMESTAMP,
    CabNumber       STRING     COMMENT 'Official Yellow Cab Number'
```

---

3 GitHub repo location: */chapter03/05 - The DeltaTableBuilder API*

```
) USING DELTA
LOCATION "/mnt/datalake/book/chapter03/YellowTaxis.delta"
COMMENT 'Table to store Yellow Taxi data'
```

We see the columns with GENERATED ALWAYS AS, which extracts the YEAR, MONTH, and DAY from the PickupTime column. The values for these columns will automatically be populated when we insert a record:

```
%sql
INSERT INTO taxidb.YellowTaxis
    (RideId, VendorId, PickupTime, DropTime, CabNumber)
VALUES
    (5, 101, '2021-7-1T8:43:28UTC+3', '2021-7-1T8:43:28UTC+3', '51-986')
```

When we select the record, we see that the generated columns are automatically populated:

```
%sql
SELECT PickupTime, PickupYear, PickupMonth, PickupDay FROM taxidb.YellowTaxis


+-------------------------+------------+-------------+-----------+
| pickupTime              | pickupYear | pickupMonth | pickupDay |
+-------------------------+------------+-------------+-----------+
| 2021-07-01 05:43:28+00:00 | 2021     | 7           | 1         |
+-------------------------+------------+-------------+-----------+
```

When we do explicitly provide a value for a generated column, the value must satisfy the constraint (<value> ⟺ generation expression) IS TRUE or the insert will fail with an error.

The expression you use in GENERATED ALWAYS AS can be any Spark SQL function that always returns the same result when given the same argument values, with a few exceptions we will touch on soon. You might think you could use a GENERATED column to generate a column with a unique ID like this:

```
%sql
CREATE OR REPLACE TABLE default.dummy
(
    ID   STRING GENERATED ALWAYS AS (UUID()),
    Name STRING
) USING DELTA
```

However, when you try to run this, you get the following error message:

```
Found uuid(). A generated column cannot use a non deterministic expression.
```

The UUID() function will return a different value for each invocation, which violates the preceding rule. There are a few exceptions to this rule for the following types of functions:

- User-defined functions

- Aggregate functions
- Window functions
- Functions returning multiple rows

GENERATED ALWAYS AS columns using the functions listed are valid, and can be very useful in several scenarios, like calculating a standard deviation of a given sample of records.

Reading a Delta Table

We have a few options when reading a table: SQL and PySpark using the DataFrameReader. When we use a notebook in the Databricks Community Edition, we tend to use both SQL and PySpark cells within the notebook. Some things, like a quick SELECT, are just easier and faster to do in SQL, while complex operations are sometimes easier expressed in PySpark and the DataFrameReader. This is of course also dependent on the experience and preferences of the engineer. We recommend a pragmatic approach using a healthy mix of both, depending on the problem you are currently solving.

Reading a Delta Table with SQL

To read a Delta table, we can simply open a SQL cell and write your SQL query. If we set up your environment as specified in the GitHub *READ.ME* file, we will have a Delta table in the */mnt/datalake/book/chapter03/YellowTaxisDelta* folder:

```
%sh
ls -al /dbfs/mnt/datalake/book/chapter03/YellowTaxisDelta
total 236955
drwxrwxrwx 2 root root      4096 Dec  4 18:04 .
drwxrwxrwx 2 root root      4096 Dec  2 19:02 ..
drwxrwxrwx 2 root root      4096 Dec  4 16:41 _delta_log
-rwxrwxrwx 1 root root 134759123 Dec  4 18:04 part-00000-...-c000.snappy.parquet
-rwxrwxrwx 1 root root 107869302 Dec  4 18:04 part-00001-...-c000.snappy.parquet
```

We can quickly register a Delta table location in the metastore, as follows:[4]

```
%sql
CREATE TABLE taxidb.YellowTaxis
USING DELTA
LOCATION "/mnt/datalake/book/chapter03/YellowTaxisDelta/"
```

Once we have created the table, we can do a quick count on the number of records:

```
%sql
SELECT
```

---

4 GitHub repo location: */chapter03/07 - Read Table with SQL*

```
    COUNT(*)
FROM
    taxidb.yellowtaxis
```

This gives us the following count:

```
+----------+
| count(1) |
+----------+
| 9999995  |
+----------+
```

We can see there are almost 10 million rows to work with. We can use another
DESCRIBE command variant to get the details of the table:

```
%sql
DESCRIBE TABLE FORMATTED taxidb.YellowTaxis;
```

DESCRIBE TABLE FORMATTED formats the output, making it a bit more readable:

```
+-----------------------------+-------------------------------------+
| col_name                    | data_type                           |
+-----------------------------+-------------------------------------+
| RideId                      | int                                 |
| VendorId                    | int                                 |
| PickupTime                  | timestamp                           |
| DropTime                    | timestamp                           |
| PickupLocationId            | int                                 |
| DropLocationId              | int                                 |
| CabNumber                   | string                              |
| DriverLicenseNumber         | string                              |
| PassengerCount              | int                                 |
| TripDistance                | double                              |
| RatecodeId                  | int                                 |
| PaymentType                 | int                                 |
| TotalAmount                 | double                              |
| FareAmount                  | double                              |
| Extra                       | double                              |
| MtaTax                      | double                              |
| TipAmount                   | double                              |
| TollsAmount                 | double                              |
| ImprovementSurcharge        | double                              |
|                             |                                     |
| # Detailed Table Information|                                     |
| Catalog                     | hive_metastore                      |
| Database                    | taxidb                              |
| Table                       | YellowTaxis                         |
| Type                        | EXTERNAL                            |
| Location                    | dbfs:/.../chapter03/YellowTaxisDelta |
| Provider                    | delta                               |
| Owner                       | root                                |
| Table Properties            | [delta.minReaderVersion=1,          |
|                             |   delta.minWriterVersion=2]         |
+-----------------------------+-------------------------------------+
```

Because Spark SQL supports most of the ANSI SQL subset, we can use any type of complex query. Following is an example that returns CabNumbers with the most expensive FareAmounts over $50:

```sql
%sql
SELECT
    CabNumber,
    AVG(FareAmount) AS AverageFare
FROM
    taxidb.yellowtaxis
GROUP BY
    CabNumber
HAVING
    AVG(FareAmount) > 50
ORDER BY
    2 DESC
LIMIT 5
```

This gives us:

```
+-----------+-------------+
| cabnumber | AverageFare |
+-----------+-------------+
| SIR104    | 111.5       |
| T628190C  | 109.0       |
| PEACE16   | 89.7        |
| T439972C  | 89.5        |
| T802013C  | 85.0        |
+-----------+-------------+
```

We can also use SQL directly in Python with spark.sql, using standard SQL as the argument. Following is a simple Python snippet that performs the same query as the previous SQL query:

```python
number_of_results = 5
sql_statement = f"""
SELECT
    CabNumber,
    AVG(FareAmount) AS AverageFare
FROM
    taxidb.yellowtaxis
GROUP BY
    CabNumber
HAVING
    AVG(FareAmount) > 50
ORDER BY
    2 DESC
LIMIT {number_of_results}"""

df = spark.sql(sql_statement)
display(df)
```

This produces the same results as the SQL:

```
+-----------+-------------+
| cabnumber | AverageFare |
+-----------+-------------+
| SIR104    | 111.5       |
| T628190C  | 109.0       |
| PEACE16   | 89.7        |
| T439972C  | 89.5        |
| T802013C  | 85.0        |
+-----------+-------------+
```

We recommend using the triple-quotes syntax, which makes it easy to span strings over multiple lines without having to use continuation lines. Also, notice how we have the variable `number_of_results`, and then convert the triple-quote string into an f-string and use the {} syntax to insert the variable for the limit.

Reading a Table with PySpark

To read the same table in PySpark, you can use the `DataFrameReader`. For example, to implement the count of records, we use:[5]

```
df = spark.read.format("delta").table("taxidb.YellowTaxis")
print(f"Number of records: {df.count():,}")
```

Output:

```
Number of records: 9,999,995
```

Note that we specify the Delta format, since our table is a Delta table and we can use the `.table()` method to specify that we want to read the entire table. Finally, we use an f-string, this time with the ":," formatter, which uses a comma separator for every three digits.

Next, let's re-create the code for the top five average fares by cab number, which we did in SQL earlier. The Python code follows:

```
# Make sure to import the functions you want to use
from pyspark.sql.functions import col, avg, desc

# Read YellowTaxis into our DataFrame
df = spark.read.format("delta").table("taxidb.YellowTaxis")

# Perform the GROUP BY, average (AVG), HAVING and order by equivalents
# in pySpark
results = df.groupBy("CabNumber")                           \
            .agg(avg("FareAmount").alias("AverageFare"))    \
            .filter(col("AverageFare") > 50)                \
            .sort(col("AverageFare").desc())                \
            .take(5)
```

---

5 GitHub repo location: */chapter03/Read Table with PySpark*

```
# Print out the result, since this is a list and not a DataFrame
# you an use list comprehension to output the results in a single
# line
[print(result) for result in results]
```

We'll get the following the output:

```
Row(CabNumber='SIR104', AverageFare=111.5)
Row(CabNumber='T628190C', AverageFare=109.0)
Row(CabNumber='PEACE16', AverageFare=89.7)
Row(CabNumber='T439972C', AverageFare=89.5)
Row(CabNumber='T802013C', AverageFare=85.0)
```

We can simply use the groupBy() function to group by a column:

> Note that the result of this is no longer a DataFrame, but a
> pyspark.sql.GroupedData instance, as illustrated in this code
> snippet:
>
> ```
> # Perform a groupBy, and print out the type
> print(type(df.groupBy("CabNumber")))
> ```
>
> This prints out:
>
> ```
> <class 'pyspark.sql.group.GroupedData'>
> ```
>
> Often, a developer new to PySpark might assume that groupBy()
> returns a DataFrame, but it returns a GroupedData instance, so you
> have to use GroupedData methods such as agg() and filter()
> instead of DataFrame functions such as avg() and where().

To calculate an average, we first have to use the .agg() method. Within the method we can specify which aggregate you want to calculate, which in this case is .avg() (average). In Python, the equivalent of the HAVING condition is the .filter() method, within which we can specify the filter using a filter expression. Finally, we use the .sort() method to sort the data, and then use .take() to extract the first five results. Note that the .take() function will return a Python list. Since we have a list here, we can use *list comprehension* to output each result in the list.

Writing to a Delta Table

There are various ways to write to a Delta table. You might want to rewrite an entire table, or you might want to append to a table. The more advanced topics, such as updates and merges, will be discussed in Chapter 4.

We first will clean out our YellowTaxis table, so that we have a clean slate, and then we will use a traditional SQL INSERT statement to insert data. Next, we will append the data from a smaller CSV file. We will also take a quick look at the overwrite mode when writing a Delta table, and finally we will use the SQL `COPY INTO` feature to merge in a large CSV file.

Cleaning Out the YellowTaxis Table

We can re-create our Delta table with a `CREATE TABLE` statement:[6]

```
%sql
CREATE TABLE taxidb.YellowTaxis
(
    RideId                  INT,
    VendorId                INT,
    PickupTime              TIMESTAMP,
    DropTime                TIMESTAMP,
    PickupLocationId        INT,
    DropLocationId          INT,
    CabNumber               STRING,
    DriverLicenseNumber     STRING,
    PassengerCount          INT,
    TripDistance            DOUBLE,
    RatecodeId              INT,
    PaymentType             INT,
    TotalAmount             DOUBLE,
    FareAmount              DOUBLE,
    Extra                   DOUBLE,
    MtaTax                  DOUBLE,
    TipAmount               DOUBLE,
    TollsAmount             DOUBLE,
    ImprovementSurcharge    DOUBLE
) USING DELTA
LOCATION "/mnt/datalake/book/chapter03/YellowTaxisDelta"
```

With the table set up, we are ready to insert data.

Inserting Data with SQL INSERT

To insert a record into the `YellowTaxis` Delta table, we can use the SQL `INSERT` command:

```
%sql
INSERT INTO taxidb.yellowtaxis
(RideId, VendorId, PickupTime, DropTime,
 PickupLocationId, DropLocationId, CabNumber,
 DriverLicenseNumber, PassengerCount, TripDistance,
 RatecodeId, PaymentType, TotalAmount,
 FareAmount, Extra, MtaTax, TipAmount,
 TollsAmount, ImprovementSurcharge)
```

---

6 GitHub repo location: */chapter03/10 - Writing to a Delta Table*

```
VALUES(9999995, 1, '2019-11-01T00:00:00.000Z',
       '2019-11-01T00:02:23.573Z', 65, 71, 'TAC304',
       '453987', 2, 4.5, 1, 1, 20.34, 15.0, 0.5,
       0.4, 2.0, 2.0, 1.1)
```

This will insert one row:

```
+---------------------+---------------------+
| num_affected_rows | num_inserted_rows |
+---------------------+---------------------+
|         1         |         1         |
+---------------------+---------------------+
```

Verify the data has loaded correctly with a SQL SELECT statement and WHERE clause for the inserted RideId:

```
%sql
SELECT count(RideId) AS count FROM taxidb.YellowTaxis
WHERE RideId = 9999995
```

Output:

```
+-------+
| count |
+-------+
|   1   |
+-------+
```

The output shows that all data has been loaded correctly.

Appending a DataFrame to a Table

Now let's append a DataFrame to our table. In this case we will load the DataFrame from a CSV file. In order to correctly load the data, we don't want to infer the schema. Instead we will use the schema of the YellowTaxis table that we know is correct.

We can easily extract the schema by loading up a DataFrame from the table:

```
df = spark.read.format("delta").table("taxidb.YellowTaxis")
yellowTaxiSchema = df.schema
print(yellowTaxiSchema)
```

This shows the table schema is as follows:

```
root
 |-- RideId: integer (nullable = true)
 |-- VendorId: integer (nullable = true)
 |-- PickupTime: timestamp (nullable = true)
 |-- DropTime: timestamp (nullable = true)
 |-- PickupLocationId: integer (nullable = true)
 |-- DropLocationId: integer (nullable = true)
 |-- CabNumber: string (nullable = true)
 |-- DriverLicenseNumber: string (nullable = true)
```

```
|-- PassengerCount: integer (nullable = true)
|-- TripDistance: double (nullable = true)
|-- RatecodeId: integer (nullable = true)
|-- PaymentType: integer (nullable = true)
|-- TotalAmount: double (nullable = true)
|-- FareAmount: double (nullable = true)
|-- Extra: double (nullable = true)
|-- MtaTax: double (nullable = true)
|-- TipAmount: double (nullable = true)
|-- TollsAmount: double (nullable = true)
|-- ImprovementSurcharge: double (nullable = true)
```

Now that we have the schema, we can load a new DataFrame (df_for_append) from the appended CSV file:

```
df_for_append = spark.read                                          \
    .option("header", "true")                                       \
    .schema(yellowTaxiSchema)                                       \
    .csv("/mnt/datalake/book/data files/YellowTaxis_append.csv")
display(df_for_append)
```

We see the following output (partial output is displayed):

```
+----------+-----------+---------------------+---------------------+
| RideId   | VendorId  | PickupTime          | DropTime            |
+----------+-----------+---------------------+---------------------+
| 9999996  | 1         | 2019-01-01T00:00:00 | 2022-03-01T00:13:13 |
+----------+-----------+---------------------+---------------------+
| 9999997  | 1         | 2019-01-01T00:00:00 | 2022-03-01T00:09:21 |
+----------+-----------+---------------------+---------------------+
| 9999998  | 1         | 2019-01-01T00:00:00 | 2022-03-01T00:09:15 |
+----------+-----------+---------------------+---------------------+
| 9999999  | 1         | 2019-01-01T00:00:00 | 2022-03-01T00:10:01 |
+----------+-----------+---------------------+---------------------+
```

We now have four additional rows, all with a VendorId of 1. We can now append this CSV file to the Delta table:

```
df_for_append.write             \
    .mode("append")             \
    .format("delta")            \
    .save("/mnt/datalake/book/chapter03/YellowTaxisDelta")
```

This appends the data directly to the Delta table. Since we had one row in the table before from the INSERT statement and we inserted four additional rows, we know that we should now have five rows in the YellowTaxis table:

```
%sql
SELECT
    COUNT(*)
FROM
    taxidb.YellowTaxis
+----------+
| count(1) |
+----------+
| 5        |
+----------+
```

We now have five rows.

Using the OverWrite Mode When Writing to a Delta Table

In the previous example we used `.mode("append")` when using the `DataFrameWriter` API to write to a Delta table. Delta Lake also supports the overwrite mode when writing to a Delta table. When you use this mode you will atomically replace all of the data in the table.

If we had used `.mode("overwrite")` in the previous code block, we would have overwritten the entire `YellowTaxis` Delta table with just the `df_for_append` DataFrame.

Even if you use `.mode("overwrite")` in your code, the old part files are not immediately physically deleted. In order to support features such as time travel, these files cannot be deleted immediately. We can use commands such as `VACUUM` to physically delete these files later when we are sure they are no longer needed. Time travel and the `VACUUM` command are covered in Chapter 6.

Inserting Data with the SQL COPY INTO Command

We can use the SQL `COPY INTO` command to append data to our table. This command is especially useful when we need to quickly append very large amounts of data.

We can use the following command to append the data from a CSV file:

```
%sql
COPY INTO taxidb.yellowtaxis
FROM (
    SELECT      RideId::Int
              , VendorId::Int
              , PickupTime::Timestamp
              , DropTime::Timestamp
              , PickupLocationId::Int
              , DropLocationId::Int
              , CabNumber::String
              , DriverLicenseNumber::String
              , PassengerCount::Int
              , TripDistance::Double
              , RateCodeId::Int
```

```
         , PaymentType::Int
         , TotalAmount::Double
         , FareAmount::Double
         , Extra::Double
         , MtaTax::Double
         , TipAmount::Double
         , TollsAmount::Double
         , ImprovementSurcharge::Double

    FROM '/mnt/datalake/book/DataFiles/YellowTaxisLargeAppend.csv'
)
FILEFORMAT = CSV
FORMAT_OPTIONS ("header" = "true")
```

All fields in a CSV file would be strings, so we need to provide some type of schema with a SQL `SELECT` statement when we load the data. This provides the type of each column, ensuring that we are loading the right schema. Note that the `FILEFORMAT`, in this case CSV, is specified. Finally, because our file has a header, we need to specify the header with `FORMAT_OPTIONS`.

The output of this statement is:

```
+---------------------+---------------------+
|  num_affected_rows  |  num_inserted_rows  |
+---------------------+---------------------+
|      9999995        |      9999995        |
+---------------------+---------------------+
```

You can see that we inserted almost 10 million rows in just a few seconds. The `COPY INTO` command also keeps track of and will not reload any previously loaded files. We can test this by running the `COPY INTO` command again:

```
+---------------------+---------------------+
|  num_affected_rows  |  num_inserted_rows  |
+---------------------+---------------------+
|          0          |          0          |
+---------------------+---------------------+
```

As you can see, no additional rows were loaded. Finally, when we check the final row count, we will see that we now have one million rows:

```
%sql
SELECT
    COUNT(*)
FROM
    taxidb.YellowTaxis
```

Output:

```
+-----------+
|  count(1) |
+-----------+
| 10000000  |
+-----------+
```

Partitions

Delta tables are often accessed with a standard query pattern. For example, data from IoT systems tends to be accessed by day, hour, or even minute. The analysts querying the yellow taxi data might want to access the data by VendorId and so on.

These use cases lend themselves well to *partitioning*. Partitioning your data to align with your query patterns can dramatically speed up query performance, especially when combined with other performance optimizations, such as Z-ordering.[7] A Delta table *partition* is composed of a folder with a subset of data rows that share the same value for one or more column(s).

 Note that this type of on-disk partitioning should *not* be confused with the partitioning that Spark applies when processing a Data-Frame. Spark applies in-memory partitioning to enable tasks to run in parallel and independently on a large number of nodes in a Spark cluster.

For example, for the yellow taxi data, the partitioning column could be VendorId. After partitioning your table, individual folders will be created for each VendorId. The last part of the folder name will have VendorId=XX:

```
drwxrwxrwx 2 root root 4096 Dec 13 15:16 VendorId=1
drwxrwxrwx 2 root root 4096 Dec 13 15:16 VendorId=2
drwxrwxrwx 2 root root 4096 Dec 13 15:16 VendorId=4
```

Once the table is partitioned, all queries with predicates that include the partition columns will run much faster, since Spark can immediately select the folder with the correct partition. You can partition data when you create a Delta table by specifying a PARTITIONED BY clause.

---

7 Z-ordering is covered in Chapter 5.

At the time of writing, partitions are the recommended approach to align data to your query patterns to increase query performance. A new feature in Delta Lake called *liquid clustering* is currently in preview, which you will learn about in Chapter 5. We felt that it was important for readers to understand how partitions work and how you can apply them manually before learning about features that automate and replace these commands. The new feature, liquid clustering, will be generally available in the near future. You can learn more and stay up-to-date on the status of liquid clustering at the Delta Lake documentation website and this feature request (*https://oreil.ly/7u3wb*).

Partitioning by a single column

Let's take our `YellowTaxis` table and create a new version that is partitioned by `VendorId`. First, create the partitioned table:[8]

```sql
%sql
CREATE TABLE taxidb.YellowTaxisPartitioned
(
    RideId                  INT,
    VendorId                INT,
    PickupTime              TIMESTAMP,
    DropTime                TIMESTAMP,
    PickupLocationId        INT,
    DropLocationId          INT,
    CabNumber               STRING,
    DriverLicenseNumber     STRING,
    PassengerCount          INT,
    TripDistance            DOUBLE,
    RatecodeId              INT,
    PaymentType             INT,
    TotalAmount             DOUBLE,
    FareAmount              DOUBLE,
    Extra                   DOUBLE,
    MtaTax                  DOUBLE,
    TipAmount               DOUBLE,
    TollsAmount             DOUBLE,
    ImprovementSurcharge    DOUBLE
) USING DELTA
PARTITIONED BY(VendorId)
LOCATION "/mnt/datalake/book/chapter03/YellowTaxisDeltaPartitioned"
```

Notice the `PARTITIONED BY(VendorId)` clause. Now that you have your table, you will load the data from our old `YellowTaxis` table, and write that data to the new table. First, read the data with the `DataFrameReader`:

---

8 GitHub repo location: */chapter03/11 - Partitions*

```
input_df = spark.read.format("delta").table("taxidb.YellowTaxis")
```

Next, use the `DataFrameWriter` to write the data to the partitioned Delta table:

```
input_df                                                              \
    .write                                                            \
    .format("delta")                                                  \
    .mode("overwrite")                                                \
    .save("/mnt/datalake/book/chapter03/YellowTaxisDeltaPartitioned")
```

Now when we look at the table's directory, we'll see a subdirectory for every `VendorID`:

```
%sh
ls -al /dbfs/mnt/datalake/book/chapter03/YellowTaxisDeltaPartitioned
drwxrwxrwx 2 root root 4096 Dec  5 17:39 .
drwxrwxrwx 2 root root 4096 Dec  2 19:02 ..
drwxrwxrwx 2 root root 4096 Dec  5 16:44 VendorId=1
drwxrwxrwx 2 root root 4096 Dec  5 16:44 VendorId=2
drwxrwxrwx 2 root root 4096 Dec  5 16:44 VendorId=4
drwxrwxrwx 2 root root 4096 Dec  5 16:44 _delta_log
```

When we look at the distinct `VendorId`, we see that you indeed only have those three IDs:

```
%sql
SELECT
    DISTINCT(VendorId)
FROM
    taxidb.YellowTaxisPartitioned;
```

We will see the same IDs:

```
+----------+
| VendorId |
+----------+
| 2        |
| 1        |
| 4        |
+----------+
```

The `VendorId` subdirectories contain the individual Parquet files, as shown here for `VendorId=4`:

```
%sh
ls -al /dbfs/mnt/datalake/book/chapter03/YellowTaxisDeltaPartitioned/VendorId=4
total 3378
drwxrwxrwx 2 root root   4096 Dec  5 17:41 .
drwxrwxrwx 2 root root   4096 Dec  5 17:39 ..
-rwxrwxrwx 1 root root 627551 Dec  5 17:41 part-00000-...parquet
-rwxrwxrwx 1 root root 618844 Dec  5 17:41 part-00001-...parquet
-rwxrwxrwx 1 root root 616377 Dec  5 17:41 part-00002-...parquet
-rwxrwxrwx 1 root root 614035 Dec  5 17:41 part-00003-...parquet
-rwxrwxrwx 1 root root 612410 Dec  5 17:41 part-00004-...parquet
-rwxrwxrwx 1 root root 360432 Dec  5 17:41 part-00005-...parquet
```

Partitioning by multiple columns

You don't have to partition by just one column. We can use multiple hierarchical columns as partitioning columns. For example, for IoT data, we might want to partition by day, hour, and minute, because that is the most commonly used query pattern.

For example, let's assume that we would not only want our YellowTaxis table partitioned by VendorId, but also by RateCodeId. First, we would have to drop the existing YellowTaxisPartitioned table and its underlying files. Next, we can re-create the table:

```
%sql
-- Create the table
CREATE TABLE taxidb.YellowTaxisPartitioned
(
    RideId                  INT,
    ...
) USING DELTA
PARTITIONED BY(VendorId, RatecodeId) -- Partition by VendorId AND rateCodeId
LOCATION "/mnt/datalake/book/chapter03/YellowTaxisDeltaPartitioned"
```

Notice the updated partition clause: PARTITIONED BY(VendorId, RatecodeId).

After this, we can reload the table the same way we did before. Once the table is loaded, we can take another look at the directory structure. The first level still looks the same:

```
%sh
ls -al /dbfs/mnt/datalake/book/chapter03/YellowTaxisDeltaPartitioned
drwxrwxrwx 2 root root 4096 Dec 13 15:33 .
drwxrwxrwx 2 root root 4096 Dec  2 19:02 ..
drwxrwxrwx 2 root root 4096 Dec 13 15:16 VendorId=1
drwxrwxrwx 2 root root 4096 Dec 13 15:16 VendorId=2
drwxrwxrwx 2 root root 4096 Dec 13 15:16 VendorId=4
drwxrwxrwx 2 root root 4096 Dec 13 15:16 _delta_log
```

When we take a look at the VendorId=1 directory, we see the partitioning by RatecodeId:

```
%sh
ls -al /dbfs/mnt/datalake/book/chapter03/YellowTaxisDeltaPartitioned/VendorId=1
drwxrwxrwx 2 root root 4096 Dec 13 15:35 .
drwxrwxrwx 2 root root 4096 Dec 13 15:33 ..
drwxrwxrwx 2 root root 4096 Dec 13 15:16 RatecodeId=1
drwxrwxrwx 2 root root 4096 Dec 13 15:16 RatecodeId=2
drwxrwxrwx 2 root root 4096 Dec 13 15:16 RatecodeId=3
drwxrwxrwx 2 root root 4096 Dec 13 15:16 RatecodeId=4
drwxrwxrwx 2 root root 4096 Dec 13 15:16 RatecodeId=5
drwxrwxrwx 2 root root 4096 Dec 13 15:16 RatecodeId=6
drwxrwxrwx 2 root root 4096 Dec 13 15:16 RatecodeId=99
```

Finally, when we query at the `RatecodeId` level:

```sh
%sh
ls -al /dbfs/.../chapter03/YellowTaxisDeltaPartitioned/VendorId=1/RatecodeId=1
```

We can see the Parquet files for that partition:

```
drwxrwxrwx 2 root root     4096 Dec 13 15:35 .
drwxrwxrwx 2 root root     4096 Dec 13 15:35 ..
-rwxrwxrwx 1 root root 10621353 Dec 13 15:35 part-00000-...parquet
-rwxrwxrwx 1 root root 10547673 Dec 13 15:35 part-00001-...parquet
-rwxrwxrwx 1 root root 10566377 Dec 13 15:35 part-00002-...parquet
-rwxrwxrwx 1 root root 10597523 Dec 13 15:35 part-00003-...parquet
-rwxrwxrwx 1 root root 10570937 Dec 13 15:35 part-00004-...parquet
-rwxrwxrwx 1 root root  6119491 Dec 13 15:35 part-00005-...parquet
-rwxrwxrwx 1 root root 13820133 Dec 13 15:35 part-00007-...parquet
-rwxrwxrwx 1 root root 24076060 Dec 13 15:35 part-00008-...parquet
-rwxrwxrwx 1 root root  6772609 Dec 13 15:35 part-00009-...parquet
```

> While this type of partitioning by multiple columns is supported, we want to point out some pitfalls. The number of files created will be the product of the cardinality of both columns, so in this case the number of vendors times the number of rate cards. This can lead to the "small file problem" where a large number of small Parquet part files are created.
>
> Sometimes other solutions, such as Z-ordering, can be more effective than partitioning. Chapter 5 covers performance tuning and this topic in greater detail.

Checking if a partition exists

To determine whether a table contains a specific partition, you can use the statement:

```
SELECT COUNT(*) > 0 FROM <table-name> WHERE <partition-column> = <value>
```

If the partition exists, `true` is returned. The following SQL statement checks if the partition for `VendorId = 1` and `RatecodeId = 99` exists:

```sql
%sql
SELECT
    COUNT(*) > 0 AS `Partition exists`
FROM
    taxidb.YellowTaxisPartitioned
WHERE
    VendorId = 2 AND RateCodeId = 99
```

This will return `true` since this partition exists as was shown earlier.

Selectively updating Delta partitions with replaceWhere

In the previous section, we saw how we can significantly speed up query operations by partitioning data. We can also selectively update one or more partitions with the `replaceWhere` option. Selectively applying updates to certain partitions is not always possible; some updates need to apply to the entire data lake. But, when applicable, these selective updates can result in significant speed gains. Delta Lake can update partitions with excellent performance, while at the same time guaranteeing data integrity.

To see `replaceWhere` in action, let's take a look at a particular partition:

```sql
%sql
SELECT
    RideId, VendorId, PaymentType
FROM
    taxidb.yellowtaxispartitioned
WHERE
    VendorID = 1 AND RatecodeId = 99 LIMIT 5
```

We see a mixture of payment types in the results:

```
+---------+---------+-------------+
| RideId  | VendorId | PaymentType |
+---------+---------+-------------+
| 1137733 | 1       | 1           |
| 1144423 | 1       | 2           |
| 1214030 | 1       | 1           |
| 1223028 | 1       | 1           |
| 1300054 | 1       | 2           |
+---------+---------+-------------+
```

Let's assume that we have a business reason that states that all `PaymentTypes` for `VendorId = 1` and `RatecodeId = 9` should be 3. We can use the following PySpark expression with `replaceWhere` to achieve that result:

```python
from pyspark.sql.functions import *
spark.read                                                              \
    .format("delta")                                                    \
    .load("/mnt/datalake/book/chapter03/YellowTaxisDeltaPartitioned")   \
    .where((col("VendorId") == 1) & (col("RatecodeId") == 99))          \
    .withColumn("PaymentType", lit(3))                                  \
    .write                                                              \
    .format("delta")                                                    \
    .option("replaceWhere", "VendorId = 1 AND RateCodeId = 99")         \
    .mode("overwrite")                                                  \
    .save("/mnt/datalake/book/chapter03/YellowTaxisDeltaPartitioned")
```

When we now look for the distinct `PaymentTypes` for this partition:

```sql
%sql
SELECT
    DISTINCT(PaymentType)
FROM
    taxidb.yellowtaxispartitioned
WHERE
    VendorID = 1 AND RatecodeId = 99
```

We see that we only have `PaymentType = 3`:

```
+-------------+
| PaymentType |
+-------------+
| 3           |
+-------------+
```

We can verify that the other partitions are not affected:

```sql
%sql
SELECT
    DISTINCT(PaymentType)
FROM
    taxidb.yellowtaxispartitioned
ORDER BY
    PaymentType
```

This shows all `PaymentTypes`:

```
+-------------+
| PaymentType |
+-------------+
| 1           |
| 2           |
| 3           |
| 4           |
+-------------+
```

`replaceWhere` can be particularly useful when you have to run an operation that can be computationally expensive, but you only need to run it on certain partitions.

In the yellow taxi scenario, let's assume that the data science team has requested that you run one of their algorithms on the `YellowTaxis` table. Initially, you can run it on your smallest partition and quickly retrieve the results and, when approved, run the algorithm on all remaining partitions overnight.

User-Defined Metadata

For auditing or regulatory purposes, we might want to add a tag to certain SQL operations. For example, our project might require that you tag INSERTs to certain tables with a General Data Protection Regulation (GDPR) tag. Once we tag the

INSERT with this tag, the auditing tool will be able to generate a complete list of statements that contain this particular tag.

We can specify these tags as user-defined strings in metadata commits made by a SQL operation. We can do this either by using the DataFrameWriter's option userMetadata, or the SparkSession configuration spark.databricks.delta.commit Info.userMetadata. If both options are specified, the DataFrameWriter's option takes precedence.

Using SparkSession to Set Custom Metadata

Let's look at the SparkSession configuration first. Assume that we have an INSERT operation, to which we want to assign a GDPR tag for auditing purposes. Following is a SQL example:

```
%sql
SET spark.databricks.delta.commitInfo.userMetadata=my-custom-metadata=
  { "GDPR": "INSERT Request 1x965383" };
```

This tag will apply to the next operation, which is a standard INSERT:

```
INSERT INTO taxidb.yellowtaxisPartitioned
(RideId, VendorId, PickupTime, DropTime,
 PickupLocationId, DropLocationId, CabNumber,
 DriverLicenseNumber, PassengerCount, TripDistance,
 RatecodeId, PaymentType, TotalAmount,
 FareAmount, Extra, MtaTax, TipAmount,
 TollsAmount, ImprovementSurcharge)
VALUES(10000000, 3, '2019-11-01T00:00:00.000Z',
       '2019-11-01T00:02:23.573Z', 65, 71, 'TAC304',
       '453987', 2, 4.5, 1, 1, 20.34, 15.0, 0.5,
       0.4, 2.0, 2.0, 1.1)
```

Note that there is nothing special in the INSERT; it is a standard operation. The GDPR tag will automatically be applied to the *commit info* in the transaction log. If we search the transaction log for the latest *.json* file, we'll see that *00004.json* is the last log entry:

```
%sh
ls -al /dbfs/.../YellowTaxisDeltaPartitioned/_delta_log/*.json
```

Output:

```
-rwxrwxrwx 1 .../_delta_log/00000000000000000000.json
-rwxrwxrwx 1 .../_delta_log/00000000000000000001.json
-rwxrwxrwx 1 .../_delta_log/00000000000000000002.json
-rwxrwxrwx 1 .../_delta_log/00000000000000000003.json
-rwxrwxrwx 1 .../_delta_log/00000000000000000004.json
```

When we look at the *00004.json* commit file, we can see the GDPR entry:

```
%sh
grep commit /dbfs/.../YellowTaxisDeltaPartitioned/_delta_log/...00004.json >
  /tmp/commit.json
python -m json.tool /tmp/commit.json
```

This is the GDPR entry:

```
{
    "commitInfo": {
        ...,
        "notebook": {
            "notebookId": "1106853862465676"
        },
        "clusterId": "0605-014705-r8puunyx",
        "readVersion": 3,
        "isolationLevel": "WriteSerializable",
        "isBlindAppend": true,
        "operationMetrics": {
            ...
        },
        "userMetadata": "my-custom-metadata=
        { \"GDPR\": \"INSERT Request 1x965383\" }",
        "engineInfo": "Databricks-Runtime/10.4.x-scala2.12",
        "txnId": "99f2f31c-8c01-4ea0-9e23-c0cbae9eb82a"
    }
}
```

 The SET statement will stay in effect for subsequent operations within your current Spark session, so if you want to continue inserting data without adding the GDPR metadata, you need to update the SET to an empty string or use the RESET operation. Be aware that RESET will reset all Spark properties, not just the metadata one!

Using the DataFrameWriter to Set Custom Metadata

We can also use DataFrameWriter with the userMetadata option to insert custom tags, as shown here:

```
df_for_append.write                                                      \
            .mode("append")                                              \
            .format("delta")                                             \
            .option("userMetadata", '{"PII": "Confidential XYZ"}') \
            .save("/mnt/datalake/book/chapter03/YellowTaxisDeltaPartitioned")
```

When we look at the corresponding JSON entry, we will see the tags in `commitInfo`:

```sh
%sh
grep commit /dbfs/.../YellowTaxisDeltaPartitioned/_delta_log/...00005.json >
  /tmp/commit.json
python -m json.tool /tmp/commit.json

{
    "commitInfo": {
        ….

        …
        "userMetadata": "{\"PII\": \"Confidential XYZ\"}",
        …
    }
}
```

Conclusion

This chapter reviewed the fundamentals for using Delta Lake by discussing the basic operations of Delta tables. Delta Lake provides a number of different ways to perform different types of operations using different types of APIs. For example, you can create Delta tables using SQL DDL, the `DataFrameWriter` API, or the `DeltaTable Builder` API, each of which has its own set of features and syntax. And when you create tables, you can specify a specific location to write the underlying data to create unmanaged tables, or you can let Spark manage both the metadata and underlying data by creating managed tables.

Once a table has been created, you can then read and write to the table using the various APIs mentioned here. This chapter primarily covered different ways to insert, append, or overwrite data using SQL or the DataFrame API, as more sophisticated write operations (e.g., `MERGE`) will be covered in subsequent chapters.

We also explored the capabilities of Delta Lake partitioning on disk. Whether partitioning on a single column or multiple, Delta tables provide simple methods for partitioning tables that allow us to achieve significant data processing improvements and efficiency. And not only can we partition tables, but powerful, built-in Delta Lake features such as `replaceWhere` allow us to selectively apply updates to certain partitions in order to apply updates faster and more efficiently.

Lastly, we learned that you can add user-defined metadata to Delta tables to aid in search and discovery, which can be particularly useful for auditing or regulatory purposes. Custom metadata allows us to compile a list of statements or operations on Delta tables that contain particular tags.

Having dipped our toes into Delta Lake and Delta table basic operations, the following chapter will dive deeper into more sophisticated Delta table DML operations.

Table Deletes, Updates, and Merges

Since Delta Lake adds a transactional layer to classic data lakes, we can perform classic DML operations, such as updates, deletes, and merges. When you perform a `DELETE` operation on a Delta table, the operation is performed at the data file level, removing and adding data files as needed. Removed data files are no longer part of the current version of the Delta table, but should not be physically deleted immediately since you might want to revert to an older version of the table with time travel (time travel is covered in Chapter 6). The same is true when you run an `UPDATE` operation. Data files will be added and removed from your Delta table as required.

The most powerful Delta Lake DML operation is the `MERGE` operation, which allows you to perform an "upsert" operation, which is a mix of `UPDATE`, `DELETE`, and `INSERT` operations, on your Delta table. You join a source and a target table, write a match condition, and then specify what should happen with the records that either match or don't match.

Deleting Data from a Delta Table

We will start with a clean `taxidb.YellowTaxis` table. This table is created by the "Chapter Initialization" script for Chapter 4.[1] It has 9,999,995 million rows:

```
%sql
SELECT
    COUNT(id)
FROM
    taxidb.YellowTaxis
```

Output:

---

1 GitHub repo location: */chapter04/00 - Chapter Initialization*

```
+----------+
| count(1) |
+----------+
| 9999995  |
+----------+
```

Table Creation and DESCRIBE HISTORY

The taxidb.YellowTaxis Delta table was created in the "Chapter Initialization" script and copied into our */chapter04* folder. Let's look at DESCRIBE HISTORY for the table:[2]

```
%sql
DESCRIBE HISTORY taxidb.YellowTaxis
```

Output (only relevant portions shown):

```
+-----------+------------------------------+---------------------+
| operation | operationParameters          | operationMetrics    |
+-----------+------------------------------+---------------------+
| WRITE     | [('mode', 'Overwrite'), (...)] | [('numFiles', '2'), |
|           |                              | ('numOutputRows',   |
|           |                              | '9999995'), ...]    |
+-----------+------------------------------+---------------------+
```

We can see that we have one transaction containing a WRITE operation, writing two data files for a total of 9,999,995 rows. Let's find out some details about both of those files.

In Chapter 2 you learned how you can use the transaction log to see the *add* and *remove* file actions. Let's take a look at the *_delta_log* directory:

```
%sh
ls /dbfs/mnt/datalake/book/chapter04/YellowTaxisDelta/_delta_log/*.json
```

As expected, we see only one transaction log entry:

```
/dbfs/mnt/datalake/book/chapter04/YellowTaxisDelta/_delta_log/....0000.json
```

This log entry should have two file *add* actions, since the numfiles entry in DESCRIBE HISTORY was two. Again, let's use our grep command to find those sections:

```
%sh
grep \"add\" /dbfs/…/chapter04/YellowTaxisDelta/_delta_log/..0000.json |
  sed -n 1p > /tmp/commit.json
python -m json.tool < /tmp/commit.json
```

One variation of the previous command is that since you now have two entries, we need to use the sed command to extract the right *add* entry.

---

2 GitHub repo location: */chapter04/01 - Delete Operations*

You can pipe the grep command output to the sed[3] command. sed is a stream editor that performs basic text transformations on an input stream and writes the result to an output stream. The -n option suppresses normal output, and the 1p command prints only the first line of the input. To find the next *add* entry, you can simply use sed -n 2p, which outputs the second line.

Produced output (only relevant portions shown):

```
{
    "add": {
        "path": "part-00000-...-c000.snappy.parquet",
        ...
        "stats": "{\"numRecords\":5530100,...}}",
        "tags": {
            ...
        }
    }
}
```

Here, we see the name of the first data file created for our table, and the number of records in that file. We can use the same command with sed -n 2p to get the second *add* action to get the second data file:

```
{
    "add": {
        "path": "part-00001-...-c000.snappy.parquet",
        "...: ""
stats": {\"numRecords\":4469895,...}}",
        "tags": {
            ...
        }
    }
}
```

Now we know that our table has the following data files:

Table 4-1. Parquet files created

Parquet filename	Number of records
part-00000-d39cbaa1-ea7a-4913-a416-e229aa1d5616-c000.snappy.parquet	5,530,100
part-00001-947cccf8-41ae-4212-a474-fedaa0f6623d-c000.snappy.parquet	4,469,895

These files correspond with our directory listing, so the transaction log and the directory listing report are consistent:

```
%sh
ls -al /dbfs/mnt/datalake/book/chapter04/YellowTaxisDelta
```

3 Manual page for sed (*https://oreil.ly/8zF82*)

```
drwxrwxrwx 2 _delta_log
-rwxrwxrwx 1 part-00000-d39cbaa1-ea7a-4913-a416-e229aa1d5616-c000.snappy.parquet
-rwxrwxrwx 1 part-00001-947cccf8-41ae-4212-a474-fedaa0f6623d-c000.snappy.parquet
```

Performing the DELETE Operation

Let's assume that we want to delete a single record, in this case the record with `RideId`
= `100000`. First, we should make sure that the record is indeed still in the table with a
SQL SELECT:[4]

```
%sql
-- First, show that you have data for RideId = 10000
SELECT
    RideId,
    VendorId,
    CabNumber,
    TotalAmount
FROM
    taxidb.YellowTaxis
WHERE
    RideId = 100000
```

Output:

```
+--------+----------+-----------+-------------+
| RideId | VendorId | CabNumber | TotalAmount |
+--------+----------+-----------+-------------+
| 100000 | 2        | T478827C  | 7.56        |
+--------+----------+-----------+-------------+
```

To delete this row, we can use a simple SQL DELETE. We can use the DELETE command
to selectively delete rows based upon a predicate, or filtering, condition:

```
%sql
DELETE FROM
    taxidb.YellowTaxis
WHERE RideId = 100000
```

Output:

```
+------------------+
|num_affected_rows |
+------------------+
| 1                |
+------------------+
```

---

4 GitHub repo location: */chapter04/01 - Delete Operations*

We can confirm that we did in fact delete one row. When we use the DESCRIBE HISTORY command to look at the different operations on the table, we get the following for version 1 (the output of the row is pivoted for readability):

```
version:                1
timestamp:              2022-12-14T17:50:23.000+0000
operation:              DELETE
operationParameters:    [('predicate',
                        '["(spark_catalog.taxidb.YellowTaxis.RideId = 100000)"]')]
operationMetrics:       [('numRemovedFiles', '1'),
                        ('numCopiedRows', '5530099'),
                        ('numAddedChangeFiles', '0'),
                        ('executionTimeMs', '32534'),
                        ('numDeletedRows', '1'),
                        ('scanTimeMs', '1524'),
                        ('numAddedFiles', '1'),
                        ('rewriteTimeMs', '31009')]
```

We can see the operation was a DELETE and the predicate we used for the deletion was WHERE RideId = 100000. Delta Lake removed one file (numRemovedFiles = 1) and added one new file (numAddedFiles = 1). If we use our trusted grep command to find out the details, things look as follows:

Table 4-2. Result of DELETE operation

Action	Filename	# of records
Add	*part-00000-96c2f047-99cc-4a43-b2ea-0d3e0e77c4c1-c000.snappy.parquet*	5,530,099
Remove	*part-00000-d39cbaa1-ea7a-4913-a416-e229aa1d5616-c000.snappy.parquet*	4,469,895

Figure 4-1 illustrates Delta Lake's actions when we deleted the record.

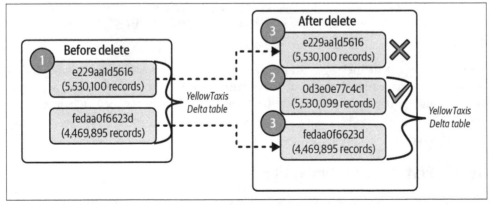

Figure 4-1. YellowTaxis Delta table before and after the DELETE operation

Delta Lake performs the following actions as part of the DELETE operation:

1. Delta Lake made the first scan of the data to identify any files containing rows matching the predicate condition. In this case, the file is the e229aa1d5616 data file; it contains the record with RideId = 100000.

2. In a second scan, Delta Lake reads the matching data files into memory. At this point Delta Lake deletes the rows in question before writing out a new clean data file to storage. This new data file is the 0d3e0e77c4c1 data file. Since Delta Lake deleted one record, this new data file contains 5,530,099 records (5,530,100 − 1).

3. As Delta Lake completes the DELETE operation, the data file e229aa1d5616 is now removed from the Delta transaction log, since it is no longer part of the Delta table. This process is called "tombstoning." However, it is important to note that this old data file is *not* deleted, because you might still need it to time travel back to an earlier version of the table. You can use the VACUUM command to delete files older than a certain time period. Time travel and the VACUUM command are covered in detail in Chapter 6.

4. The data file fedaa0f6623d remains part of the Delta table, since no changes applied to it.

We can see the one data file (0d3e0e77c4c1) that has been added to the directory in our directory listing:

```
%sh
ls -al /dbfs/mnt/datalake/book/chapter04/YellowTaxisDelta/

drwxrwxrwx _delta_log
-rwxrwxrwx part-00000-96c2f047-99cc-4a43-b2ea-0d3e0e77c4c1-c000.snappy.parquet
-rwxrwxrwx part-00000-d39cbaa1-ea7a-4913-a416-e229aa1d5616-c000.snappy.parquet
-rwxrwxrwx part-00001-947cccf8-41ae-4212-a474-fedaa0f6623d-c000.snappy.parquet
```

The data file e229aa1d5616 was not physically deleted.

The most important message to take away from this is that the delete transaction occurs at the data file level. Delta Lake will create new partitions and insert new *add file* and r*emove file* actions in the transaction log, as needed. Chapter 6 on performance tuning will cover the VACUUM command and other ways to clean up tombstoned data files that are no longer required.

DELETE Performance Tuning Tips

The main way to improve the performance of a DELETE operation on Delta Lake is to add more predicates to narrow the search spectrum. For example, if you have partitioned data, and know the partition that the to-be-deleted records are part of, you can add their partition clause to the DELETE predicate.

Delta Lake also provides a number of other optimization conditions, such as *data skipping and z-order optimization*. Z-ordering reorganizes the layout of each data file so that similar column values are strategically colocated near one another for maximum efficiency. Please refer to Chapter 5 for more details.

Updating Data in a Table

Now that you have seen the impact of a DELETE operation on the YellowTaxis table, let's take a quick look at an UPDATE operation. You can use the UPDATE operation to selectively update any rows matching a filtering condition, also known as a *predicate*.

Use Case Description

Let's assume there was an error with the DropLocationId for the record where RideId = 9999994. First, let's ensure this record is present in our table with the following SELECT:

```
SELECT
    INPUT_FILE_NAME(),
    RideId,
    VendorId,
    DropLocationId
FROM
    taxidb.YellowTaxis
WHERE
    RideId = 9999994
```

The Spark SQL INPUT_FILE_NAME() function is a handy function that gives us the filename in which the record is located:

```
+--------------------------+---------+----------+----------------+
| input_file_name()        | RideId  | VendorId | DropLocationId |
+--------------------------+---------+----------+----------------+
| .../part-00001-...parquet | 9999994 | 1        | 243            |
+--------------------------+---------+----------+----------------+
```

The INPUT_FILE_NAME function shows that our record is located in the fedaa0f6623d data file, which makes sense, since it is one of the last records, so logically it is located in the last-created data file. We can see that the existing DropLocationId is currently 243. Let's assume that we want to update this field to have a value of 250. We'll take a look at the actual DELETE operation next.

Updating Data in a Table

We can now write the UPDATE SQL statement as follows:

```
%sql

UPDATE
    taxidb.YellowTaxis
SET
    DropLocationId = 250
WHERE
    RideId = 9999994
```

We see that we updated a single row:

```
+-------------------+
| num_affected_rows |
+-------------------+
|    1              |
+-------------------+
```

Let's first verify that we updated the table successfully:

```
%sql
SELECT
    RideId,
    DropLocationId
FROM
    taxidb.YellowTaxis
WHERE
    RideId = 9999994


+---------+----------------+
| RideId  | DropLocationId |
+---------+----------------+
| 9999994 | 250            |
+---------+----------------+
```

The output shows the record was updated successfully. When we use the DESCRIBE HISTORY command on the table, we see the UPDATE operation on version 3 of the table (output pivoted for clarity):

```
version:             3
timestamp:           2022-12-23 17:20:45+00:00
operation:           UPDATE
operationParameters: [('predicate', '(RideId = 9999994)')]
operationMetrics:    [('numRemovedFiles', '1'),
                      ('numCopiedRows', '4469894'),
                      ('numAddedChangeFiles', '0'),
                      ('executionTimeMs', '25426'),
                      ('scanTimeMs', '129'),
                      ('numAddedFiles', '1'),
```

```
('numUpdatedRows', '1'),
('rewriteTimeMs', '25293')]
```

One file was removed (`'numRemovedFiles'`, `'1'`), and one was added (`'numAdded Files'`, `'1'`). We can also see our UPDATE predicate [(`'predicate'`, `'(RideId = 9999994)'`)]. If we use the `grep` command to find out the details, things look as follows:

Table 4-3. Actions taken as a result of the UPDATE operation

Action	Filename	# of records
Add	*part-00000-da1ef656-46e-4de5-a189-50807db851f6-c000.snappy.parquet*	4,469,895
Remove	*part-00001-947cccf8-41ae-4212-a474-fedaa0f6623d-c000.snappy.parquet*	4,469,895

Figure 4-2 illustrates the actions that Delta Lake took when we deleted the record.

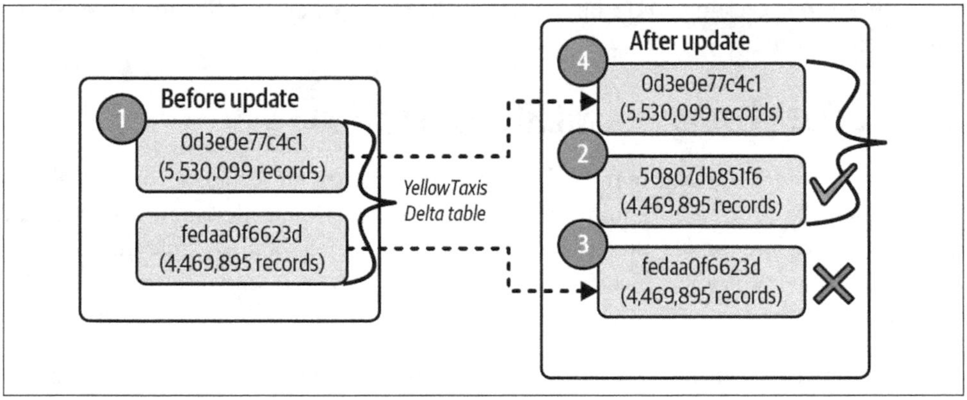

Figure 4-2. Before and after an UPDATE operation

Delta Lake performs an UPDATE on a table in two steps:

1. It finds and selects the data files containing data that match the predicate and therefore need to be updated. Delta Lake uses data skipping whenever possible to speed up this process. In this case, that is the `fedaa0f6623d` data file. We could also verify that with the `INPUT_FILE_NAME()` SQL function.

2. Next, Delta Lake reads each matching file into memory, updates the relevant rows, and writes out the result in a new data file. The new data file in this case is the `50807db851f6` file. It now contains all the records of the `fedaa0f6623d` partition, but with the applied updates, which in this case is the update for `RideId = 9999994`. This data file is `50807db851f6`. This data file continues to hold 4,469,895 records. Once Delta Lake has executed the UPDATE successfully, it adds an *add* file action for the new data file.

Since it is no longer required, the data file `fedaa0f6623d` is removed from the Delta table with a *remove* commit action in the transaction log. However, like the `DELETE` operation, the file is not physically deleted, in case we might want to look at an old version of the table with time travel.

The data file `0d3e0e77c4c1` was unaffected by our update, so it remains part of the Delta table and continues to hold 5,530,099 records.

UPDATE Performance Tuning Tips

Like the `DELETE` operation, the main way to improve the performance of an `UPDATE` command on Delta Lake is to add more predicates to narrow the search scope. The more specific the search, the fewer files Delta Lake needs to scan and/or modify.

As mentioned in the previous section, other Delta Lake features, such as Z-ordering, can be used to speed up `UPDATE` operations further. See Chapter 5 for details on Delta Lake optimization.

Upsert Data Using the MERGE Operation

The Delta Lake `MERGE` command allows you to perform upserts on your data. An upsert is a mix of an `UPDATE` and an `INSERT` command. To understand upserts, let's assume that we have an existing table (the *target* table) and a *source* table that contain a mix of new records and updates to existing records. Here is how an upsert actually works:

1. When a record from the source table *matches a preexisting record* in the target table, Delta Lake *updates* the record.
2. When there is *no* such *match*, Delta Lake *inserts* the new record.

Use Case Description

Let's apply a `MERGE` operation to our `YellowTaxis` table. Let's perform a count of our `YellowTaxis` table:

```
%sql
SELECT
    COUNT(*)
FROM
    taxidb.YellowTaxis
```

We see that we have 9,999,994 records.

```
+----------+
| count(1) |
+----------+
| 9999994  |
+----------+
```

We want to reinsert the record with RideId = 100000 that we deleted in the DELETE section of this chapter. So, in our source data, we need one record with a RideId set to 100000.

For this example, let's assume we also want to update the records with RideId = 999991 because the VendorId was inserted wrong, and it needs to be updated to 1 (VendorId = 1) for these five records. Finally, we want to bring the record count to an even 10,000,000 records, so we have 5 more records, with RideIds ranging from 999996 through 10000000.

The MERGE Dataset

In our companion source data files for the book, we have a file named *YellowTaxis-MergeData.csv*, which has these records. Since we need to supply a schema, we first read the schema from our existing table:

```
df = spark.read.format("delta").table("taxidb.YellowTaxis")
yellowTaxiSchema = df.schema
print(yellowTaxiSchema)
```

Once we have loaded the schema, we can load our merge data CSV file:

```
yellowTaxisMergeDataFrame = spark          \
            .read                          \
            .option("header", "true")      \
            .schema(yellowTaxiSchema)      \
            .csv("/mnt/datalake/book/chapter04/YellowTaxisMergeData.csv")
            .sort(col("RideId"))

yellowTaxisMergeDataFrame.show()
```

A partial output is shown here:

```
+-----------+-----------+-----------------------------+
| RideId    | VendorId  | PickupTime                  |
+-----------+-----------+-----------------------------+
|    100000 | 2         | 2022-03-01T00:00:00.000+0000 |
|   9999991 | 1         | 2022-04-04T20:54:04.000+0000 |
|   9999992 | 1         | 2022-04-04T20:54:04.000+0000 |
|   9999993 | 1         | 2022-04-04T20:54:04.000+0000 |
|   9999994 | 1         | 2022-04-04T20:54:04.000+0000 |
|   9999995 | 1         | 2022-04-04T20:54:04.000+0000 |
|   9999996 | 3         | 2022-03-01T00:00:00.000+0000 |
|   9999997 | 3         | 2022-03-01T00:00:00.000+0000 |
|   9999998 | 3         | 2022-03-01T00:00:00.000+0000 |
|   9999999 | 3         | 2022-03-01T00:00:00.000+0000 |
|  10000000 | 3         | 2022-03-01T00:00:00.000+0000 |
+-----------+-----------+-----------------------------+
```

We can see our record with RideId = 100000, the five records (9999991 through 9999995) with their new VendorId of 1, and the five new records, starting at 9999996.

We want to write our MERGE statement in SQL, so we need to have our DataFrame available in SQL. The DataFrame class has a handy method called createOrReplace TempView, which does exactly that:

```
# Create a Temporary View on top of our DataFrame, making it
# accessible to the SQL MERGE statement below
yellowTaxisMergeDataFrame.createOrReplaceTempView("YellowTaxiMergeData")
```

We can now just use the view name in SQL:

```
%sql
SELECT
    *
FROM
    YellowTaxiMergeData
```

This shows exactly the same output as shown with the display() method of the DataFrame.

The MERGE Statement

You can now write your MERGE statement as follows:

```
%sql
MERGE INTO taxidb.YellowTaxis AS target
    USING YellowTaxiMergeData AS source
        ON target.RideId = source.RideId

-- You need to update the VendorId if the records
-- matched
WHEN MATCHED
    THEN
```

```
          -- If you want to update all columns,
          -- you can say "SET *"
          UPDATE SET target.VendorId = source.VendorId
   WHEN NOT MATCHED
      THEN
          -- If all columns match, you can also do a "INSERT *"
          INSERT(RideId, VendorId, PickupTime, DropTime, PickupLocationId,
                 DropLocationId, CabNumber, DriverLicenseNumber, PassengerCount,
                 TripDistance, RateCodeId, PaymentType, TotalAmount, FareAmount,
                 Extra, MtaTax, TipAmount, TollsAmount, ImprovementSurCharge)
          VALUES(RideId, VendorId, PickupTime, DropTime, PickupLocationId,
                 DropLocationId, CabNumber, DriverLicenseNumber, PassengerCount,
                 TripDistance, RateCodeId, PaymentType, TotalAmount, FareAmount,
                 Extra, MtaTax, TipAmount, TollsAmount, ImprovementSurCharge)
```

Let's analyze this statement:

1. We are going to MERGE INTO the YellowTaxis Delta table. Notice that we give the table an alias of source.

2. Using the USING clause we specify the source dataset, which in this case is the view YellowTaxiMergeData, and give it an alias of source.

3. Define the join condition between the source and target dataset. In our case, we simply want to join on the VendorId. If you have partitioned data, and want to target a partition, you might want to add that condition here with an AND statement.

4. Specify the action when the RideId matches between the source and target. In this use case, we want to update the source with the VendorId of the source, which is set to 1. Here, we are only updating one column, but if we need to, we can supply a column list, separated by commas. If we want to update all columns, we simply say UPDATE SET *.

5. Define the action when the record exists in the source, but not in the target. We do not have any additional condition with the WHEN NOT MATCHED, but you can add any additional clauses if the use case calls for it. Most of the time you will provide an INSERT statement as an action. Since our source and target column names are identical, we could have also used a simple INSERT *.

When we execute this MERGE statement, we get the following output:

```
+-------------------+-------------------+-------------------+-------------------+
| num_affected_rows | num_updated_rows  | num_deleted_rows  | num_inserted_rows |
+-------------------+-------------------+-------------------+-------------------+
|        11         |        5          |        0          |        6          |
+-------------------+-------------------+-------------------+-------------------+
```

This output is exactly what you expected:

- We update five rows (VendorIds 9999991 through 9999995)
- We insert six rows:
  - One row with a RideId of 100000
  - The five rows at the end (9999996 through 10000000)

We can see the updates on the first five rows:

```sql
%sql
-- Make sure that the VendorId has been updated
-- for the records with RideId between
-- 9999991 and 9999995
SELECT
    RideId,
    VendorId
FROM
    taxidb.YellowTaxis
WHERE RideId BETWEEN 9999991 and 9999995
```

```
+---------+----------+
| RideId  | VendorId |
+---------+----------+
| 9999991 | 1        |
| 9999992 | 1        |
| 9999993 | 1        |
| 9999994 | 1        |
| 9999995 | 1        |
+---------+----------+
```

All rows now have the source VendorId of 1.

We can see the inserted record with RideId = 100000:

```sql
%sql
--Make sure that you have a record with VendorId = 100000
SELECT
    *
FROM
    taxidb.YellowTaxis
WHERE
    RideId = 100000
```

Output (partial output shown):

```
+---------+----------+---------------------------+---------------------------+
| RideId  | VendorId | PickupTime                | DropTime                  |
+---------+----------+---------------------------+---------------------------+
| 100000  | 2        | 2022-03-01 00:00:00+00:00 | 2022-03-01 00:12:01+00:00 |
+---------+----------+---------------------------+---------------------------+
```

And finally, we can see the new rows with `RideId > 9999995`:

```
%sql
SELECT
    *
FROM
    taxidb.YellowTaxis
WHERE
    RideId > 9999995
```

```
+----------+----------+--------------------------+
| RideId   | VendorId | PickupTime               |
+----------+----------+--------------------------+
| 9999996  | 3        | 2022-03-01 00:00:00+00:00 |
| 9999997  | 3        | 2022-03-01 00:00:00+00:00 |
| 9999998  | 3        | 2022-03-01 00:00:00+00:00 |
| 9999999  | 3        | 2022-03-01 00:00:00+00:00 |
| 10000000 | 3        | 2022-03-01 00:00:00+00:00 |
+----------+----------+--------------------------+
```

And a grand total of 10 million records:

```
%sql
SELECT
    COUNT(RideId)
FROM
    taxidb.YellowTaxis
```

```
+----------+
| count(1) |
+----------+
| 10000000 |
+----------+
```

Modifying unmatched rows using MERGE

An important addition to the Delta Lake MERGE operation is the recently released WHEN
NOT MATCHED BY SOURCE clause. This clause can be used to UPDATE or DELETE records
in the target table that do not have corresponding records in the source table. This
can be a useful operation for deleting records in the target table that no longer exist
in the source table, or for flagging records that indicate the data should be considered
deleted or inactive, while still keeping the records in the target table (i.e., soft delete).

> WHEN NOT MATCHED BY SOURCE clauses are supported by the Scala,
> Python, and Java Delta Lake APIs in Delta 2.3 and above. SQL is
> supported in Delta 2.4 and above.

To delete records that exist in the source tables and not in the target table (i.e., hard delete), use the WHEN NOT MATCHED BY SOURCE clause, as seen in the following code example:

 The WHEN NOT MATCHED BY SOURCE code is for demonstration purposes only and is not meant to be executed in sequence with the earlier code examples. Please note that if you execute the WHEN NOT MATCHED BY SOURCE code examples, then the remaining code outputs in this chapter will not align with the examples and expected outputs in this chapter.

```
%sql
MERGE INTO taxidb.YellowTaxis AS target
    USING YellowTaxiMergeData AS source
        ON target.RideId = source.RideId
WHEN MATCHED
        UPDATE SET *
WHEN NOT MATCHED
        INSERT *
-- DELETE records in the target that are not matched by the source
WHEN NOT MATCHED BY SOURCE
    DELETE
```

If you wish to flag records in the target table that no longer exist in the source table (i.e., soft delete) that satisfy a certain condition, you can specify a MERGE condition and an UPDATE:

```
%sql
MERGE INTO taxidb.YellowTaxis AS target
    USING YellowTaxiMergeData AS source
        ON target.RideId = source.RideId
WHEN MATCHED
        UPDATE SET *
WHEN NOT MATCHED
        INSERT *
-- Set target.status = 'inactive' when records in the target table
-- don't exist in the source table and condition is met
WHEN NOT MATCHED BY SOURCE target.PickupTime >=
  (current_date() - INTERVAL '5' DAY)
THEN
        UPDATE SET target.status = 'inactive'
```

It is best practice to add an optional MERGE condition when you add the WHEN NOT MATCHED BY SOURCE clause to UPDATE or DELETE target rows. This is because when there is no specified MERGE condition, this can lead to a large number of target rows being modified. Therefore, for best performance, apply a MERGE condition to the WHEN NOT MATCHED BY SOURCE clause (e.g., target.PickupTime >= (current_date() - INTERVAL '5' DAY in the previous code example) to limit the number of target rows being updated or deleted, because then a target row is only modified if that condition is true for that row.

You can also add multiple WHEN NOT MATCHED BY SOURCE clauses to a MERGE operation. When there are multiple clauses, they are evaluated in the order they are specified and all WHEN NOT MATCHED BY SOURCE clauses, except the last one, must have conditions.

Analyzing the MERGE operation with DESCRIBE HISTORY

When we run DESCRIBE HISTORY on the YellowTaxis table in the operationsParameters section of the output, we can see our MERGE predicate:

```
operation: MERGE

[('predicate',
  '(target.RideId = source.RideId)'),
  ('matchedPredicates', '[{"actionType":"update"}]'),
  ('notMatchedPredicates', '[{"actionType":"insert"}]')]
```

We can see the join condition (target.RideId = source.RideId), the matchedPredicate that specifies an update, and the notMatchedPredicate, which specifies an insert.

The operationMetrics output sections show the details of the different actions:

```
[('numTargetRowsCopied', '4469890'),
  ('numTargetRowsDeleted', '0'),
  ('numTargetFilesAdded', '4'),
  ('executionTimeMs', '91902'),
  ('numTargetRowsInserted', '6'),
  ('scanTimeMs', '8452'),
  ('numTargetRowsUpdated', '5'),
  ('numOutputRows', '4469901'),
  ('numTargetChangeFilesAdded', '0'),
  ('numSourceRows', '11'),
  ('numTargetFilesRemoved', '1'),
  ('rewriteTimeMs', '16782')]
```

Here, we can again see that six rows were inserted (numTargetRowsInserted), and five rows were updated (numTargetRowsUpdated). Four new data files were added to our Delta table, and one data file was removed.

Inner Workings of the MERGE Operation

Internally, Delta Lake completes a MERGE operation like this in two steps:

1. It first performs an `inner join` between the target table and the source table to select all data files containing matches. This prevents the operation from unnecessarily shuffling data that can be safely ignored.

2. Next, it performs an `outer join` between the selected files in the target and source tables, and applies the appropriate INSERT, DELETE, or UPDATE clause as specified by the user.

The main way that a MERGE differs from an UPDATE or a DELETE under the hood is that Delta Lake uses joins to complete a MERGE. This allows you to use some unique strategies when trying to improve performance.

Conclusion

DML operations like DELETE, UPDATE, and MERGE are essential operations for any table format and ETL operations, all of which are enabled through the transaction log. By leveraging these operations, you can start efficiently handling data changes and maintaining data integrity in your data platform.

Similar to tables in a traditional RDBMS, you read in this chapter that with Delta tables you can perform DELETE, UPDATE, and MERGE operations, but you can also apply these operations using SQL or the DataFrame API. More importantly, you learned what happens under the hood in Delta Lake with the underlying files in the Delta table directory, and how the transaction log records and tracks these different types of entries. Using the DESCRIBE HISTORY command, we can view details about the output of a table's transactions. Each of these operations can also leverage predicates to reduce the number of files scanned and improve performance. Outside of using predicates during operations, there are other performance tuning techniques that can be applied to Delta tables that you will learn about in the following chapter.

Performance Tuning

Any time you are storing and retrieving data, whether with a traditional RDBMS or with Delta tables, how you organize the data in the underlying storage format can significantly affect the time it takes to perform table operations and queries. In general, performance tuning refers to the process of optimizing the performance of a system, and in the context of Delta tables this involves optimizing how the data is stored and retrieved. Historically, retrieving data is accomplished by either increasing RAM or CPU for faster processing, or reducing the amount of data that needs to be read by skipping nonrelevant data. Delta Lake provides a number of different techniques that can be combined to accelerate data retrieval by efficiently reducing the amount of files and data that needs to be read during operations.

An additional problem that can contribute to slower reads and inefficient processing in Apache Spark and Delta Lake is the small file problem, briefly mentioned in Chapter 1. The small file problem is an issue that can arise when the underlying data files are divided into numerous small files, as opposed to larger, more efficient files. It can occur for several different reasons, primarily due to frequent writes, but can be addressed through a variety of techniques in Delta Lake that include compacting small files into larger files.

By leveraging good performance tuning strategies to reduce the effects of the small file problem and better enable data skipping on Delta tables, you can significantly improve the performance of execution times, especially when dealing with large tables or resource-intensive data lake operations and queries.

Data Skipping

Skipping nonrelevant data is ultimately the foundation for most performance tuning features, as it aims to reduce the amount of data that needs to be read. This feature, called data skipping, can be enhanced through a variety of different techniques in Delta Lake.

Delta Lake automatically maintains the minimum and maximum value for up to 32 fields for files, and stores those values as part of the metadata. Delta Lake uses these minimum and maximum ranges to skip the files that are out of the range of the querying field values. This is a key aspect that enables data skipping through what is called *data skipping statistics*.

You do not need to configure or specify data skipping and data statistics as this feature is activated whenever applicable in Delta Lake, but the effectiveness greatly depends on the layout of your data. In order to maximize the effectiveness of data skipping, data can be consolidated, clustered, and colocated using commands such as OPTIMIZE and ZORDER BY, which will be discussed in further detail in subsequent sections, so that minimum and maximum ranges are narrow and, ideally, nonoverlapping.

Delta Lake collects the following data skipping statistics for each data file:

- Number of records
- Minimum values for each of the first 32 columns
- Maximum values for each of the first 32 columns
- Number of null values for each of the first 32 columns

Delta Lake collects these statistics on the first 32 columns defined in your table schema. Please note, each field within nested columns (e.g., StructType[1]) counts as a column. You can configure statistics collection on certain columns by reordering columns in the schema, or you can increase the number of columns to collect statistics on by using delta.dataSkippingNumIndexedCols, but adding additional columns also adds additional overhead that can adversely affect write performance. Typically, you want to collect data skipping statistics on columns that are commonly used in filters, WHERE clauses, joins, and columns that you tend to perform aggregations on. Conversely, avoid collecting data skipping statistics on long strings as they are far less efficient for data skipping purposes.

Figure 5-1 shows that by default only statistics for the first 32 columns are collected on a table. And for the purpose of collecting statistics, each field within a nested column is considered an individual column.

---

1 Apache Spark data types (*https://oreil.ly/VuXdF*)

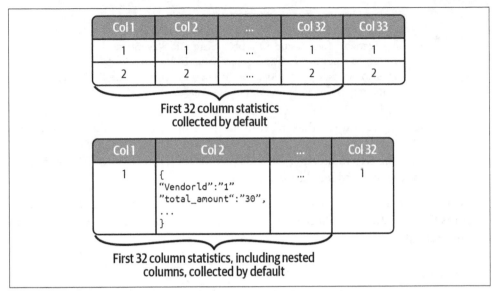

Col 1	Col 2	...	Col 32	Col 33
1	1	...	1	1
2	2	...	2	2

First 32 column statistics
collected by default

Col 1	Col 2	...	Col 32

1	{
	"VendorId":"1"
	"total_amount":"30",
	...
	}
		...	1

First 32 column statistics, including nested
columns, collected by default

Figure 5-1. Data skipping statistics collected on the first 32 columns

The following example can be found in the "Data Skipping" notebook, which should be run after executing the "Chapter Initialization" notebook for Chapter 5, which creates a Delta table at a specified location. The script in the "Data Skipping" notebook uses a shell command to look at the last *add file* action in the transaction log of the Delta table that was created. This will show you examples of the data skipping statistics collected in the last transaction entry:

```
%sh
# define path to Delta table
delta_table_path='mnt/datalake/book/chapter05/YellowTaxisDelta/'

# find the last transaction entry and search for "add"
# the output will show you the file stats stored in the json
# transaction entry for the last file added
grep "\"add"\" "$(ls -1rt /dbfs/$delta_table_path/_delta_log/*.json |
  tail -n1)" | sed -n 1p > /tmp/commit.json
python -m json.tool < /tmp/commit.json
```

This produces the following output (only relevant portions shown):

```
stats:"{\"numRecords\":12177114,\"minValues\":{\"VendorID\":1,
  \"tpep_pickup_datetime\":\"2022-01-01\"...."maxValues\":{\"VendorID\":6,
  \"tpep_pickup_datetime\":\"2022-11-01\"...."nullCount\":{\"VendorID\":0,
  \"tpep_pickup_datetime\":0
```

We are displaying the *add file* command in the transaction log using a shell command to show the appropriate item in a JSON file in a readable format and in a programmatic way. Since this file is written to a storage location where your Delta table is stored, you can also navigate to that location to open the appropriate JSON file in the transaction log to view the information that way as well.

From this output, we can see that the minimum values and maximum values were captured in the last file, along with the number of nulls, or null count. Statistics were collected on all columns in the table because it contains fewer than 32. This metadata is collected for every file added during the operation.

If the table contains more than 32 columns, we can also change the number of columns that statistics are collected for using the table property `delta.dataSkipping NumIndexedCols`:

```sql
%sql
ALTER TABLE
  table_name
SET
  TBLPROPERTIES ('delta.dataSkippingNumIndexedCols' = '<value>');
```

Delta Lake properties such as `delta.dataSkippingNumIndexed Cols` can also be set using the Spark configuration settings.

It may not be effective to collect minimum and maximum values on some columns because collecting statistics on long values like strings or binary can be an expensive operation. We can either configure the table property `delta.dataSkipping NumIndexedCols` to avoid columns containing long values or move columns containing long values to a column greater than `delta.dataSkippingNumIndexedCols` using `ALTER TABLE ALTER COLUMN`.[2] Chapter 7 discusses updating a table's schema and changing ordering in more detail.

Partitioning

In an effort to further reduce the amount of data that needs to be read during operations (i.e., data skipping) and to increase performance on large tables, Delta Lake partitioning allows you to organize a Delta table by dividing the data into smaller chunks called *partitions*.

---

2 `ALTER TABLE` Delta Lake documentation (*https://oreil.ly/z4NIk*)

The partitioning described in this section does not describe the partitioning that Spark applies when processing a DataFrame. Rather, the partitioning in this chapter is referring to on-disk, or Hive-style, partitioning where data is organized with paths that contain key value pairs such as Year=2023.

You can create partitions based on the values in one or more columns of the table (the most common being date) which can speed up queries against the table, as well as with data manipulation commands such as INSERT, UPDATE, MERGE, and DELETE.

 At the time of writing, partitions are the recommended approach to enable data skipping in regard to data layout. A new feature in Delta Lake called liquid clustering, which you will learn about in the last section of this chapter, is currently in preview and is not compatible with partitions. This will replace partitions as the recommended approach to optimize query performance in regard to data layout. We felt it was important to understand how partitions work and how you can apply them manually before learning about features that automate and replace these commands. The new feature, liquid clustering, will be generally available in the near future. You can learn more and stay up-to-date on the status of liquid clustering by reviewing the Delta Lake documentation website (*https://oreil.ly/MQzTk*) and this feature request (*https://oreil.ly/tFsNL*).

When you partition a table, the underlying dataset is organized into different directories and subdirectories for each partition (Figure 5-2).

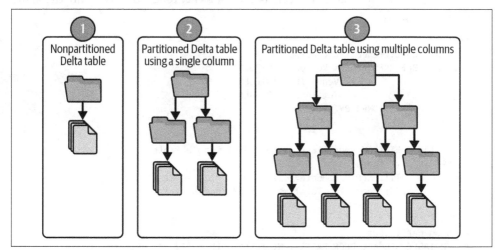

Figure 5-2. The underlying data files of a Delta table organized into different directories and subdirectories

The numbered steps in Figure 5-2 show:

1. A Delta table with no partitions is organized into a single directory.
2. A Delta table partitioned on a single column has a directory created for each of the partition values.
3. A Delta table partitioned on multiple columns has a directory created for each partition value, and then subdirectories are created for each of the additional columns defined for the partition.

 In Delta Lake, partitions run the risk of *decreasing* performance in many cases, as opposed to not partitioning a Delta table. This is because partitions can create the small file problem, discussed earlier in this book and later on in this chapter, especially when partitioning on multiple columns. Partitioning is seldom advisable; please refer to "Partitioning Warnings and Considerations" on page 108 before applying partitions to Delta tables.

When you can selectively query a partition, rather than scanning all of the files in the dataset, Delta Lake quickly scans the appropriate directory (or directories), or partitions, to perform your operation, which results in faster operations. Delta Lake automatically tracks the sets of partitions present in a table and updates the list as data is added or removed, so there is no need to run ALTER TABLE to account for new partitions.

To create a partitioned table, we can use the PARTITIONED BY clause in the table definition using SQL:

```
%sql
--create partitioned table using SQL
CREATE TABLE tripData(PickupMonth INTEGER,
                      VendorID   INTEGER,
                      TotalAmount DOUBLE)
        PARTITIONED BY(PickupMonth)


--use the PARTITION specification to INSERT into a table
INSERT INTO tripData
        PARTITION(PickupMonth= '12') (VendorId, TotalAmount)
        SELECT VendorId, TotalAmount FROM decemberTripData;


-- drop partitions
ALTER TABLE student DROP PARTITION(PickupMonth = '12');
```

The following script,[3] which can be found in the notebook "02 - Partitioning," demonstrates how to write a partitioned Delta table from a Parquet file, while also adding a column to partition on:

```
# import modules
from pyspark.sql.functions import (month, to_date)

## UPDATE destination_path WITH YOUR PATH ##
# define Delta table destination path
destination_path = '/mnt/datalake/book/chapter05/YellowTaxisPartitionedDelta/'

# read the Delta table, add columns to partition on,
# and write it using a partition
# make sure to overwrite the existing schema if the table already exists
# since we are adding partitions
spark.table('taxidb.tripData')                          \
.withColumn('PickupMonth', month('PickupDate'))         \
.withColumn('PickupDate', to_date('PickupDate'))        \
.write                                                   \
.partitionBy('PickupMonth')                             \
.format("delta")                                        \
.option("overwriteSchema", "true")                      \
.mode("overwrite")                                      \
.save(destination_path)

# register table in Hive
spark.sql(f"""CREATE TABLE IF NOT EXISTS taxidb.tripDataPartitioned
        USING DELTA LOCATION '{destination_path}' """ )
```

 If you are following along using the GitHub repository, please note that your file locations may differ from the file locations in the notebooks in the repository. Please update them accordingly.

To view the partitions of a Delta table, we can use the SHOW PARTITIONS command:

```
%sql
--list all partitions for the table
SHOW PARTITIONS taxidb.tripDataPartitioned
```

---

3 GitHub repo location: /chapter05/01 - Compaction

This produces the following output:

```
+-------------+
| PickUpMonth |
+-------------+
| 1           |
| 2           |
| ...         |
| 12          |
+-------------+
```

In this output we can see that the Delta table is partitioned by `PickUpMonth`, and there is a partition for each month.

 To overwrite the schema or change partitioning on an existing Delta table, set `.option("overwriteSchema", "true")`.

To view how the partitions are organized in the underlying filesystem, we can also view the directories created where the Delta table is located. Keep in mind that since we are looking at the actual file system, this could also show you old or nonexistent partitions. Since this table was created using the scripts in the chapter, it should only have the relevant partitions:

```
# import OS module
import os

# create an environment variable so we can use this variable in the
# following bash script
os.environ['destination_path'] = '/dbfs' + destination_path

# list files and directories in directory
print(os.listdir(os.getenv('destination_path')))
```

This produces the following output:

```
['PickupMonth=1','PickupMonth=10','PickupMonth=11','PickupMonth=12',
 'PickupMonth=2', 'PickupMonth=3','PickupMonth=4','PickupMonth=5',
 'PickupMonth=6','PickupMonth=7', 'PickupMonth=8','PickupMonth=9',
 '_delta_log']
```

In this output, the Delta table not only contains the transaction log directory, _delta_log, but also a directory for each of the values in the partition, in this case months 1 to 12.

The values of the directories for each partition are also contained in the transaction log as metadata entries that are part of each *add file* action. This metadata entry can be seen in your current table when looking at the *add file* action in the transaction log and looking at `partitionValues`:

```
%sh
# find the last transaction entry and search for "add" to find an added file
# the output will show you partitionValues
grep "\"add"\" "$(ls -1rt $destination_path/_delta_log/*.json | tail -n1)" |
    sed -n 1p > /tmp/commit.json | sed -n 1p > /tmp/commit.json
python -m json.tool < /tmp/commit.json
```

This produces the following output (only showing relevant portions):

```
{
    "add": {
        "path": "PickupMonth=12/part-00000-....c000.snappy.parquet",
        "partitionValues": {
            "PickupMonth": "12"
        }
```

Due to this metadata, partitioning is essentially the same thing as data skipping. But rather than basing data skipping on data statistics, a topic you will learn more about later on in this chapter, the data skipping is based on exact matches of a string, the partition value, which helps filter files.

Delta Lake also makes it easy to update only specified partitions using `replaceWhere`, which you learned about in Chapter 3. Let's assume that we have a business require-ment that says when the payment type is 4 in the month of December, it needs to be updated to 5. We can use the following PySpark expression with `replaceWhere` to achieve that result:

```
# import month from SQL functions
from pyspark.sql.functions import lit
from pyspark.sql.types import LongType

# use replaceWhere to update a specified partition
spark.read                                                      \
    .format("delta")                                            \
    .load(destination_path)                                     \
    .where("PickupMonth == '12' and PaymentType == '3' ")       \
    .withColumn("PaymentType", lit(4).cast(LongType()))         \
    .write                                                      \
    .format("delta")                                            \
    .option("replaceWhere", "PickupMonth = '12'")               \
    .mode("overwrite")                                          \
    .save(destination_path)
```

> The Delta table schema cannot be overwritten when using `replace Where`.

In the preceding command, notice that we loaded just a single partition using a WHERE clause. Reading partitions directly is not necessary, but using a WHERE clause (Spark SQL) or a .where() function (DataFrame API) enables data skipping, such as:

```
# read a partition from the Delta table into a DataFrame
df = spark.read.table("<delta_table_path>").where("PickupMonth = '12'"
```

While using .where() for reading data can be very effective, you can also use .where() in combination with performance tuning commands, such as compaction, OPTIMIZE, and ZORDER BY, to perform those operations only on a specified partition(s). This can be especially helpful when you are writing new data to specific partitions (e.g., inserting data for the current month). If the WHERE clause or .where() function is not used, then the entire table is scanned by default.

For example, we can perform compaction on a single partition:

```
# read a partition from the Delta table and repartition it
spark.read.format("delta")              \
.load(destination_path)                 \
.where("PickupMonth = '12' ")           \
.repartition(5)                         \
.write                                  \
.option("dataChange", "false")          \
.format("delta")                        \
.mode("overwrite")                      \
.save(destination_path)
```

We can also perform OPTIMIZE and ZORDER BY on specified partitions easily using SQL:

```
%sql
OPTIMIZE taxidb.tripData WHERE PickupMonth = 12 ZORDER BY tpep_pickup_datetime
```

Partitioning Warnings and Considerations

Partitions can be very beneficial, especially for very large tables, but there are a few things to consider when partitioning tables:

- Select your partition column(s) carefully. If the cardinality of a column is very high, do not use that column for partitioning. For example, partitioning by a column timestamp that may have one million distinct timestamps is a bad partitioning strategy. High cardinality columns are great for Z-ordering, but not partitioning, because it can lead to the same small file problem discussed at the beginning of the chapter. This is why we added date columns in the earlier examples—they help serve as appropriate partitioning columns.

  The most commonly used partition column is typically a date.

- You can partition by a column if you expect data in that partition to be at least 1 GB. Tables with fewer, larger partitions tend to outperform tables with many smaller partitions, otherwise you run into the small file problem.

- Columns used for partitioning are always moved to the end of the table unless the partition columns are explicitly defined in the column specification (the name and data type for each column) when creating the table.

- Once you create a table with partitions, you cannot change those partitions even as query patterns or partition requirements change. Partitions are considered a *fixed data layout* and do not support partition evolution.

- There is no magic recipe for partitioning strategies—simply guidelines to consider. It depends on the data, granularity, ingestion and update pattern, etc.

Compact Files

When performing DML operations on a Delta table, often new data is written in many small files across partitions. Due to the additional volume of file metadata and the total number of data files that need to be read, queries and operation speed can be reduced. As an important reminder, this is the small file problem mentioned previously.

To avoid this issue, you should rewrite a large number of small files into a small number of larger files greater than 16 MB. Delta Lake supports the ability to optimize this layout of data in storage with various ways to coalesce small files into larger ones.

Compaction

The consolidation of files is called compaction, or bin-packing. To perform compaction using your own specifications, for example, specifying the number of files to compact the Delta table into, you can use a DataFrame writer with dataChange = false. This indicates that the operation does not change the data; it simply rearranges the data layout.

> When data is compacted, Delta Lake sets dataChange = true by default. This can break concurrent operations on the table, such as downstream streaming consumers, when the table is used as a streaming source.
>
> Conversely, when using dataChange = false, an operation that changes data can corrupt the underlying data in the table. It is best to only use dataChange = false when there are no data changes, as this option lets any downstream consumers know that the operation only rearranges the data and thus those consumers can ignore the event in the transaction log.

The following example can be found in step 1 in the "03 - Compaction, Optimize and ZOrder" notebook. The script in the notebook demonstrates how we can use the DataFrame writer with `repartition`, a method used to increase or decrease the number of partitions in a Spark DataFrame, and the option `dataChange = False` to compact the data into five files using our own algorithm:

```
# define the path and number of files to repartition
path = "/mnt/datalake/book/chapter05/YellowTaxisDelta"
numberOfFiles = 5


# read the Delta table and repartition it
spark.read                          \
 .format("delta")                   \
 .load(path)                        \
 .repartition(numberOfFiles)        \
 .write                             \
 .option("dataChange", "false")     \
 .format("delta")                   \
 .mode("overwrite")                 \
 .save(path)
```

OPTIMIZE

Compaction allows you to specify how to consolidate small files into larger ones. In Delta Lake, a more optimal way to trigger this compaction and let Delta Lake determine the optimal number of large files you want is with the `OPTIMIZE` command.

The `OPTIMIZE` command aims to remove unnecessary files from the transaction log while also producing evenly balanced data files in terms of file size. The smaller files are compacted into new, larger files up to 1 GB.

Figure 5-3 shows how `OPTIMIZE` consolidates smaller files into larger files. Keep in mind, `OPTIMIZE` does not take into account how the data is organized within the files; it only rearranges and consolidates files. You will learn more about how to organize data within the files in the next section.

As you can see in Figure 5-3:

1. The Delta table is comprised of small files containing data with no particular order. In this case there are four files with two rows each.

2. You run `OPTIMIZE` to reduce the number of files that need to be read during operations.

3. The small files in your Delta table are compacted into new, larger files up to 1 GB. In this case, we have two files with four rows each.

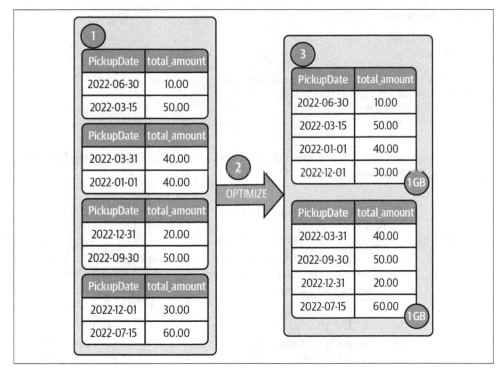

Figure 5-3. Data files before and after OPTIMIZE

Unlike compaction achieved through the repartition method, there is no need to specify the dataChange option. OPTIMIZE uses snapshot isolation when performing the command so concurrent operations and downstream streaming consumers remain uninterrupted.

Let's walk through an example of OPTIMIZE. Using the notebook "03 - Compaction, Optimize and ZOrder," we will execute step 2 (step 1 was executed in the compaction section) to repartition the existing table into 1,000 files to simulate a scenario where we consistently insert data into a table.[4] In step 3 in the notebook, run the OPTIMIZE command. The output will provide metrics of the operation.

```
%sql
OPTIMIZE taxidb.YellowTaxis
```

---

4 GitHub repo location: */chapter05/03 - Compaction, Optimize and ZOrder*

Output (only relevant portions shown):

```
+------------------------------------------------------------+
| metrics                                                    |
+------------------------------------------------------------+
| {"numFilesAdded": 9, "numFilesRemoved": 1000              |
| "filesAdded":{..."totalFiles": 9,                         |
| "totalSize": 2096274374...                                |
| "filesRemoved":{..."totalFiles": 1000, "totalSize": 2317072851 |
+------------------------------------------------------------+
```

After running the OPTIMIZE command on the table, we can see that 1,000 files were removed and 9 files were added.

 When comparing the total size of files removed to files added, you will notice that the size of the file stayed relatively the same, even increasing slightly. The NYC Taxi dataset we are using is mainly integers, so you see little compression from organizing the data. If your data contains many string values, you will see much better compression after running OPTIMIZE.

It is important to note that the 1,000 files that were removed were not physically removed from the underlying storage; rather, they were only logically removed from the transaction log. These files will be physically removed from the underlying storage next time you run VACUUM, which is covered in detail in Chapter 6.

Optimization using OPTIMIZE is also idempotent, meaning that if it is run twice on the same table or subset of data, the second run has no effect. If you run the same command again on the taxidb.YellowTaxis table, the data skipping statistics, which you will learn more about later in this chapter, indicate that 0 files were added and 0 files were removed:

```
%sql
OPTIMIZE taxidb.YellowTaxis
```

Output (only relevant portions shown):

```
+----------------------------------------------------------+
| metrics                                                  |
+----------------------------------------------------------+
| {"numFilesAdded": 0, "numFilesRemoved": 0 "filesAdded": |
| {..."totalFiles": 0, "totalSize": 0...                  |
+----------------------------------------------------------+
```

We can also optimize on specific subsets of data rather than optimizing the entire table. This can be useful when we are only performing DML operations on a specific partition (you will learn more about partitions later in this chapter) and need to optimize just that partition(s). We can specify an optional partition predicate using a WHERE clause. Suppose we are only adding and updating data on a regular basis in the partition for the current month; in this case, that is month 12. After adding 12 to the partition predicate, you will notice that after running the following command, only 17 files were removed and 4 files were added in the specified partition:

```
%sql
OPTIMIZE taxidb.YellowTaxis WHERE PickupMonth = 12
```

Output (only relevant portions shown):

```
+----------------------------------------------------------+
| metrics                                                  |
+----------------------------------------------------------+
| {"numFilesAdded": 4, "numFilesRemoved": 17 "filesAdded": |
| {..."totalFiles": 4, "totalSize":1020557526             |
+----------------------------------------------------------+
```

OPTIMIZE considerations

While OPTIMIZE can help improve the speed of queries, there are a few things to consider before running this command on all tables to help ensure its effectiveness:

- The OPTIMIZE command is effective for tables, or table partitions, that you write data continuously to and thus contain large amounts of small files.

- The OPTIMIZE command is not effective for tables with static data or tables where data is rarely updated because there are few small files to coalesce into larger files.

- The OPTIMIZE command can be a resource-intensive operation that takes time to execute. You can incur costs from your cloud provider while running your compute engine to perform the operation. Balancing these resource-intensive operations with the ideal query performance for your tables is important.

ZORDER BY

While OPTIMIZE aims to consolidate files, Z-ordering allows us to read the data in those files more efficiently by optimizing the data layout. ZORDER BY is a parameter of the command and refers to the way that data is arranged in files based on their values. Specifically, this technique clusters and colocates related information in the same set of files to allow for faster data retrieval. This colocality is automatically used by Delta Lake in data-skipping algorithms, which you will learn more about in the next section of this chapter.

Z-order indexes can improve the performance of queries that filter on the specified Z-order columns. Performance is improved because it allows queries to more efficiently locate the relevant rows, and it also allows joins to more efficiently locate rows with matching values. This efficiency can ultimately be attributed to the reduction in the amount of data that needs to be read during queries.

Similar to partitions, Z-order indexes will soon be replaced by the new Delta Lake feature, liquid clustering, as the preferred technique to simplify data layout and optimize query performance. Delta Lake liquid clustering is not compatible with user-specified table partitions or Z-ordering. This feature is currently in preview and will be generally available in the near future. You can learn more and stay up-to-date on the status of liquid clustering by reviewing the Delta Lake documentation website (*https://oreil.ly/MQzTk*) and this feature request (*https://oreil.ly/72cGH*).

To demonstrate OPTIMIZE combined with Z-ordering, we will reset and clear the optimization we did on taxidb.YellowTaxis earlier in the chapter by repartitioning the existing table into 1,000 smaller files once again by running step 6:

```
# define the path and number of files to repartition
path = "/mnt/datalake/book/chapter05/YellowTaxisDelta"
numberOfFiles = 1000

# read the Delta table and repartition it
spark.read.format("delta").load(path).repartition(numberOfFiles)   \
  .write                                                            \
  .option("dataChange", "false")                                   \
  .format("delta")                                                  \
  .mode("overwrite")                                                \
  .save(path)
```

To get a baseline for the initial query, execute the baseline query in the script:

```
%sql
-- baseline query
-- take note how long it takes to return results
SELECT
  COUNT(*) as count,
  SUM(total_amount) as totalAmount,
  PickupDate
FROM
  taxidb.tripData
WHERE
  PickupDate BETWEEN '2022-01-01' AND '2022-03-31'
GROUP BY
  PickupDate
```

This query will give us a general baseline for how long the execution will take when the underlying Delta table has many small files and the data is not organized in any particular order. We can apply `ZORDER BY` with the `OPTIMIZE` command to consolidate files and effectively order the data in those files. This will, in turn, significantly decrease the time it takes to fetch the query results since the data is easier to locate. This is generally most effective when used on a high-cardinality column and a column used frequently in query predicates, which means that the column that we apply Z-ordering to impacts how well the data is retrieved:

```sql
%sql
OPTIMIZE taxidb.tripData ZORDER BY PickupDate
```

Now that we added Z-ordering, we can see the detailed `zOrderStats` highlighted in the output, which includes the strategy name, input cube files, and other statistics about the `ZORDER BY` operation.

When we run the same baseline query that was executed before the `OPTIMIZE` and `ZORDER BY` command, we should notice a significant increase in the time it takes to retrieve the query results. The time it takes to retrieve the results will vary depending on the cluster configuration, but we consistently noticed around a 70% decrease in time it took to return the query results due to the optimizations.

In this case, adding Z-ordering increased the query engine's efficiency in reading the data, and `OPTIMIZE` coalesced the small files into larger ones. This can be difficult to show using large datasets, but Figure 5-4 illustrates how consolidation and ordering occur using the `taxidb.YellowTaxis` table.

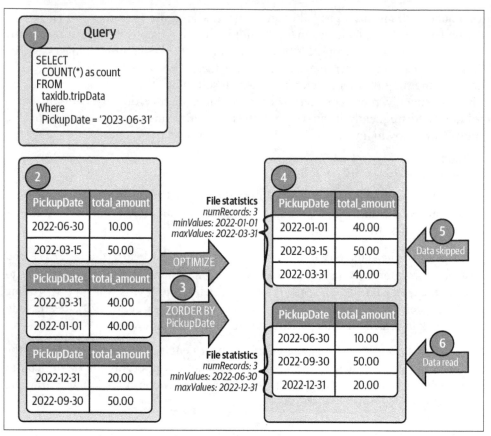

Figure 5-4. `taxidb.tripData` *Delta table files before and after* OPTIMIZE *and* ZORDER BY, *along with how data is retrieved using data skipping*

The numbered steps in Figure 5-4 show:

1. Query the Delta table called `taxiDb.YellowTaxis` and count the number of records `WHERE PickupDate = '2022-06-30'`.

2. The Delta table is comprised of small files containing data with no particular order.

3. We run `OPTIMIZE` with `ZORDER BY` for better performance during query executions.

4. Small files are coalesced into larger ones, and the data is sorted by the Z-order column, which is `PickupDate`.

5. Data skipping is leveraged since we are looking for the query predicate `Pickup Date = '2022-06-30'`. The first file is skipped because Delta Lake knows that the query predicate is not contained in this file since it falls outside the range of the min and max values in the data skipping statistics.

6. Data is quickly read from the second file because Delta Lake knows to scan this file since the search predicate falls inside the range of the min and max values.

You can see that before we ran any optimization on the table, the data was organized into smaller files with no order to the data. When running the baseline query, the query engine had to scan all the Delta Lake files to find our query predicate `WHERE PickupDate BETWEEN '2022-01-01' AND '2022-03-31'`. Once we applied `OPTIMIZE` with `ZORDER BY`, the data was coalesced into larger files, and the data was sorted by the column `PickupDate` in ascending order. This allowed the query engine to read the first file based on the query predicate, and ignore, or skip, the second file to gather the results.

ZORDER BY Considerations

You can specify multiple columns for `ZORDER BY` as a comma-separated list in the command. However, the effectiveness of the locality drops with each additional column:

```sql
%sql
OPTIMIZE taxidb.tripData ZORDER BY PickupDate, VendorId
```

Similar to `OPTIMIZE`, you can apply Z-ordering to specific subsets of data, such as partitions, rather than applying it to the entire table:

```sql
%sql
OPTIMIZE taxidb.tripData ZORDER BY PickupDate, VendorId
WHERE PickupMonth = 2022
```

> You cannot use `ZORDER BY` on fields used for partitioning. You have learned that `ZORDER BY` works in tandem with the `OPTIMIZE` command. However, you cannot combine files across partition boundaries, so Z-order clustering can only occur within a partition. For unpartitioned tables, files can be combined across the entire table.

If you expect a column to be commonly used in query predicates, and if that column has high cardinality (that is, a large number of distinct values), then use `ZORDER BY`.

Unlike OPTIMIZE, Z-ordering is not idempotent but aims to be an incremental operation. The time it takes for Z-ordering is not guaranteed to reduce over multiple runs. However, if no new data was added to a partition that was just Z-ordered, another Z-ordering of that partition will not have any effect.[5]

Liquid Clustering

Liquid clustering is a new feature in Delta Lake that is currently in preview at the time of writing. This feature will be generally available in the near future. You can learn more and stay up-to-date on the status of liquid clustering by reviewing the Delta Lake documentation website (*https://oreil.ly/MQzTk*) and this feature request (*https://oreil.ly/72cGH*).

While some of the performance tuning techniques mentioned throughout this chapter aim to optimize data layouts and thus improve read and write performance, there are some shortcomings:

Partitioning
>   Partitions run the risk of introducing the small file problem, where data is stored across many different small files, which inevitably results in poor performance. And once a table is partitioned, this partition cannot be changed and can cause challenges for new use cases or new query patterns. While Delta Lake supports partitioning, there are challenges with partition evolution, as partitioning is considered a *fixed data layout*.

ZORDER BY
>   Anytime data is inserted, updated, or deleted on a table, OPTIMIZE ZORDER BY must be run again for optimization. And when ZORDER BY is applied again, the user must remember the columns used in the expression. This is because the columns used in ZORDER BY are not persisted and can cause errors or challenges when attempting to apply it again. Since OPTIMIZE ZORDER BY is not idempotent, this will result in reclustering data when it is run.

Many of the shortcomings with partitioning and Z-ordering can be addressed through Delta Lake's liquid clustering feature. The following scenarios for Delta tables benefit greatly from liquid clustering

- Tables often filtered by high cardinality columns
- Tables with substantial skew in data distribution
- Tables that require large amounts of tuning and maintenance

---

5 See "Optimizations" in the Delta Lake documentation (*https://oreil.ly/Etmjy*).

- Tables with concurrent write requirements
- Tables with partition patterns that change over time

Delta Lake's liquid clustering feature aims to address limitations found with partitioning and Z-ordering, and revamp both read and write performance through a more dynamic data layout. Ultimately, liquid clustering helps reduce performance tuning overhead while also supporting efficient query access.

Enabling Liquid Clustering

To enable liquid clustering on a table, you can specify the CLUSTER BY command when creating a table. You must specify liquid clustering using the CLUSTER BY command when you create the table; you cannot add clustering to an existing table (e.g., using ALTER TABLE) that does not have liquid clustering enabled.

 If you are using Databricks to follow along in this book and run the notebooks from the GitHub repo, Databricks Runtime 13.2 and above is required to run the code related to liquid clustering.

To demonstrate how to create a table with liquid clustering enabled, we can use the notebook "04 - Liquid Clustering" and the following command:

```sql
%sql
CREATE EXTERNAL TABLE taxidb.tripDataClustered CLUSTER BY (VendorId)
LOCATION '/mnt/datalake/book/chapter05/YellowTaxisLiquidClusteringDelta'
AS SELECT * FROM taxiDb.tripData LIMIT 1000;
```

The preceding command creates an external table with liquid clustering enabled, clustered by VendorId, and populated with data from the taxiDb.tripData table that was created earlier.

To trigger clustering, run the OPTIMIZE command on the newly created table:

```sql
%sql
OPTIMIZE taxidb.tripDataClustered;
```

Output (only relevant portions shown):

```
+--------------------------------------------------------------------------+
| metrics                                                                  |
+--------------------------------------------------------------------------+
| {"sizeOfTableInBytesBeforeLazyClustering": 43427, "isNewMetadataCreated": |
| true…"numFilesClassifiedToLeafNodes": 1,                                  |
| "sizeOfFilesClassifiedToLeafNodesInBytes": 43427,                        |
| "logicalSizeOfFilesClassifiedToLeafNodesInBytes": 43427,                 |
| "numClusteringTasksPlanned": 0,  "numCompactionTasksPlanned": 0,         |
| "numOptimizeBatchesPlanned": 0, "numLeafNodesExpanded": 0,               |
```

```
|   "numLeafNodesClustered": 0, "numLeafNodesCompacted": 0,                       |
|   "numIntermediateNodesCompacted": 0, "totalSizeOfDataToCompactInBytes": 0,     |
|   "totalLogicalSizeOfDataToCompactInBytes": 0,                                  |
|   "numIntermediateNodesClustered": 0, "numFilesSkippedAfterExpansion": 0,       |
|   "totalSizeOfFilesSkippedAfterExpansionInBytes": 0,                            |
|   "totalLogicalSizeOfFilesSkippedAfterExpansionInBytes": 0,                     |
|   "totalSizeOfDataToRewriteInBytes": 0,                                         |
|   "totalLogicalSizeOfDataToRewriteInBytes": 0…                                  |
+---------------------------------------------------------------------------------+
```

Earlier in the chapter you saw the metrics displayed after running the OPTIMIZE command on a table. In the output of the OPTIMIZE command for a table with liquid clustering enabled, you will see clusterMetrics are now included in the metrics of the output. These clusterMetrics display detailed information about the underlying data files (e.g., size and number), compaction details, and cluster node information so that you can view the results of clustering.

It is important to note that only a few operations automatically cluster data on write when writing data to a table with liquid clustering. The following operations support automatically clustering data on write, provided the size of the data being inserted does not exceed 512 GB:

- INSERT INTO
- CREATE TABLE AS SELECT (CTAS) statements
- COPY INTO
- Write appends such as spark.write.format("delta").mode("append")

Since only these specific operations support clustering data on write, you should trigger clustering on a regular basis by running OPTIMIZE. Running this command frequently will ensure that data is properly clustered.

It is also worth noting that liquid clustering is incremental when triggered by OPTIMIZE, meaning that only the necessary data is rewritten to accommodate data that needs to be clustered. Since not all write operations automatically cluster data, and since OPTIMIZE is an incremental operation, it is recommended to regularly schedule OPTIMIZE jobs to cluster data, especially since this incremental process helps these jobs run quickly.

Operations on Clustered Columns

By enabling liquid clustering, you learned how to specify what columns a table is clustered on by using the CLUSTER BY command. Once a table is clustered by particular columns, you can read data more efficiently by leveraging the clustered columns, while also being able to view, change, and remove those columns.

Changing clustered columns

While you must specify how a table is clustered when it is initially created, you can still change the columns used for clustering on the table using ALTER TABLE and CLUSTER BY. To change the cluster columns of the table that we created earlier to be clustered on both VendorId and RateCodeId, run the following command:

```
%sql
ALTER TABLE taxidb.tripDataClustered CLUSTER BY (VendorId, RateCodeId);
```

 You can specify up to four columns as clustering keys.

When changing clustered columns, liquid clustering does not require the entire table to be rewritten. This clustering evolution is due to the dynamic data layout feature of liquid clustering and offers a significant advantage over partition features mentioned earlier in the chapter. Traditional partitioning is a fixed data layout and does not support changing how a table is partitioned without having to rewrite the entire table. This clustering evolution can be essential as query patterns for a table can often change over time, and this allows you to dynamically adapt to new query patterns without any significant overhead or challenges.

Viewing clustered columns

Now that we have changed how the table is clustered, we can view the table metadata using DESCRIBE TABLE to confirm these changes and see the clustered columns:

```
%sql
DESCRIBE TABLE taxidb.tripDataClustered;
```

Output (only relevant portions shown):

```
+-----------------------------+-----------+---------+
| col_name                    | data_type | comment |
+-----------------------------+-----------+---------+
| # Clustering Information    |           |         |
+-----------------------------+-----------+---------+
| # col_name                  | data_type | comment |
+-----------------------------+-----------+---------+
| VendorId                    | bigint    | null    |
+-----------------------------+-----------+---------+
| RateCodeId                  | double    | null    |
+-----------------------------+-----------+---------+
```

The DESCRIBE TABLE command returns basic metadata information about the table, which shows the cluster information and that the table is now clustered on both VendorId and RateCodeId.

Reading data from a clustered table

Now that we have confirmed the clustered columns, we can specify the clustered columns in query filters (e.g., WHERE clause) to achieve the best (i.e., fastest) query results. For example, add VendorId and RateCodeId to a WHERE clause on the taxidb.tripDataClustered table to achieve the best query results:

```
%sql
SELECT * FROM taxidb.tripDataClustered WHERE VendorId = 1 and RateCodeId = 1
```

Removing clustered columns

If we choose to remove the columns that a table is clustered by, we can simply specify CLUSTER BY NONE:

```
%sql
ALTER TABLE taxidb.tripDataClustered CLUSTER BY NONE;
```

Liquid Clustering Warnings and Considerations

Given that liquid clustering is currently in preview at the time of writing, there are several factors to take into account prior to enabling and utilizing liquid clustering:

- Check your environment runtime to ensure it supports OPTIMIZE on Delta tables with liquid clustering enabled.

  If you are using Databricks to follow along in this book and run the notebooks from the GitHub repo, Databricks Runtime 13.2 and above is required.

- Tables created with liquid clustering enabled have numerous Delta table features enabled at creation and use Delta version 7 and reader version 3. Table protocol versions cannot be downgraded, and tables with clustering enabled are not readable by Delta Lake clients that do not support all enabled Delta reader protocol table features.

- You must enable Delta Lake liquid clustering when first creating a table. You cannot alter an existing table to add clustering without clustering being enabled when the table is first created.

- You can only specify columns with statistics collected for clustered columns. Remember, only the first 32 columns in a Delta table have statistics collected by default.

- Structured Streaming workloads do not support clustering-on-write.
- Run `OPTIMIZE` frequently to ensure new data is clustered.

 Liquid clustering is not compatible with partitioning or `ZORDER BY`.

Conclusion

In this chapter, you learned about different techniques to store and organize data, both physically and dynamically, and the significant effects that it can have on how data is read and retrieved during operations. As the types of data points captured continue to grow, along with the sheer volume of data, tables will continue to get larger and larger. Performance tuning on large datasets has been, and always will be, considered a good strategy and best practice. Understanding the Delta Lake features that enable this will help significantly reduce overhead.

We discussed the small data files problem, the impact that it can have on performance, and how it can be solved using compaction strategies, including optimal file consolidation using `OPTIMIZE`. After you `OPTIMIZE` a table's files, you can arrange the values within those files using `ZORDER BY`, which allows you to leverage data skipping more effectively through data skipping statistics. You can take data skipping one step further by partitioning Delta tables and breaking the data into distinct parts to further reduce the amount of data that needs to be read.

Then we looked at new Delta Lake features that address some of the challenges that partitioning and Z-ordering can still have. Liquid clustering offers clustering evolution through dynamic data layouts that don't require you to rewrite an entire table as query patterns evolve over time. This largely automated feature is not compatible with partitioning and Z-ordering, but requires less tuning effort compared to other performance optimization features, and greatly enhances the read and write performance of tables.

Using the Delta Lake features mentioned in this chapter can reduce the amount of nonrelevant data that needs to be read, and improve performance, especially as the number of data files in your Delta table grows. In the next chapter, you will learn how Delta Lake leverages old data files to allow you to version your data and travel back to a certain point in time.

Using Time Travel

Having worked with databases and tables before, odds are you have had that immediate sense of panic when you forgot a WHERE clause and accidentally ran a DELETE or UPDATE statement against an entire table. We have all been there. Or you may have wondered what your data or schema looked like at a specific point in time for auditing, tracking, or analysis purposes.

Given how data is constantly changing, the following scenarios are common occurrences that, historically, have been difficult to solve or answer:

Regulatory
> Auditing and regulatory compliance can require that data be stored and retrieved for many years or can require that you track certain changes to your data (e.g., GDPR).

Reproduce experiments and reports
> There are often requirements for data scientists or analysts to re-create reports or machine learning experiments and model outputs given a specific set of data at a specific point in time.

Rollbacks
> Accidental or bad DML operations on your data, such as INSERT, UPDATE, DELETE, and MERGE, can require fixes and rollbacks to a previous state.

Time-series analysis
> Reporting needs can require you to look back or analyze data over time, for example, how many new customers were added over the course of a month.

Debugging
> Troubleshooting ETL pipelines, data quality issues, or broken processes where the specific cause may only be observable in a historical state.

The ability to easily traverse through different versions of data at specific points in time is a key feature in Delta Lake called Delta Lake time travel. You learned in Chapter 2 that the transaction log automatically versions data in a Delta table, and this versioning helps you access any historical version of that data. Through versioning and data retention, you will learn how to use these powerful Delta Lake features while also leveraging data management and storage optimization.

Delta Lake Time Travel

Delta Lake time travel allows you to access and revert to previous versions of data stored in Delta Lake, easily providing a powerful mechanism for version control, auditing, and data management. You can then track changes over time and roll back to previous versions if needed.

Let's walk through an example. First, execute the "Chapter Initialization" notebook for Chapter 6[1] to create the `taxidb.tripData` Delta table. Next, open the "01 - Time Travel" notebook for Chapter 6. Let's assume that we need to update `VendorId` from 1 to 10. Then, we need to delete all occurrences `WHERE VendorId = 2`. Using the scripts in the notebook for "01 - Time Travel," execute the following command to apply those changes:

```
%sql
--update records in table
UPDATE taxidb.tripData
SET VendorId = 10
WHERE VendorId = 1;

--delete records in table
DELETE FROM taxidb.tripData
WHERE VendorId = 2;

--describe the table history
DESCRIBE HISTORY taxidb.tripData;
```

You will see this output (only relevant portions shown):

```
+---------+-----------+----------------------------------------------------------+
| version | operation | operationParameters                                      |
+---------+-----------+----------------------------------------------------------+
| 2       | DELETE    | {"predicate":                                            |
|         |           | "[\"(spark_catalog.taxidb.tripData.VendorId = 2L)\"]"}   |
+---------+-----------+----------------------------------------------------------+
| 1       | UPDATE    | {"predicate": "(VendorId#5081L = 1)"}                    |
+---------+-----------+----------------------------------------------------------+
| 0       | WRITE     | {"mode": "Overwrite", "partitionBy": "[]"}               |
+---------+-----------+----------------------------------------------------------+
```

---

1 GitHub repo location: */chapter06/00 - Chapter Initialization*

Output continued and modified to show `operationMetrics` (only relevant portions shown):

```
+--------------------+-----------+-------------------------------------------------------+
| version | operation | operationMetrics                                          |
+--------------------+-----------+-------------------------------------------------------+
| 2       | DELETE    | {"numRemovedFiles": "10", "numCopiedRows": "9643805",  |
|         |           | "numAddedChangeFiles": "0",                            |
|         |           | ..."numDeletedRows": "23360027"...,                    |
|         |           | "numAddedFiles": "10"...}                              |
+--------------------+-----------+-------------------------------------------------------+
| 1       | UPDATE    | {"numRemovedFiles": "10", "numCopiedRows": "23414817", |
|         |           | "numAddedChangeFiles": "0","..."numAddedFiles": "10".} |
+--------------------+-----------+-------------------------------------------------------+
| 0       | WRITE     | {"numFiles": "10", "numOutputRows": "33003832"...}     |
+--------------------+-----------+-------------------------------------------------------+
```

Looking at the output, we can see that there are a total of three versions of the table, one for each commit, with version 2 being the most recent change:

- Version 0: wrote the initial Delta table using overwrite and no partitions
- Version 1: updated the Delta table using the predicate `VendorId = 1`
- Version 2: deleted data from the Delta table using the predicate `VendorId = 2`

Notice that the `DESCRIBE HISTORY` command shows details about the version, transaction timestamp, operation, operation parameters, and operation metrics. The `operationMetrics` in the output also shows the number of rows and files changed from the operation.

Figure 6-1 illustrates the different versions of the table and examples of the underlying data.

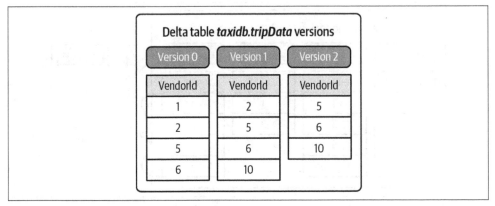

Figure 6-1. `taxidb.tripData` *version history*

Restoring a Table

Now, let's say that we want to roll back the previous UPDATE and DELETE operations we performed on taxidb.tripData and restore it back to its original state (i.e., version 0). We can use the RESTORE command to roll back the table to the desired version:

```
%sql
--restore table to previous version
RESTORE TABLE taxidb.tripData TO VERSION AS OF 0;

--describe the table history
DESCRIBE HISTORY taxidb.tripData;
```

Output (only relevant portions shown):

```
+------------------------------------------------------------------------+
| version | operation | operationParameters                              |
+------------------------------------------------------------------------+
| 3       | RESTORE   | {"version": "0", "timestamp": null}              |
+------------------------------------------------------------------------+
| 2       | DELETE    | {"predicate":                                    |
|         |           | "[\"(spark_catalog.taxidb.tripData.VendorId IN 5,6L) |
|         |           | \"]"}                                            |
+------------------------------------------------------------------------+
| 1       | UPDATE    | {"predicate": "(VendorId#5081L = 1)"}            |
+------------------------------------------------------------------------+
| 0       | WRITE     | {"mode": "Overwrite", "partitionBy": "[]"}       |
+------------------------------------------------------------------------+
```

After restoring the table to version 0 and running the DESCRIBE HISTORY command, you will see that there is now an additional version of the table, version 3, which captures the RESTORE operation. Figure 6-2 illustrates the different versions of the table and examples of the underlying data.

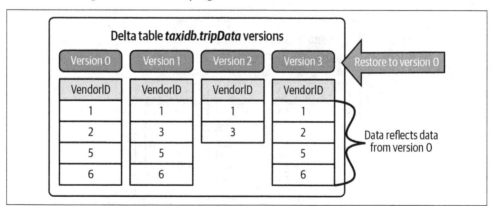

Figure 6-2. taxidb.tripData *versions after restoring back to version 0*

You can now see in the data and Figure 6-2 that the latest version of the table now reflects the data from version 0.

 You can restore a table that has already been restored. You can also restore a table to a version that was previously restored.

When data files are deleted either manually or through VACUUM (you will learn more about VACUUM later in this chapter), restoring a table to a version that references those data files will fail. Use the Spark configuration spark.sql.files.ignoreMissingFiles = True to partially restore the table. As the name indicates, this Spark configuration will simply ignore missing files when reading data.

Restoring via Timestamp

In the previous examples we restored the table to a specific version, but we can also restore a table to a specific timestamp. The timestamp format for restoring to an earlier state is yyyy-MM-dd HH:mm:ss. Providing only a *date* (yyyy-MM-dd) string is also supported.

```
%sql
--restore table to a specific timestamp
RESTORE TABLE taxidb.tripData TO TIMESTAMP AS OF '2023-01-01 00:00:00';

--restore table to the state it was in an hour ago
RESTORE TABLE taxidb.tripData
TO TIMESTAMP AS OF current_timestamp() - INTERVAL '1' HOUR;
```

We can also import the delta module to use PySpark and the DataFrame API for restoring a table. We can use the method restoreToVersion(version: int) to restore to a specific version like we did earlier, or we can use the restoreToTimestamp(timestamp: str) method to restore to a specified timestamp:

```
--import delta module
from delta.tables import *

--restore table to a specific timestamp using PySpark
deltaTable = DeltaTable.forName(spark, "taxidb.tripData")
deltaTable.restoreToTimestamp("2023-01-01")
```

Time Travel Under the Hood

Version history can be kept on a Delta table because the transaction log keeps track of which files should or should not be read when performing operations on a table. When the DESCRIBE HISTORY command is executed, it will also return the operationMetrics, which tells you the number of files added and removed during an operation. When performing an UPDATE, DELETE, or MERGE on a table, that data is not physically removed from the underlying storage. Rather, these operations update the transaction log to indicate which files should or should not be read. Similarly, when you restore a table to a previous version, it does not physically add or remove data; it only updates the metadata in the transaction log to tell it which files to read.

In Chapter 2 you learned about JSON files within the _delta_log_ directory and checkpoint files. Checkpoint files save the state of the entire table at a point in time, and are automatically generated to maintain read performance by combining JSON commits into Parquet files. The checkpoint file and subsequent commits can then be read to get the current state, and previous states in the case of time travel, of the table, avoiding the need to list and reprocess all of the commits.

The transaction log commits checkpoint files, and the fact that data files are only logically removed as opposed to being physically removed is the foundation for how Delta Lake easily enables time travel on your Delta table. Figure 6-3 shows the transaction log entries for each of the operations on the `taxidb.tripData` table throughout the different transactions and versions.

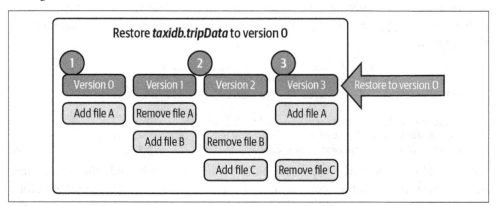

Figure 6-3. `taxidb.tripData` *transaction log files*

The numbered steps in Figure 6-3 show:

1. Version 0: the initial table is created and files are added in the transaction log.

2. Version 1 and 2: *add file* and *remove file* act as metadata entries that Delta Lake uses to determine which files should be read for each version. *Remove file* does not physically delete data; it just logically removes files from the table.

3. Version 3: this version was restored back to version 0, so the transaction log restores file A, the original file added in version 0, and logically removes file C.

If you look at the table history of the `taxidb.tripData` table that we previously restored to version 0, you will notice the number of restored, added, and removed files captured in the `operationMetrics`:

```
%sql
--describe table history
DESCRIBE HISTORY taxidb.tripData
```

Output (only relevant portions shown):

```
+---------------------------------------------------------------------+
| version | operation | operationMetrics                              |
+---------------------------------------------------------------------+
| 3       | RESTORE   | {"numRestoredFiles": "10"…"numRemovedFiles":  |
|         |           | "10"…"numOfFilesAfterRestore": "10"           |
+---------------------------------------------------------------------+
| 2       | DELETE    | {"numRemovedFiles": "10"…"numAddedChangeFiles":|
|         |           | "0"…"numAddedFiles": "10"                     |
+---------------------------------------------------------------------+
| 1       | UPDATE    | {"numRemovedFiles": "10"…"numAddedChangeFiles":|
|         |           | "0"…"numAddedFiles": "10"                     |
+---------------------------------------------------------------------+
| 0       | WRITE     | {"numFiles": "10", "numOutputRows": "33003832",|
|         |           | "numOutputBytes": "715810450"}                |
+---------------------------------------------------------------------+
```

You will learn more about how to retain and remove previous versions of data in later sections of this chapter.

RESTORE Considerations and Warnings

It is important to note that RESTORE is a data-changing operation, meaning data Change = true. This means it can potentially affect downstream jobs, such as Structured Streaming jobs, which you will learn more about in Chapter 8.

Consider a situation where the streaming query only processes updates to a Delta table. If we RESTORE the table to a previous version, then previous updates to the table could be processed again by your streaming job since the transaction log restores previous versions of the data using the *add file* action with dataChange = true. The streaming job recognizes the records as new data.

Table 6-1. Operations resulting from RESTORE

Table version	Operation	Delta log updates	Records in data change log updates
0	INSERT	AddFile(/path/to/file-1, dataChange = true)	(VendorId = 1, passenger_count = 2, (VendorId = 2, passenger_count = 3)
1	INSERT	AddFile(/path/to/file-2, dataChange = true)	(VendorId = 2, passenger_count = 4)
2	OPTIMIZE	AddFile(/path/to/file-3, dataChange = false), RemoveFile(/path/to/file-1), RemoveFile(/path/to/file-2)	(No records change during OPTIMIZE)

Table version	Operation	Delta log updates	Records in data change log updates
3	RESTORE	RemoveFile(/path/to/file-3), AddFile(/path/to/file-1, dataChange = true), Add File(/path/to/file-2, data Change = true)	(VendorId = 1, passenger_count = 2, (VendorId = 2, passenger_count = 3), (VendorId = 2, passenger_count = 4)

In Table 6-1, notice that the OPTIMIZE operation removed files related to versions 1 and 2, and added a file for version 3. After running the RESTORE command, the operation added back file 1 and file 2 for their respective versions, which was considered a dataChange operation.

Querying an Older Version of a Table

By default, whenever you query a Delta table you always query the table's latest version. But Delta Lake time travel allows you to also perform read operations on a table's previous versions without needing to restore them. Remember, the data itself is not physically deleted from the underlying storage, it is just logically removed. Logical removal rather than physical deletion means that time travel not only allows you to restore a table to a specific point in time, but you can easily query previous versions of a table directly, without restoring.

You can access previous versions of the data in two different ways:

1. Using a timestamp
2. Using a version number

Similar to how we restored the table to a previous version using the version number, we can also use the version number to query the table at a specific point in time. In the earlier example, we restored the table back to its previous state, but we had deleted records in version 2 using the predicate WHERE VendorId = 2. We can search for the count of those VendorId records in version 2 of the table using time travel:

```sql
%sql
--count records where VendorId = 1 using version number
SELECT COUNT(*) AS count FROM taxidb.tripData VERSION AS OF 2 WHERE VendorId = 1;

--count records where VendorId = 1 using operation timestamp
SELECT COUNT(*) AS count FROM taxidb.tripData
VERSION AS OF '2023-01-01 00:00:00' WHERE VendorId = 1;

--count records where VendorId = 1 using operation timestamp and using @ syntax
--timestamp must be in yyyyMMddHHmmssSSS format
SELECT COUNT(*) AS count FROM taxidb.YellowTaxi@20230101000000000
WHERE VendorId = 1;
```

```
--count records where VendorId = 1 using version number and using @ syntax
SELECT COUNT(*) AS count FROM taxidb.tripData@v2 WHERE VendorId = 1;
```

Output:

```
+-------+
| count |
+-------+
| 0     |
+-------+
```

As seen in the preceding examples, we can access the different versions of the data using different types of syntax, we can either use a timestamp or the version number with the syntax specifying VERSION AS OF or appending "@" after the table name.

Time travel is not only accessible via SQL, but we can also time travel via the DataFrame API using the .option() method:

```
# count records where VendorId = 1 using version number
spark.read.option("versionAsOf", "0").table("taxidb.tripData").filter(
    "VendorId = 1"
).count()
```

```
# count records where VendorId = 1 using timestamp
spark.read.option("timestampAsOf", "0").table("taxidb.tripData").filter(
    "VendorId = 1"
).count()
```

Querying by timestamp makes it easy to perform time-series analysis because we can compare the data of the same table to itself at two different points in time. And while there are other ETL patterns we can follow to capture historical data and enable time-series analysis (e.g., slowly changing dimensions and change data feeds), time travel provides a quick and easy way to perform ad hoc analysis for tables that may not have these ETL patterns in place. For example, if we wanted to quickly see how many passengers were picked up this week compared to last week using the version history of taxidb.tripData, we could run the following query:

```
%sql
--count number of new passengers from 7 days ago
SELECT sum(passenger_count) - (
  SELECT sum(passenger_count)
  FROM taxidb.tripData TIMESTAMP AS OF date_sub(current_date(), 7)
)
FROM taxidb.tripData
```

While time travel enables time-series analysis as demonstrated, there are more efficient ways to perform similar operations. These time-series examples are illustrated for the purposes of demonstrating the capabilities of time travel. Later on in this chapter you will learn about Delta Lake's Change Data Feed, which supports a recommended approach for performing time-series analysis due to its efficiency.

Data Retention

The data files backing a Delta table are never deleted automatically, but log files are automatically cleaned up after checkpoints are written. Ultimately, what enables time travel to a specific version of a table is the retention of *both* the data and log files for that version of a table. By default, Delta tables retain the commit history, or log files, for 30 days. So you can access time travel on Delta tables for up to 30 days unless you have modified the data or log files.

In this and following sections, you will see the term *retention thresholds*. The retention threshold refers to the interval (e.g., days) a file must be kept before it is a candidate to be physically removed from storage. For example, if the retention threshold for a table is seven days, then a file must be *at least* seven days older than the current table version before becoming eligible to be removed. The following sections will cover the two types of retention that this book will discuss, data and log file retention.

Data File Retention

Data file retention refers to how long data files are retained in a Delta table. The default retention is seven days for files that are candidates to be removed by VACUUM, a command used for physically deleting data files. In brief, VACUUM removes data files no longer referenced by the Delta table and older than the retention period. Unless removed manually, data files will only be removed when you run VACUUM. This command does not delete Delta log files, only data files. You will learn more about the VACUUM command and how it works later on in this chapter.

Data files commonly need to be retained for longer than the default retention period. The table property `delta.deletedFileRetentionDuration = "interval <interval>"` controls how long ago a file must have been deleted before being a candidate for VACUUM.

To retain data files for a certain period of time even if you run VACUUM, use the table property `delta.deletedFileRetentionDuration = "interval <interval>"`. This will control how long ago a file must have been deleted before being a candidate for

VACUUM. For example, if you need to retain and access historical data for one year, set
`delta.deletedFileRetentionDuration = "interval 365 days"`.

 Once you remove a data file(s), you will be unable to time travel to versions of the table that used that data file(s).

However, retaining excess data files can cause cloud storage costs to grow over time, along with potential impacts on performance for processing metadata.

To demonstrate how data files can grow over time, using `DESCRIBE HISTORY` on the `taxiDb.tripData` table, we can use the metrics `numFiles` and `numAddedFiles` in `operationMetrics` to show how many files were added during each operation:

```
%sql
--describe table history
DESCRIBE HISTORY taxidb.tripData
```

Output (only relevant portions shown):

```
+------------------------------------------------------------------------+
| version | operation | operationMetrics                                 |
+------------------------------------------------------------------------+
| 3       | RESTORE   | {"numRestoredFiles": "10"…"numRemovedFiles":     |
|         |           | "10"…"numOfFilesAfterRestore": "10"              |
+------------------------------------------------------------------------+
| 2       | DELETE    | {"numRemovedFiles": "10"…"numAddedChangeFiles": |
|         |           | "0"…"numAddedFiles": "10"                        |
+------------------------------------------------------------------------+
| 1       | UPDATE    | {"numRemovedFiles": "10"…"numAddedChangeFiles": |
|         |           | "0"…"numAddedFiles": "10"                        |
+------------------------------------------------------------------------+
| 0       | WRITE     | {"numFiles": "10", "numOutputRows": "33003832", |
|         |           | "numOutputBytes": "715810450"}                   |
+------------------------------------------------------------------------+
```

Based on the `numFiles` and `numAddedFiles` metrics, you can see that 30 files have been added to this table. If you have an ETL process that runs each day and performs INSERTs, UPDATEs, or DELETEs on a single table, then after one year you could have *10,950 (30 x 365) files*! And this is just the number of files for a single table. Imagine the number of files you can have across your entire data platform. The number of files added during each operation obviously depends on the operations performed, number of rows contained during each operation, and other variables, but this helps demonstrate how your data files can grow over time.

Fortunately, cloud data lakes are very cost-effective when it comes to storing data, but these costs can grow as your data files do. This is why it is still important to be economical when retaining data files for extended periods of time, and take costs and business requirements into consideration when setting retention periods.

Log File Retention

Log file retention refers to how long the log files are retained in the Delta table. The default retention is 30 days. You can change how long files are retained using the table property `delta.logRetentionDuration`. For example, if you need to retain commit history on a table for one year, set `delta.logRetentionDuration = "interval 365 days"`.

In Chapter 2 you learned that every 10 commits, a checkpoint is written (at the time of writing; this is subject to change in future versions of Delta Lake). Delta Lake automatically cleans up log files based on the retention interval each time a new checkpoint is generated.

 In order to time travel to a specific version of the table, *all* of the consecutive log entries up until a new checkpoint is written are required. Checkpoints are written every 10 commits, which means that if you want to time travel to version 0-9 of a table, then there must be log entries for all versions 0, 1, 2, ..., 9. You will be unable to time travel to version 0-9 of the table if the log for version 0 is removed due to Delta automatically cleaning up log entries older than the retention interval.

There is minimal downside to retaining log files, as log files do not affect performance on read/writes on the table; they only affect performance on operations that leverage table history. You should always consider storage costs when retaining files, but log files are generally small in nature.

 Delta Lake properties such as `delta.deletedFileRetentionDura tion` and `delta.logRetentionDuration` can also be set using the Spark configuration properties.

Setting File Retention Duration Example

Using the `taxidb.tripData` table, let's say, for example, there is a requirement to maintain the entire history of a table for one year for either time-series analysis or regulatory purposes. To ensure that we can time travel to this table at any point in the last year, we can set the following table properties:

```
%sql
--set log retention to 365 days
```

```
ALTER TABLE taxidb.tripData
SET TBLPROPERTIES(delta.logRetentionDuration = "interval 365 days");

--set data file retention to 365 days
ALTER TABLE taxidb.tripData
SET TBLPROPERTIES(delta.deletedFileRetentionDuration = "interval 365 days");

--show the table properties to confirm data and log file retention
SHOW TBLPROPERTIES taxidb.tripData;
```

Output (only relevant portions shown):

```
+--------------------------------------+--------------------+
| key                                  | value              |
+--------------------------------------+--------------------+
| delta.deletedFileRetentionDuration   | interval 365 days  |
+--------------------------------------+--------------------+
| delta.logRetentionDuration           | interval 365 days  |
+--------------------------------------+--------------------+
```

Since `delta.deletedFileRetentionDuration` and `delta.logRetentionDuration` are table properties, we can set these properties when we initially create the table, or we can alter the table's properties after it has been created.

You can see in the preceding example that after altering the table's properties and then executing the command `SHOW TBLPROPERTIES`, it returns the intervals for retention on deleted files and log files for `taxidb.tripData`. By setting both intervals to 365 days, we can now ensure that we can time travel to this table at any point in time during the last year to satisfy both business requirements and regulatory requirements.

Data Archiving

In the case of regulatory or archival purposes where you may need to retain data for a certain number of years, storing this data using time travel and file retention can become expensive due to storage costs. To help minimize costs, an alternative solution can be to archive your data in a daily, weekly, or monthly manner by creating a new table using a `CREATE TABLE AS SELECT` pattern:

```
%sql
--archive table by creating or replace
CREATE OR REPLACE TABLE archive.tripData USING DELTA AS
SELECT
  *
FROM
 taxidb.tripData
```

Tables created in this way will have independent history compared to the source table; therefore time travel queries on the source table and the new table may return different results based on your archiving frequency.

VACUUM

In the previous section you learned that you can set retention thresholds and remove data files that have been logically deleted and are no longer referenced by a Delta table. This is a reminder: these data files are *never* automatically physically deleted from storage unless the VACUUM command is run. VACUUM is designed to allow users to physically delete old versions of data files and directories that are no longer needed, while also taking into account the retention threshold of the table.

Physically deleting old versions of data files using VACUUM is important for primarily two reasons:

Cost

    Storing old and unused data files can cause cloud storage costs to grow exponentially, especially for data that changes often. Minimize these costs by removing unused data files.

Regulatory

    Auditing and regulatory compliance (e.g., GDPR) can require that some records are permanently removed and no longer available. Physically deleting files containing these records can help satisfy those regulatory requirements.

Figure 6-4 illustrates a condensed version of both the log and data files in a Delta table between different versions to show the effects of VACUUM.

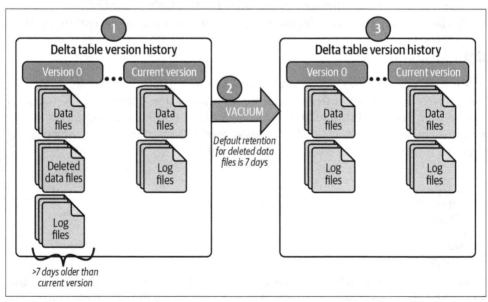

Figure 6-4. Results of running the VACUUM *command on a Delta table*

The numbered steps in the figure show:

1. Version 0 of the table is past the retention threshold (greater than seven days old). This version of the table contains log files, data files that are used in the table's current version, and deleted data files that are no longer used by the current version of the table.

2. The VACUUM command is run on the table.

   - The default retention for deleted data files is seven days.

3. After running the VACUUM command, logically deleted data files from version 0 are physically removed from storage because they were greater than the default deleted file retention period of seven days.

   - Log files were not removed, only deleted data files.
   - Data files still used in the current version of the table were not removed.

VACUUM Syntax and Examples

When vacuuming a table, you can specify VACUUM without any parameters to vacuum files that are not required by version older than the default retention period. You can also use the RETAIN num HOURS parameter to vacuum files that are not required by versions greater than the number of hours specified in the parameter.

To vacuum a table, specify the table name or filepath and then add any additional parameters:

```sql
%sql
--vacuum files not required by versions older than the default retention period
VACUUM taxidb.tripData;

VACUUM './chapter06/YellowTaxisDelta/'; --vacuum files in path-based table

VACUUM delta.`./chapter06/YellowTaxisDelta/`;

--vacuum files not required by versions more than 100 hours old
VACUUM delta.`./chapter06/YellowTaxisDelta/` RETAIN 100 HOURS;
```

Before attempting to vacuum the table, we can also run VACUUM using the parameter DRY RUN to view the list of files that are to be deleted before deleting them:

```sql
%sql
VACUUM taxidb.tripData DRY RUN --dry run to get the list of files to be deleted
```

Output (only relevant portions shown):

```
+-------------------------------------------------------------------+
| path                                                              |
+-------------------------------------------------------------------+
| dbfs:/xxx/chapter06/YellowTaxisDelta/part-xxxx.c000.snappy.parquet |
| dbfs:/xxx/chapter06/YellowTaxisDelta/part-xxxx.c000.snappy.parquet |
| dbfs:/xxx/chapter06/YellowTaxisDelta/part-xxxx.c000.snappy.parquet |
+-------------------------------------------------------------------+
```

You can see the list of files from the output that will be deleted from the Delta table `taxidb.tripData` if you were to run VACUUM.

VACUUM also commits to the Delta transaction log, which means that you can also view previous VACUUM commits and `operationMetrics` using DESCRIBE HISTORY:

```
%sql
DESCRIBE HISTORY taxidb.tripData --view the previous vacuum commit(s)
```

Output (only showing relevant portions):

```
+-------+-------------+-------------------------+--------------------------+
|version| operation   |  operationParameters    |  operationMetrics        |
+-------+-------------+-------------------------+--------------------------+
| x     |VACUUM END   |{"status": "COMPLETED"}  | {"numDeletedFiles": "100"|
|       |             |                         | "numVacuumedDirectories":|
|       |             |                         | "1"}                     |
+-------+-------------+-------------------------+--------------------------+
| x     |VACUUM START|{"retentionCheckEnabled":|                           |
|       |             |"true"...}               | {"numFilesToDelete":     |
|       |             |                         | "100"}                   |
+-------+-------------+-------------------------+--------------------------+
```

In the output, notice that the `operationParameters` show if `retentionCheckEnabled` is `true` or `false`. You will also notice that the `operationMetrics` show the number of files that were deleted and the number of directories that were vacuumed.

How Often Should You Run VACUUM and Other Maintenance Tasks?

It is recommended to regularly run VACUUM on all tables, outside of your main ETL workflow, to reduce excess cloud data storage costs. There is no exact science that indicates exactly how often you should run VACUUM. Rather, your decision on frequency should primarily be based on your budgeted storage costs, and business and regulatory needs. Scheduling a regularly occurring maintenance job to VACUUM your tables is strongly recommended to appropriately satisfy these factors.

This maintenance job, which can also include other file cleanup operations such as OPTIMIZE, should be run as a separate workflow outside of your main ETL workflow for several reasons:

Resource utilization

File cleanup operations can be resource intensive and can compete for resources with your main workflow, leading to a decline in overall performance. Therefore, you should specify maintenance windows outside of off-peak hours. These types of operations also require different cluster sizing recommendations, such as autoscaling, as opposed to regular workflows that typically use a fixed cluster size. You will read more about cluster-sizing recommendations at the end of this chapter.

Isolation

It is best to isolate processes that perform file cleanup and consolidation so that they have exclusive access to the Delta table to avoid any potential conflicts.

Monitoring

By isolating these processes, it is much easier to monitor performance so that you can track progress and resource consumption for tuning. Having an isolated process also reduces any debugging complexities when processes run in parallel, and also makes it easier to identify any bottlenecks.

By scheduling separate workflows for maintenance tasks such as VACUUM, you can have greater resource management, isolation, monitoring, and overall control of your jobs and workflows.

Related to the frequency of your maintenance jobs, an important setting to remember is the default retention period. The default retention threshold for VACUUM is seven days. You can always increase the retention threshold for a Delta table(s) based on needs. Decreasing the retention threshold is not recommended. Even if you regularly run VACUUM on all tables, it will only remove data files that are eligible to be removed based on your table's retention settings. Setting a higher threshold gives you access to a greater history for your table, but increases the number of data files stored, incurring greater storage costs from your cloud provider. Therefore, it is always important to balance retention thresholds with your needs and your budget.

VACUUM Warnings and Considerations

Although VACUUM is designed to be a low-impact operation that can be performed without interrupting normal data operations since it physically removes old and unused data from storage, there are a few things to consider to avoid conflicts or even corrupt tables:

- It is not recommended that you set a retention interval shorter than seven days. It is possible that if you run VACUUM on a table with a short retention interval, files that are still active, such as uncommitted files that are needed by readers or writers, could be deleted. If VACUUM deletes files that haven't been committed, it can cause read operations to fail or even corrupt your table.

- Delta Lake has a safety check to prevent you from running a dangerous `VACUUM` command. If you are certain that there are no operations being performed on this table that take longer than the retention interval you plan to specify, you can turn off this safety check by setting the Spark configuration property `spark.data bricks.delta.retentionDurationCheck.enabled = false`.

  — If you do set `spark.databricks.delta.retentionDurationCheck.enabled` to `false`, you must choose an interval that is longer than the longest running concurrent transaction and the longest period that any stream can lag behind the most recent update to the table.

  — Do not disable `spark.databricks.delta.retentionDurationCheck.enabled` and run `VACUUM` configured to `RETAIN 0 HOURS`.

  — If you run `VACUUM RETAIN num HOURS`, then you must set `RETAIN num HOURS` to an interval greater than or equal to the retention period. Otherwise you will receive an error if `spark.databricks.delta.reten tionDurationCheck.enabled = true`. If you are certain that there are no operations being performed on this table, such as `INSERT/UPDATE/ DELETE/OPTIMIZE`, then you may turn off this check by setting `spark.data bricks.delta.retentionDurationCheck.enabled = false` to avoid the exception error.

- When you run `VACUUM` on a Delta table, it removes the following files from the underlying filesystem:

  — Any data files that are not maintained by Delta Lake, ignoring directories beginning with an underscore, like _delta_log_. If you are storing additional metadata like Structured Streaming checkpoints within a Delta table directory, which you will learn more about in Chapter 8, use a directory name such as _checkpoints_.

  — Stale data files (files that are no longer referenced by a Delta table) that are older than the retention period.

- Since vacuuming removes files, it is important to note that the process can take some time, depending on the size of the table and the number of files to be removed.

  Run `OPTIMIZE` regularly to eliminate small files and reduce the number of files that need to be removed. When you combine `OPTIMIZE` with regular `VACUUM` runs, you ensure that the number of stale data files is minimized.

- The ability to time travel back to a version older than the retention period is lost after running `VACUUM`.

  — Set a deleted file retention duration equal to your log retention duration to maintain full compatibility of the entire history that you can time travel to.

— This means that if you run VACUUM with the default settings, you will only be able to time travel seven days into the past from the time you run VACUUM.

- Depending on how many unused files need to be identified and removed, the VACUUM command can take a while to execute. To optimize the cost and performance of your Spark cluster, it is recommended to use a cluster that auto-scales and configures based on the following steps that VACUUM follows to perform the operation:

  — Step 1 of the VACUUM operation *identifies* unused files using the *worker nodes* on the Spark cluster while the driver node sits idle. Therefore you should use 1 to 4 worker nodes with at least 8 cores each.

  — Step 2 of the VACUUM operation *deletes* the identified files using the *driver node* on the Spark cluster. Therefore you should use a driver node that has between 8 and 32 cores to avoid out-of-memory errors.

Changing Data Feed

So far in this chapter you have learned that through data and file retention, time travel enables you to traverse through different versions of data at specific points in time. But time travel does not track row-level changes, or rather, how row-level data is inserted, updated, or deleted across different versions. And Delta Lake offers more efficient ways to view these changes across different versions rather than just comparing entire versions of tables. This efficient tracking of row-level changes across versions is called the Change Data Feed (CDF).

When enabled on a Delta table, the Delta Lake records "change events" for all the data written into the table. This includes the row data and metadata indicating whether the specified row was inserted, deleted, or updated. Downstream consumers can also read the change events in batch queries using SQL and DataFrame APIs, and in streaming queries with .readStream. You will read more about how streaming queries can consume the CDF in Chapter 9.

With the CDF, you can capture changes to the data without having to process every single record in your Delta table file or query an entire version of a table. So, if just one record changed, you no longer have to read all records in the file or a table. The CDF is stored in a separate directory called *_change_data* that sits alongside *_delta_log* and maintains the changes to the Delta table file. The CDF supports several use cases that supplement Delta Lake time travel and versioning:

ETL operations
Identifying and processing only records that require row-level changes following operations can greatly accelerate and simplify ETL operations. Incrementally loading records during ETL operations is essential for any efficient ETL process.

For example, if you have a large, denormalized table that contains all sales order information used for reporting and is created by joining from several upstream tables, you want to avoid processing all records each time the table processes. With the CDF, you can track the row-level changes from the upstream tables to determine what information, or sales order records, are new, updated, or deleted, and subsequently use that to incrementally process your table containing sales order information.

Transmit changes for downstream consumers

Other downstream systems and consumers, such as Spark Structured Streaming or Kafka, can consume the CDF to process data. For example, streaming queries, which you will learn more about in Chapter 8, can read the change feed to stream data for near-real-time analytics and reporting.

If you have an event-driven application, an event-streaming platform such as Kafka could read the change feed and trigger actions for a downstream application or platform. For instance, if you have an ecommerce platform, Kafka could read the change feed and trigger near-real-time actions in the platform based on product inventory changes that were captured in the Delta table.

Audit trail table

The CDF provides enhanced efficiency, especially compared to time travel, with querying changes to row-level data over time so that you can easily see data that was updated or deleted and when. This provides a full audit trail of your data.

Many regulatory requirements may require certain industries to track these row-level changes and keep an entire audit trial. In healthcare, for example, HIPAA and audit controls require systems to track activity, or changes, around electronic protected health information (ePHI).[2] The CDF in Delta Lake helps support regulatory requirements for tracking changes.

Enabling the CDF

We can enable the CDF for all new tables by setting this Spark configuration property as follows:

```
%sql
set spark.databricks.delta.properties.defaults.enableChangeDataFeed = true
```

If you don't wish to enable the CDF for all tables in your environment, you can specify it using table properties when you create a table or alter existing ones. At the start of this chapter when we executed the "Chapter Initialization" notebook, an external Delta table containing aggregate information about passenger counts and

---

2 "45 CFR § 164.312 - Technical Safeguards." Cornell Law School. January 25, 2013. *https://oreil.ly/qWFDe*.

fare amounts for vendors, or taxis, was created. In the following example that can be found in the notebook for "02 - Change Data Feed,"[3] we create a new table and enable the CDF:

```
%sql
--create new table with change data feed
CREATE TABLE IF NOT EXISTS taxidb.tripAggregates
(VendorId INT, PassengerCount INT, FareAmount INT)
TBLPROPERTIES (delta.enableChangeDataFeed = true);


--alter existing table to enable change data feed
ALTER TABLE myDeltaTable SET TBLPROPERTIES (delta.enableChangeDataFeed = true);
```

 Only changes made after you enable the CDF will be recorded, so any changes made to a table prior to enabling the CDF will not be captured.

Modifying Records in the CDF

To demonstrate the CDF, first let's INSERT, UPDATE, and DELETE some data in the taxidb.tripAggregates table we just created so that we can view the CDF later on:

```
%sql
--insert record in the table
INSERT INTO taxidb.tripAggregates VALUES
(4, 500, 1000);

--update records in the table
UPDATE taxidb.tripAggregates SET TotalAmount = 2500 WHERE VendorId = 1;

-- delete record in the table
DELETE FROM taxidb.tripAggregates WHERE VendorId = 3;
```

Now that there have been changes to the table, the CDF has captured the row-level changes. If we look at the location where the Delta table is stored, we will notice the new _change_data_ directory:

```
%sh
ls -al /dbfs/mnt/datalake/book/chapter06/TripAggregatesDelta/
```

Output (only relevant portions shown):

```
drwxrwxrwx 2 root _change_data
drwxrwxrwx 2 root _delta_log
-rwxrwxrwx 1 root part-00000-...-c000.snappy.parquet
```

---

3 GitHub repo location: _/chapter06/02 - Change Data Feed_

```
-rwxrwxrwx 1 root part-00000-....snappy.parquet
-rwxrwxrwx 1 root part-00000-...-c000.snappy.parquet
-rwxrwxrwx 1 root part-00001-....snappy.parquet
```

Now that we can see the new *_change_data* directory, we can look in the directory to see the data files that contain the data changes:

```
%sh
ls -al /dbfs/mnt/datalake/book/chapter06/TripAggregatesDelta/_change_data
```

Output:

```
-rwxrwxrwx 1 root cdc-00000-....snappy.parquet
-rwxrwxrwx 1 root cdc-00001-....snappy.parquet
```

The *_change_data* directory is another metadata directory containing the change capture data contained in the data files. Every time you make a change to the data going forward, you will not only update the current version's data files, but also the files in the *_change_data* directory. It is important to note that the CDF directory will only store updates and deletes in the *_change_data* directory, whereas for inserts it is more efficient to compute the CDF directly from the transaction log. This does not mean that inserts are not captured in the CDF; they are simply not stored in the *_change_data* directory.

> The data files in the *_change_data* directory adhere to the same retention policy of the table. This means that CDF data that is outside of the table's retention policy *will be deleted* when you run VACUUM.

Viewing the CDF

To help identify the row-level changes that occurred, the CDF contains additional metadata to label the type of event and commit information. The following table shows the schema of the additional metadata columns.

Table 6-2. CDF metadata

Column name	Type	Values
_change_type	String	insert, update_preimage, update_postimage, delete
_commit_version	Long	The table version containing the change
_commit_timestamp	Timestamp	Timestamp of when the commit occurred

Using the additional metadata columns from the CDF, we can easily view the row-level changes of a table. To view these changes and the CDF metadata columns, we can use the TABLE_CHANGES(table_str, start [, end]) SQL command. The following table details the arguments for this command.

Table 6-3. TABLE_CHANGES Arguments

Argument	Type	Definition
table_str	String	Represents the optionally qualified name of the table.
start	BIGINT or Timestamp	The first version or timestamp of change to return.
end	BIGINT or Timestamp	An optional argument for the last version or timestamp of change to return. If not specified, all changes from the start up to the current change are returned.

Now circling back to the `taxidb.tripAggregates` table, there have been several DML operations to INSERT, UPDATE, and DELETE data on the existing table. You can indicate a version or timestamp, similar to time travel, to view the table changes using the TABLE_CHANGES() SQL command:

```
%sql
SELECT *
FROM table_changes('taxidb.tripAggregates', 1, 4)
ORDER BY _commit_timestamp
```

Output:

```
+----------------+-------------+------------------+-----------------+
| PassengerCount | FareAmount  | _change_type     | _commit_version |
+----------------+-------------+------------------+-----------------+
|      1000      |    2000     | update_preimage  |        2        |
+----------------+-------------+------------------+-----------------+
|      1000      |    2500     | update_postimage |        2        |
+----------------+-------------+------------------+-----------------+
|      7000      |    10000    | delete           |        3        |
+----------------+-------------+------------------+-----------------+
|      500       |    1000     | insert           |        4        |
+----------------+-------------+------------------+-----------------+


+----------+------------------------+
| VendorId | _commit_timestamp      |
+----------+------------------------+
|    1     | 2023-07-09T19:17:54    |
+----------+------------------------+
|    1     | 2023-07-09T19:17:54    |
+----------+------------------------+
|    3     | 2023-07-09T19:17:54    |
+----------+------------------------+
|    4     | 2023-07-09T19:17:54    |
+----------+------------------------+
```

When looking at the row-level changes in this example, you can see the versions that correspond to when a particular record was inserted, updated, or deleted by looking at the _commit_version. The _change_type indicates the type of operation on the record, and for updated records notice that it indicates the row-level data *before* the update, as indicated by update_preimage, and the row-level data *after* the update, as indicated by update_postimage.

The same table changes can be viewed using the DataFrame API as well by using the .option() method and setting "readChangeFeed" to "true":

```python
%python
# view CDF table changes using versions
spark.read.format("delta") \
  .option("readChangeFeed", "true") \
  .option("startingVersion", 1) \
  .option("endingVersion", 4) \
  .table("taxidb.tripAggregates")

# view CDF table changes using timestamps
spark.read.format("delta")\
  .option("readChangeFeed", "true")\
  .option("startingTimestamp", "2023-01-01 00:00:00")\
  .option("endingTimestamp", "2023-01-31 00:00:00")\
  .table("taxidb.tripAggregates")
```

Now, if we want to see the audit trail of a record and see how it has changed over time, we can simply use the CDF and TABLE_CHANGES() to capture this efficiently. For example, if we wanted to see how the values of a specific vendor in taxidb.tripAggregates have changed over time, let's say WHERE VendorId = 1, we could use the following query:

```sql
%sql
SELECT *
FROM table_changes('taxidb.tripAggregates', 1, 4)
WHERE VendorId = 1 AND _change_type = 'update_postimage'
ORDER BY _commit_timestamp
```

Output:

```
+------------+-------------+------------------+-----------------+
| FareAmount | TotalAmount | _change_type     | _commit_version |
+------------+-------------+------------------+-----------------+
|   10000    |    25000    | update_postimage |        2        |
+------------+-------------+------------------+-----------------+

+----------+----------------------------+
| VendorId | _commit_timestamp          |
+----------+----------------------------+
|    1     | 2023-07-09T19:17:54.000+000 |
+----------+----------------------------+
```

This provides an audit trail of how data for a particular vendor has been updated over time. While this is a simple example, you can see that this can be extremely powerful and much more efficient than time travel for large tables with many values that are consistently updated.

Or, let's say we want to perform a time-series analysis and see how many new vendors have been added (assuming the granularity of this table is VendorId) and what their

FareAmount generated has been since a particular point in time. We can use a WHERE clause to specify this information and efficiently read the CDF:

```sql
%sql
SELECT *
FROM table_changes('taxidb.tripAggregates', '2023-01-01')
WHERE VendorId = 1 AND _change_type = 'insert'
ORDER BY _commit_timestamp
```

Output:

```
+------------+-------------+----------------+-----------------+
| FareAmount | TotalAmount | _change_type   | _commit_version |
+------------+-------------+----------------+-----------------+
|    500     |    1000     | insert         |       4         |
+------------+-------------+----------------+-----------------+


+----------+----------------------------+
| VendorId | _commit_timestamp          |
+----------+----------------------------+
|    4     | 2023-07-09T19:17:54.000+000 |
+----------+----------------------------+
```

This demonstrates that you can see the table changes, specifically WHERE VendorId = 1 AND _change_type = 'insert', since a commit timestamp, which in this case is 2023-01-01.

The CDF is an efficient, powerful feature that can capture changes to data over time. This can be used with other ETL operations to easily build type 2 slowly changing dimensions, or you can process only row-level changes following MERGE, UPDATE, or DELETE operations to accelerate ETL operations and incrementally load data downstream. As mentioned previously, there are other use cases for the CDF, one of which is streaming, which you will learn more about in Chapter 9.

CDF Warnings and Considerations

While the CDF is a powerful feature, there are some things to consider:

- Change records follow the same retention policy as the data files of the table. This means that if a CDF file is outside the table's retention policy, it is a candidate for VACUUM and will be deleted if VACUUM is run.

- The CDF does not add any significant overhead to table processing, as everything is generated inline as the DML operations. And typically the data files written in the *_change_data* directory are much smaller in size compared to the total size of rewritten files of a table operation since they only contain operations for records that were updated or deleted. As mentioned previously, records inserted into a table are not captured in the *_change_data* directory.

Since the change data happens inline with other operations, the change data is available as the new data is committed and available in the table.

- The CDF does not record changes to records that occurred prior to the CDF being enabled.
- Once you enable the CDF for a table, you can no longer write to the table using Delta Lake 1.2.1 or below, but you can still read the table.

Conclusion

In this chapter, you read about how Delta Lake uses version control and how that enables you to traverse through different versions of data at specific points in time, while also using the CDF to track row-level changes to data over time. Time travel and the CDF in Delta Lake are powerful features that allow users to track changes over time and can be leveraged for enabling downstream consumers, ETL operations, time-series analysis, version control, auditing, and data management.

After reading about how you can easily restore or query previous versions of a table, you learned that you can use either version numbers or timestamps to roll back, audit, and satisfy a variety of use cases. By using commands like DESCRIBE HISTORY, you can easily view a table's commit history. This is all made possible through the transaction log and file retention. You can further define these retention settings, if you wish to change the default settings, for both log and data files using Spark configuration or table properties. Then, since data files are not automatically removed, you can remove old data files using the VACUUM command.

To supplement time travel, Delta Lake also offers the Change Data Feed (CDF) for tables. This feature allows you to capture row-level changes in an efficient manner for numerous different use cases, rather than needing to compare entire versions of each table's history to identify changes.

Using built-in Delta Lake features for time travel, retention, maintenance, and the CDF, you can save valuable time and resources, and satisfy regulatory and audit requirements. These features are made possible through the _change_data directory and more importantly the transaction log, and in the next chapter you will learn more about how the transaction log also stores a table's schema and uses that to update and modify table schemas.

Schema Handling

Traditionally, data lakes have always operated under the principle of schema on read, but have always had challenges enforcing schema on write. This means there is no predefined schema when data is written to storage, and a schema is only adapted when the data is processed. It is imperative for the case of analytics and data platforms that your table formats enforce the schema on write to prevent introducing change-breaking processes, and to maintain proper data quality and integrity.

And while it is essential to adhere to schema on write, we must also acknowledge that in today's fast-paced business climate and evolving landscape of data management, data sources, analytics, and simply just data and its overall structure are constantly changing. These changes need to be accounted for with schemas that are flexible enough to evolve over time in order to capture new, changing information.

The schematic challenges often seen from traditional data lakes can be further classified into two key schema handling features that any data platform and table format, regardless of the storage layer, must support:

Schema enforcement
> This is the process of ensuring that all data being added to a table conforms to that specific schema, where the schema defines a table structure by a list of column names, their data types, and any optional constraints. Enforcing data to fit to the structure of a defined schema helps to maintain the quality and consistency of the data, as any write to the table that does not comply with the schema is rejected. In turn, this helps prevent data quality issues that can arise from having data in different formats where it can be difficult to ensure that the data in the table is accurate and consistent.

Schema evolution

This allows the data stored in the data lake to be flexible and adaptable to address the changing business requirements and data landscape. Schema evolution should be performed in a very conscious, controlled, and organized manner, and is mostly limited to the addition of columns to the schema.

Fortunately, Delta Lake has excellent schema handling features that allow for both flexible schema evolution and rigid enforcement. This chapter will demonstrate how Delta Lake performs validation and enforcement, along with schema evolution scenarios and how Delta Lake can handle them.

Schema Validation

Every DataFrame that you create in Apache Spark will have a schema. The best way to look at a schema is as a blueprint or structure that defines the shape of your data. This includes the name of each column, its data type, whether or not the column can be NULL, and any metadata associated with each column.

Delta Lake will store the schema of a Delta Table as a schemaString in the metaData action of the transaction log entries. In this section we will take a look at these entries. Next, we look at the validation rules that Delta Lake applies during a schema on write operation. We will close out this section with a use case for each of the schema validation rules.

To follow along with the code, first execute the "00 - Chapter Initialization" notebook (*https://oreil.ly/RrFRf*) for Chapter 7 to create the TaxiRateCode Delta table.

Viewing the Schema in the Transaction Log Entries

Delta Lake will store the schema in JSON format inside the transaction log. For example, the initialization notebook writes a Delta table like this:

```
# Write in Delta Lake format
df.write.format("delta")    \
        .mode("overwrite") \
        .save("/mnt/datalake/book/chapter07/TaxiRateCode")
```

To take a look at how the schema is saved, open the "01 - Schema Enforcement" notebook. In this notebook, we see that the table's schema is saved in JSON format inside the transaction log when we view the transaction log file:

```
%sh
# The schemaString is part of the metaData action of the Transaction Log entry
# The schemaString contains the full schema of the Delta table file
# at the time that the log entry was written
grep "metadata" /dbfs/mnt/datalake/.../TaxiRateCode.delta/_delta_log/...000.json
> /tmp/commit.json
python -m json.tool < /tmp/commit.json
```

We see the following output:

```
{
    "metaData": {
        "id": "8f348474-0288-440a-a76e-2358ccf45a96",
        "format": {
            "provider": "parquet",
            "options": {}
        },
        "schemaString": "{\"type\":\"struct\",\"fields\":[{\"name\":\
                        "RateCodeId\",\"type\":\"integer\",\"nullable\
                        ":true,\"metadata\":{}},{\"name\":\"RateCodeDesc\
                        ",\"type\":\"string\",\"nullable\":true,\
                        "metadata\":{}}]}",
        "partitionColumns": [],
        "configuration": {},
        "createdTime": 1681161987269
    }
}
```

The schema is a structure (struct), with a list of fields representing the columns, where each field has a `name`, a `type`, and a `nullable` indicator that tells us whether the field is mandatory or not.

Each column also contains a `metadata` field. The `metadata` field is a JSON string that can contain various types of information, depending on the transaction being performed, for example:

- The username of the person who executed the transaction
- The timestamp of the transaction
- The version of Delta Lake used
- The schema partition columns
- Any additional application-specific metadata that may be relevant to the transaction

Schema on Write

Schema validation rejects writes to a table that does not match a table's schema. Delta Lake performs schema validation on write, so it will check the schema of the data that is being written to the table. If the schema is compatible, the validation will pass and the write will succeed; if the schema of the data is not compatible, Delta Lake will cancel the transaction and no data is written.

Note that this operation will always be atomic, so you will never have a condition where only a part of the data is written to the table. All source data is written when the transaction succeeds, and no source data is written when the validation fails.

When schema validation fails, Delta Lake will raise an exception to let the user know about the mismatch.

To determine whether a write to a table is compatible, Delta Lake uses the following rules:

The source DataFrame to be written:

Cannot contain any columns that are not present is the target table's schema
Note that it is allowed that the new data does not contain every column in the table, as long as the missing columns are marked as `nullable` in the target table's schema. If a missing column was not marked as nullable in the target schema, the transaction will fail.

Cannot have column data types that differ from the column data types in the target table
For example, if the target table's column contains `StringType` data, but the corresponding source column contains `IntegerType` data, schema enforcement will raise an exception and prevent the write operation from taking place.

Cannot contain column names that differ only by case
For example, if the source data contains a column named `Foo` and the source data has a column named `foo`, the transaction will fail. There is a bit of history behind this particular rule:

- Spark can be used in case-sensitive or case-insensitive (default) mode.
- Parquet, on the other hand, is case-sensitive when storing and returning column information.
- Delta Lake is case preserving but insensitive when storing the schema.

The preceding rules combined get rather complex. Therefore, to avoid potential mistakes, data corruption, or loss issues, Delta Lake will *not* allow column names that only differ in case.

Schema Enforcement Example

Let's take a look at the details of schema enforcement. We will start out by appending a DataFrame with a matching schema, which will succeed without any issues. Next, we will add an additional column to the DataFrame and attempt to append it to the Delta table. We will validate that this results in an exception, and no data has been written.

Matching schema

To illustrate schema enforcement, we will first append a DataFrame with the correct schema to the `TaxiRateCode` table, as shown in step 2 in the "01 - Schema Enforcement" notebook:

```
# Define the schema for the DataFrame
# Notice that the columns match the table schema
schema = StructType([
    StructField("RateCodeId", IntegerType(), True),
    StructField("RateCodeDesc", StringType(), True)
])

# Create a list of rows for the DataFrame
data = [(10, "Rate Code 10"), (11, "Rate Code 11"), (12, "Rate Code 12")]

# Create a DataFrame, passing in the data rows
# and the schema
df = spark.createDataFrame(data, schema)

# Perform the write. This write will succeed without any
# problems
df.write                \
  .format("delta") \
  .mode("append")   \
  .save("/mnt/datalake/book/chapter07/TaxiRateCode")
```

Since the source and target schema align, the DataFrame is successfully appended to the table.

Schema with an additional column

In step 3 of the notebook, we will attempt to add one more column to the source schema:

```
# Define the schema for the DataFrame
# Notice that we added an additional column
schema = StructType([
    StructField("RateCodeId", IntegerType(), True),
    StructField("RateCodeDesc", StringType(), True),
    StructField("RateCodeName", StringType(), True)
])

# Create a list of rows for the DataFrame
data = [
    (15, "Rate Code 15", "C15"),
    (16, "Rate Code 16", "C16"),
    (17, "Rate Code 17", "C17")]

# Create a DataFrame from the list of rows and the schema
df = spark.createDataFrame(data, schema)

# Attempt to append the DataFrame to the table
df.write                \
  .format("delta") \
  .mode("append")   \
  .save("/mnt/datalake/book/chapter07/TaxiRateCode")
```

This code will fail with the following exception:

```
AnalysisException: A schema mismatch detected when writing to the Delta table
(Table ID: 8f348474-0288-440a-a76e-2358ccf45a96).
```

When we scroll down, we see that Delta Lake provided a detailed explanation of what happened:

```
To enable schema migration using DataFrameWriter or DataStreamWriter, please set:
'.option("mergeSchema", "true")'.
For other operations, set the session configuration
spark.databricks.delta.schema.autoMerge.enabled to "true". See the documentation
specific to the operation for details.

Table schema:
root
-- RateCodeId: integer (nullable = true)
-- RateCodeDesc: string (nullable = true)


Data schema:
root
-- RateCodeId: integer (nullable = true)
-- RateCodeDesc: string (nullable = true)
-- RateCodeName: string (nullable = true)
```

Delta Lake informs us that we can evolve the schema with the mergeSchema option set to true, which is something we will examine in the next section. It then shows us the table and source data schema, which is very helpful for debugging.

When we look at the transaction log entries, we see the following:

```
# Create a listing of all transaction log entries.
# We notice that there are only two entries.
# The first entry represents the creation of the table
# The second entry is the append of the valid dataframe
# There is no entry for the above code since the exception
# occurred, resulting in a rollback of the transaction
ls -al /dbfs/mnt/datalake/book/chapter07/TaxiRateCode/_delta_log/*.json


-rwxrwxrwx 1 Apr 10 21:26 /dbfs/.../TaxiRateCode.delta/_delta_log/...000.json
-rwxrwxrwx 1 Apr 10 21:27 /dbfs/.../TaxiRateCode.delta/_delta_log/...001.json
```

The first entry (0000…0.json) represents the creation of the table, and the second entry (0000…1.json) is the append with the valid DataFrame. There is no entry for the preceding code, since the schema mismatch exception was thrown, and no data was written at all, illustrating the atomic behavior of Delta Lake transactions.

A run of the DESCRIBE HISTORY command for the table confirms this:

```
%sql
-- Look at the history for the Delta table
DESCRIBE HISTORY delta.`/mnt/datalake/book/chapter07/TaxiRateCode`
```

Output (only relevant data shown):

```
+-------+----------+------------------------------------------+
|version|operation |     operationParameters                  |
+-------+----------+------------------------------------------+
|1      | WRITE    | {"mode":"Append","partitionBy":"[]"}     |
|0      | WRITE    | {"mode":"Overwrite","partitionBy":"[]"}  |
+-------+----------+------------------------------------------+
```

In this section, we have seen schema enforcement at work. It provides peace of mind that your table's schema will not change unless you choose to change it. Schema enforcement ensures data quality and consistency for your Delta Lake tables, and keeps the developer honest and the tables clean.

However, if you consciously decide that you really need the additional column in your table to facilitate your business, then you can leverage schema evolution, which we will cover in the next section.

Schema Evolution

Schema evolution in Delta Lake refers to the ability to evolve the schema of a Delta table over time, while preserving the existing data in the table. In other words, schema evolution allows us to add, remove, or modify columns in an existing Delta table without losing any data or breaking any downstream jobs that depend on the table. This is important as your data and business needs change over time and you may need to add new columns to your table or modify the existing columns to support new use cases.

Schema evolution is enabled on the table level by using .option("mergeSchema", "true") during a write operation. You can also enable schema evolution for the entire Spark cluster by setting spark.databricks.delta.schema.auto Merge.enabled to true. By default, this setting will be set to false.

When schema evolution is enabled, the following rules are applied:

- If a column exists in the source DataFrame being written but not in the Delta table, a new column is added to the Delta table with the same name and data type. All existing rows will have a null value for the new column.
- If a column exists in the Delta table but not in the source DataFrame being written, the column is not changed and retains its existing values. The new records will have a null value for the missing columns in the source DataFrame.

- If a column with the same name but a different data type exists in the Delta table, Delta Lake attempts to convert the data to the new data type. If the conversion fails, an error is thrown.

- If a `NullType` column is added to the Delta table, all existing rows are set to null for that column.

Let's look at a number of schema evolution scenarios, starting with the most common: adding a column to the table.

Adding a Column

Returning to our schema enforcement example, we can use schema evolution to add the `RateCodeName` column to the schema that was previously rejected due to schema mismatch. Recall that the rule states:

> If a column exists in the DataFrame being written but not in the Delta table, a new column is added to the Delta table with the same name and data type. All existing rows will have a null value for the new column.

You can follow along with the code in the "02 - Schema Evolution" notebook. In step 2 of the notebook, schema evolution is activated by adding `.option("mergeSchema", "true")` to the `.write` Spark command:

```
# Define the schema for the DataFrame
# Notice the additional RateCodeName column, which
# is not part of the target table schema
schema = StructType([
    StructField("RateCodeId", IntegerType(), True),
    StructField("RateCodeDesc", StringType(), True),
    StructField("RateCodeName", StringType(), True)
])

# Create a list of rows for the DataFrame
data = [
    (20, "Rate Code 20", "C20"),
    (21, "Rate Code 21", "C21"),
    (22, "Rate Code 22", "C22")
]

# Create a DataFrame from the list of rows and the schema
df = spark.createDataFrame(data, schema)

# Append the DataFrame to the Delta Table
df.write                              \
  .format("delta")                    \
  .option("mergeSchema", "true")      \
  .mode("append")                     \
  .save("/mnt/datalake/book/chapter07/TaxiRateCode")
```

```
# Print the schema
df.printSchema()
```

We see the new schema:

```
root
 |-- RateCodeId: integer (nullable = true)
 |-- RateCodeDesc: string (nullable = true)
 |-- RateCodeName: string (nullable = true)
```

Now, the write operation will complete successfully, and the data will be added to the Delta table:

```
%sql
SELECT
        *
FROM
        delta.`/mnt/datalake/book/chapter07/TaxiRateCode`
ORDER BY
    RateCodeId
```

We get the following output:

```
+-----------+---------------------+-----------+
|RateCodeId |     RateCodeDes      |RateCodeName|
+-----------+---------------------+-----------+
|1          |Standard Rate        | null      |
|2          |JFK                  | null      |
|3          |Newark               | null      |
|4          |Nassau or Westchester| null      |
|5          |Negotiated fare      | null      |
|6          |Group ride           | null      |
|20         |Rate Code 20         | C20       |
|21         |Rate Code 21         | C21       |
|22         |Rate Code 22         | C22       |
+-----------+---------------------+-----------+
```

The new data has been added, and the RateCodeName for the existing rows has been set to null, which is expected. When we look at the corresponding transaction log entry, we can see that a new metadata entry has been written with the updated schema:

```
{
    "metaData": {
        "id": "ac676ac9-8805-4aca-9db7-4856a3c3a55b",
        "format": {
            "provider": "parquet",
            "options": {}
        },
        "schemaString": "{\"type\":\"struct\",\"fields\":[
            {\"name\":\"RateCodeId\",\"type\":\"integer\",\"nullable\
            ":true,\"metadata\":{}},
            {\"name\":\"RateCodeDesc\",\"type\":\"string\",\"nullable\
            ":true,\"metadata\":{}},
```

```
                {\"name\":\"RateCodeName\",\"type\":\"string\",\"nullable\
                ":true,\"metadata\":{}}]}",
            "partitionColumns": [],
            "configuration": {},
            "createdTime": 1680650616156
        }
    }
```

This validates the schema evolution rules for adding columns.

Missing Data Column in Source DataFrame

Next, let's take a look at the impact of removing a column. Recall that the rule states:

> If a column exists in the Delta table but not in the DataFrame being written, the
> column is not changed and retains its existing values. The new records will have a null
> value for the missing columns in the source DataFrame.

In the "02 - Schema Evolution" notebook in step 3, there is a code example where we
left the RateCodeDesc column out of the DataFrame:

```
# Define the schema for the DataFrame
schema = StructType([
    StructField("RateCodeId", IntegerType(), True),
    StructField("RateCodeName", StringType(), True)
])

# Create a list of rows for the DataFrame
data = [(30, "C30"), (31, "C31"), (32, "C32")]

# Create a DataFrame from the list of rows and the schema
df = spark.createDataFrame(data, schema)

# Append the DataFrame to the table
df.write                                  \
  .format("delta")                        \
  .option("mergeSchema", "true") \
  .mode("append")                         \
  .save("/mnt/datalake/book/chapter07/TaxiRateCode")
```

When we now look at the data in the Delta table, we see the following:

```
+-----------+---------------------+-----------+
|RateCodeId |    RateCodeDes      |RateCodeName|
+-----------+---------------------+-----------+
|1          |Standard Rate        | null      |
|2          |JFK                  | null      |
|3          |Newark               | null      |
|4          |Nassau or Westchester| null      |
|5          |Negotiated fare      | null      |
|6          |Group ride           | null      |
|20         |Rate Code 20         | C20       |
|21         |Rate Code 21         | C21       |
```

```
|22          |Rate Code 22        | C22        |
|30          |null                | C30        |
|31          |null                | C31        |
|32          |null                | C32        |
+------------+--------------------+------------+
```

Observe the following behavior:

- The schema of the Delta table remains unchanged.

- The RateCodeDesc column values for the existing rows are not changed.

- The values for the RateCodeDesc column of the new DataFrame are set to NULL, since they do not exist in the DataFrame.

When we look at the corresponding transaction log entry, you can see the commitInfo and three add sections (one for each new source record), but no new schemaString, implying that the schema was not changed:

```
{
    "commitInfo": {
        ...
    }
}
{
    "add": {
        ...
        "stats": "{\"numRecords\":1,\"minValues\":{\"RateCodeId\":30,
                \"RateCodeName\":\"C30\"},\"maxValues\":
                {\"RateCodeId\":30,\"RateCodeName\":\"C30\"},\"nullCount\"
                :{\"RateCodeId\":0,\"RateCodeDesc\":1,
                \"RateCodeName\":0}}",
        ...
    }
}
{
    "add": {
        ...
        "stats": "{\"numRecords\":1,\"minValues\":{\"RateCodeId\":31,
                \"RateCodeName\":\"C31\"},\"maxValues\":
                {\"RateCodeId\":31,\"RateCodeName\":\"C31\"},\"nullCount\"
                :{\"RateCodeId\":0,\"RateCodeDesc\":1,
                \"RateCodeName\":0}}",
        "tags": {
            ...
        }
    }
}
{
    "add": {
        ...
```

```
    "stats": "{\"numRecords\":1,\"minValues\":{\"RateCodeId\":32,
            \"RateCodeName\":\"C32\"},\"maxValues\":
              {\"RateCodeId\":32,\"RateCodeName\":\"C32\"},\"nullCount\"
              :{\"RateCodeId\":0,\"RateCodeDesc\":1,
              \"RateCodeName\":0}}",
    "tags": {
        ...
    }
  }
}
```

This validates our rule for removing columns, as stated in the introduction.

Changing a Column Data Type

Next, let's take a look at the impact of changing a column's data type. Recall that the rule states:

> If a column with the same name but a different data type exists in the Delta table, Delta Lake attempts to convert the data to the new data type. If the conversion fails, an error is thrown.

In step 4 of the "02 -Schema Evolution" notebook, we will first reset the table by removing the directory:

```
dbutils.fs.rm("dbfs:/mnt/datalake/book/chapter07/TaxiRateCode", recurse=True)
```

And then we can drop the table:

```
%sql
drop table taxidb.taxiratecode;
```

Next, we re-create the table, but this time we use a short data type for the RateCodeId:

```
# Read our CSV data, and change the data type of
# the RateCodeId to short
df = spark.read.format("csv")        \
        .option("header", "true") \
        .load("/mnt/datalake/book/chapter07/TaxiRateCode.csv")
df = df.withColumn("RateCodeId", df["RateCodeId"].cast(ShortType()))

# Write in Delta Lake format
df.write.format("delta")   \
        .mode("overwrite") \
        .save("/mnt/datalake/book/chapter07/TaxiRateCode")

# Print the schema
df.printSchema()
```

We can see the new schema, and verify that RateCodeId is now indeed a short data type:

```
root
 |-- RateCodeId: short (nullable = true)
 |-- RateCodeDesc: string (nullable = true)
```

Next, we will attempt to change the data type of the `RateCodeId` column from a `ShortType` to an `IntegerType`, which is one of the supported conversions for schema evolution:

```
# Define the schema for the DataFrame
# Note that we now define the RateCodeId to be an
# Integer type
schema = StructType([
    StructField("RateCodeId", IntegerType(), True),
    StructField("RateCodeDesc", StringType(), True)
])

# Create a list of rows for the DataFrame
data = [(20, "Rate Code 20"), (21, "Rate Code 21"), (22, "Rate Code 22")]

# Create a DataFrame from the list of rows and the schema
df = spark.createDataFrame(data, schema)

# Write the DataFrame with Schema Evolution
df.write                              \
  .format("delta")                    \
  .option("mergeSchema", "true") \
  .mode("append")                     \
  .save("/mnt/datalake/book/chapter07/TaxiRateCode")

# Print the schema
df.printSchema()
```

This code will successfully execute and print the following schema:

```
root
 |-- RateCodeId: integer (nullable = true)
 |-- RateCodeName: string (nullable = true)
```

A new `schemaString` is written in the corresponding transaction log entry with the `IntegerType`:

```
{
    "metaData": {
        "id": "7af3c5b8-0742-431f-b2d5-5634aa316e94",
        "format": {
            "provider": "parquet",
            "options": {}
        },
        "schemaString": "{\"type\":\"struct\",\"fields\":[
            {\"name\":\"RateCodeId\",\"type\":\"integer\",\"nullable\":
            true,\"metadata\":{}},
            {\"name\":\"RateCodeDesc\",\"type\":\"string\",\"nullable\":
            true,\"metadata\":{}}]}",
```

```
        "partitionColumns": [],
        "configuration": {},
        "createdTime": 1680658999999
    }
}
```

Currently, Delta Lake only supports a limited number of conversions:

- You can convert from a `NullType` to any other type.

- You can upcast from a `ByteType` to a `ShortType`.

- You can upcast from a `ShortType` to an `IntegerType` (which is our use case from earlier).

Adding a NullType Column

In Delta Lake, the `NullType()` type is a valid data type that is used to represent a column that can contain a null value, as shown in step 5 of the "02 - Schema Evolution" notebook:

```python
# Define the schema for the DataFrame
schema = StructType([
    StructField("RateCodeId", IntegerType(), True),
    StructField("RateCodeDesc", StringType(), True),
    StructField("RateCodeExp", NullType(), True)
])

# Create a list of rows for the DataFrame
data = [
    (50, "Rate Code 50", None),
    (51, "Rate Code 51", None),
    (52, "Rate Code 52", None)]

# Create a DataFrame from the list of rows and the schema
df = spark.createDataFrame(data, schema)

df.write                               \
  .format("delta")                     \
  .option("mergeSchema", "true") \
  .mode("append")                      \
  .save("/mnt/datalake/book/chapter07/TaxiRateCode")

# Print the schema
df.printSchema()
```

The schema for this DataFrame is:

```
root
 |-- RateCodeId: integer (nullable = true)
 |-- RateCodeDesc: string (nullable = true)
 |-- RateCodeExp: void (nullable = true)
```

When we look at the metadata entry for the corresponding transaction log entry, we see the nullable type reflected:

```
"schemaString": "{\"type\":\"struct\",\"fields\":[
    {\"name\":\"RateCodeId\",\"type\":\"integer\",\"nullable\"
    :true,\"metadata\":{}},
    {\"name\":\"RateCodeDesc\",\"type\":\"string\",\"nullable\"
    :true,\"metadata\":{}},
    {\"name\":\"RateCodeExp\",\"type\":\"void\",\"nullable\"
    :true,\"metadata\":{}}]}",
```

We can see the data type reflected as void. Note that if we try to query this table with a SELECT *, we will get an error:

```
%sql
SELECT
    *
FROM
    delta.`/mnt/datalake/book/chapter07/TaxiRateCode`
```

We get the following exception:

```
java.lang.IllegalStateException: Couldn't find RateCodeExp#26346
in [RateCodeId#26344,RateCodeDesc#26345]
```

The reason for this error is that NullType columns in Delta Lake do not have a defined schema, so Spark cannot infer the data type of the column. Therefore, when we try to run a SELECT * query, Spark is unable to map the NullType column to a specific data type, and the query fails.

If you want to query the table, we can list the columns you need without the NullType column:

```
%sql
SELECT
    RateCodeId,
    RateCodeDesc
FROM
    delta.`/mnt/datalake/book/chapter07/TaxiRateCode`
```

This will succeed without any issues.

Explicit Schema Updates

So far we have leveraged schema evolution to allow the schema to evolve according to a number of rules. Let's look at how we can explicitly manipulate a Delta table's schema. First, we will add a column to a Delta table using both the SQL ALTER TABLE and ADD COLUMN commands. Next, we will use the SQL ALTER COLUMN statement to add comments to a table column. Next, we will use a variation of the ALTER TABLE command to change the column ordering for the table. We will review Delta Lake column mapping, since it is required for the following.

Adding a Column to a Table

In step 3 of the "03 - Explicit Schema Updates" notebook, we have an example of how to use the SQL ALTER TABLE...ADD COLUMN command to add a column to a Delta table:

```sql
%sql
ALTER TABLE delta.`/mnt/datalake/book/chapter07/TaxiRateCode`
ADD COLUMN RateCodeTaxPercent INT AFTER RateCodeId
```

Note that we used the AFTER keyword, so the column will be added after the RateCodeId field, and not at the end of the column list, as is the standard practice without the AFTER keyword. Similarly, we can use the FIRST keyword to add the new column at the first position in the column list.

Looking at the schema with the DESCRIBE command, we see that the new column is indeed inserted after the RateCodeId column:

```
+-------------------+----------+--------+
|col_name           | data_type|comment |
+-------------------+----------+--------+
|RateCodeId         |int       | null   |
|RateCodeTaxPercent |int       | null   |
|RateCodeDesc       |string    | null   |
+-------------------+----------+--------+
```

By default, nullability is set to true, so all of the values for the newly added column will be set to null:

```
+----------+------------------+--------------------+
|RateCodeId|RateCodeTaxPercent|RateCodeDesc        |
+----------+------------------+--------------------+
|1         |    null          |Standard Rate       |
|2         |    null          |JFK                 |
|3         |    null          |Newark              |
|4         |    null          |Nassau or Westchester|
|5         |    null          |Negotiated fare     |
|6         |    null          |Group ride          |
+----------+------------------+--------------------+
```

When we look at the transaction log entry for the ADD COLUMN operation, you see:

- A commitInfo action with the ADD COLUMN operator.

- A metaData action with the new schemaString. In the schemaString, we see the new RateTaxCodePercent column:

```
{
    "commitInfo": {
        ...
        "operation": "ADD COLUMNS",
        "operationParameters": {
            "columns": "[{\"column\":{\"name\":\"RateCodeTaxPercent\",\"type\":
                        \"integer\",\"nullable\":true,
                        \"metadata\":{}},\"position\":\"AFTER RateCodeId\"}]"
        },
        ...
    }
}
{
    "metaData": {
        ...
        "schemaString": "{\"type\":\"struct\",\"fields\":[
            {\"name\":\"RateCodeId\", \"type\":\"integer\",\"nullable\":
            true,\"metadata\":{}},
            {\"name\":\"RateCodeTaxPercent\",\"type\":\"integer\",\"nullable\":
            true,\"metadata\":{}},
            {\"name\":\"RateCodeDesc\",\"type\":\"string\",\"nullable\":
            true,\"metadata\":{}}]}",
        "partitionColumns": [],
        "configuration": {},
        "createdTime": 1681168745910
    }
}
```

Note that there are no add or remove actions, so no data had to be rewritten for ADD COLUMN to succeed; the only operation Delta Lake had to perform is to update the schemaString in the metaData transaction log action.

Adding Comments to a Column

In step 3 of the "Explicit Schema Updates" notebook, we see how to add comments to a Delta table using SQL with the ALTER COLUMN statement. For example, if we have the standard taxidb.TaxiRateCode table, we can add a comment to a column:

```
%sql
--
-- Add a comment to the RateCodeId column
--
ALTER TABLE taxidb.TaxiRateCode
ALTER COLUMN RateCodeId COMMENT 'This is the id of the Ride'
```

We see a commitInfo entry in the corresponding transaction log entry with a CHANGE COLUMN operation, and the addition of the comment:

```
{
    "commitInfo": {
        ...
        "userName": "bennie.haelen@insight.com",
        "operation": "CHANGE COLUMN",
        "operationParameters": {
            "column": "{\"name\":\"RateCodeId\",\"type\":\"integer\",
                \"nullable\":
                true,\"metadata\":
                {\"comment\":\"This is the id of the Ride\"}}"
        },
        ...
    }
}
```

In the metadata entry, we see the updated metadata for the column:

```
"schemaString": "{\"type\":\"struct\",\"fields\":[
    {\"name\":\"RateCodeId\",\"type\":\"integer\",\"nullable\":
    true,\"metadata\":
        {\"comment\":\"This is the id of the Ride\"}},
    {\"name\":\"RateCodeDesc\",\"type\":\"string\",\"nullable\":
    true,\"metadata\":{}}]}",
```

We can also see the column change with the DESCRIBE HISTORY command:

```
DESCRIBE HISTORY taxidb.TaxiRateCode
```

Changing Column Ordering

By default, Delta Lake collects statistics on only the first 32 columns. Therefore, if there is a specific column that we would like to have included in the statistics, we might want to move that column in the column order. In step 4 of the "03 - Explicit Schema Updates" notebook, we can see how to use ALTER TABLE and ALTER COLUMN to change the order of the table. Right now, the table looks as follows:

```
%sql
DESCRIBE taxidb.TaxiRateCode
```

```
+------------------+----------+------------------------+
|col_name          | data_type|comment                 |
+------------------+----------+------------------------+
|RateCodeId        |int       |This is the id of the Ride|
|RateCodeTaxPercent|int       | null                   |
|RateCodeDesc      |string    | null                   |
+------------------+----------+------------------------+
```

Let's assume that we want to move the RateCodeDesc column up so it appears after the RateCodeId. We can use the ALTER COLUMN syntax:

```
%sql
ALTER TABLE taxidb.TaxiRateCode  ALTER COLUMN RateCodeDesc AFTER RateCodeId
```

After executing this statement, the schema will look as follows:

```
+------------------+---------+----------------------+
|col_name          |  data_type|comment             |
+------------------+---------+----------------------+
|RateCodeId        |int      |This is the id of the Ride|
|RateCodeDesc      |string   | null                 |
|RateCodeTaxPercent|int      | null                 |
+------------------+---------+----------------------+
```

You can combine column ordering and adding a comment within a single ALTER COLUMN statement. This operation will preserve all data in the table.

Delta Lake Column Mapping

Column mapping allows Delta Lake tables and the underlying Parquet file columns to use different names. This enables Delta Lake schema evolution such as RENAME COLUMN and DROP COLUMN on a Delta Lake table without the need to rewrite the underlying Parquet files.

> At the time of writing, Delta Lake column mapping is in experimental support mode, but this is an important, powerful feature to discuss that supports many common scenarios. You can find more information about column mapping at the Delta Lake documentation website (*https://oreil.ly/1gQpy*).

Delta Lake supports column mapping for Delta Lake tables, which enables metadata-only changes to mark columns as deleted or renamed without rewriting data files. It also allows users to name Delta table columns using characters that are not allowed by Parquet, such as spaces, so that users can directly ingest CSV or JSON data into Delta Lake without the need to rename columns due to previous character constraints.

Column mapping requires the following Delta Lake protocols:

- Reader version 2 or above
- Writer version 5 or above

Once a Delta table has the required protocol versions, you can enable column mapping by setting delta.columnmapping.mode to name.

In step 4 of the "03 - Explicit Schema Updates" notebook, we can see that to check the reader and writer protocol versions of our table, we can use the DESCRIBE EXTENDED command:

```
%sql
DESCRIBE EXTENDED taxidb.TaxiRateCode
+-----------------+-----------------------------------------------------+
|col_name         |data_type                                            |
+-----------------+-----------------------------------------------------+
|RateCodeId       |int                                                  |
|  .........      |                                                     |
|Table Properties |[delta.minReaderVersion=1,delta.minWriterVersion=2]  |
+-----------------+-----------------------------------------------------+
```

We see that the table is not at the protocol version required by column mapping. We can update both the versions and `delta.columnmapping.mode` with the following SQL statement:

```
%sql
ALTER TABLE taxidb.TaxiRateCode  SET TBLPROPERTIES (
    'delta.minReaderVersion' = '2',
    'delta.minWriterVersion' = '5',
    'delta.columnMapping.mode' = 'name'
 )
```

When we look at the corresponding log entry for the SET TBLPROPERTIES statement, we see quite a few changes.

First, we see a `commitInfo` action with the SET TBLPROPERTIES entry:

```
{
    "commitInfo": {
        ...
        "operation": "SET TBLPROPERTIES",
        "operationParameters": {
            "properties": "{\"delta.minReaderVersion\":\"2\",
                            \"delta.minWriterVersion\":\"5\",
                            \"delta.columnMapping.mode\":\"name\"}"
        },
        ...
    }
}
```

Next, we see a protocol action, informing us that the `minReader` and `minWriter` versions have been updated:

```
{
    "protocol": {
        "minReaderVersion": 2,
        "minWriterVersion": 5
    }
}
```

And finally, we see a `metaData` entry with a `schemaString`. But now, column mapping has been added to the `schemaString`:

```
{
    "metaData": {
        ...,
        "schemaString": "{\"type\":\"struct\",\"fields\":[
            {\"name\":\"RateCodeId\",\"type\":\"integer\",\"nullable\":true,
                \"metadata\":{\"comment\":\"This is the id of the Ride\",
                \"delta.columnMapping.id\":1,\"delta.columnMapping.physicalName\
                ":\"RateCodeId\"}},
            {\"name\":\"RateCodeDesc\",\"type\":\"string\",\"nullable\":true,
                \"metadata\":{\"delta.columnMapping.id\":2,
                \"delta.columnMapping.physicalName\":\"RateCodeDesc\"}},
            {\"name\":\"RateCodeTaxPercent\",\"type\":\"integer\",\"nullable\":
            true,
                \"metadata\":{\"delta.columnMapping.id\":3,
                \"delta.columnMapping.physicalName\":\"RateCodeTaxPercent\"}}]}",
        ..,
        "configuration": {
            "delta.columnMapping.mode": "name",
            "delta.columnMapping.maxColumnId": "3"
        },
        ..
    }
}
```

For each column, you have:

- The name, which is the official Delta Lake column name (e.g., `RateCodeId`).

- `delta.columnMapping.id`, which is the ID of the column. This ID will remain stable.

- `delta.columnMapping.physicalName`, which is the physical name in the Parquet file.

Renaming a Column

You can use `ALTER TABLE...RENAME COLUMN` to rename a column without rewriting any of the column's existing data. Note that *column mapping* needs to be in place for this to be enabled. Assume we want to rename the `RateCodeDesc` column to a more descriptive `RateCodeDescription`:

```
%sql
-- Perform our column rename
ALTER TABLE taxidb.taxiratecode RENAME COLUMN RateCodeDesc to RateCodeDescription
```

When we look at the corresponding log entry, we see the rename reflected in the schemaString:

```
"schemaString": "{\"type\":\"struct\",\"fields\":[
        ...
        {\"name\":\"RateCodeDescription\",\"type\":\"string\",\"nullable\"
        :true,
            \"metadata\":{\"delta.columnMapping.id\":
            2,\"delta.columnMapping.physicalName\":\"RateCodeDesc\"}},
        ...
```

We see that the Delta Lake column name has been changed to RateCodeDescription, but the physicalName is still RateCodeDesc in the Parquet file. This is how Delta Lake can perform a complex DDL operation, such as RENAME COLUMN, without needing to rewrite any files, as a simple metadata operation.

Replacing the Table Columns

In Delta Lake, the ALTER TABLE REPLACE COLUMNS command can be used to replace all the columns of an existing Delta table with a new set of columns. Note that in order to do this, you need to enable Delta Lake column mapping, as described in the previous section.

Once column mapping is enabled, we can use the REPLACE COLUMNS command:

```
%sql
ALTER TABLE taxidb.TaxiRateCode
REPLACE COLUMNS (
  Rate_Code_Identifier   INT     COMMENT 'Identifies the code',
  Rate_Code_Description STRING COMMENT 'Describes the code',
  Rate_Code_Percentage  INT     COMMENT 'Tax percentage applied'
)
```

When we look at the schema, we see the following:

```
%sql
DESCRIBE EXTENDED taxidb.TaxiRateCode


+---------------------+--------------------------------------------------------+
|col_name             |data_type                                               |
+---------------------+--------------------------------------------------------+
|Rate_Code_Identifier | int                                                    |
|Rate_Code_Description| string                                                 |
|Rate_Code_Percentage | int                                                    |
| .........           |  ......                                                |
|Table Properties     |[delta.columnMapping.maxColumnId=6,                     |
|                     |  delta.columnMapping.mode=name,                        |
|                     |delta.minReaderVersion=2,delta.minWriterVersion=5]      |
+---------------------+--------------------------------------------------------+
```

In the DESCRIBE output, we can see the new schema, and we can also see the minimum reader and writer versions.

When we look at the corresponding transaction log entry, we see the commitInfo with the REPLACE COLUMNS operation:

```
"commitInfo": {
        ...
        "operation": "REPLACE COLUMNS",
        "operationParameters": {
            "columns": "[
                {\"name\":\"Rate_Code_Identifier\",\"type\":\"integer\",\
                "nullable\":true,
                    \"metadata\":{\"comment\":\"Identifies the code\"}},
                {\"name\":\"Rate_Code_Description\",\"type\":\"string\",\
                "nullable\":true,
                    \"metadata\":{\"comment\":\"Describes the code\"}},
                {\"name\":\"Rate_Code_Percentage\",\"type\":\"integer\",\
                "nullable\":true,
                    \"metadata\":{\"comment\":\"Tax percentage applied\"}}]"
        },
        ...
    }
}
```

In the metaData section, we see the new schemaString with some interesting information. The new Delta Lake columns are now mapped to guide-based column names with new IDs (starting with 4):

```
{
    "metaData": {
    ...,
    "schemaString": "{\"type\":\"struct\",\"fields\":[
        {\"name\":\"Rate_Code_Identifier\",\"type\":\"integer\",
        \"nullable\":true,
            \"metadata\":{\"comment\":\"Identifies the code\",
            \"delta.columnMapping.id\":4,
                \"delta.columnMapping.physicalName\":
                \"col-72397feb-3cb0-4613-baad-aa78fff64a40\"}},
        {\"name\":\"Rate_Code_Description\",\"type\":
        \"string\",\"nullable\":true,
    \"metadata\":{\"comment\":\"Describes the code\",
    \"delta.columnMapping.id\":5,
    \"delta.columnMapping.physicalName\":
    \"col-67d47d0c-5d25-45d8-8d0e-c9b13f5f2c6e\"}},
        {\"name\":\"Rate_Code_Percentage\",\"type\":\"integer\",\"nullable\":true,
    \"metadata\":{\"comment\":\"Tax percentage applied\",
    \"delta.columnMapping.id\":\"delta.columnMapping.physicalName\":
    \"col-3b8f9847-71df-4e64-a921-64c918de328d\"}}]}", ...
    "configuration": {
    "delta.columnMapping.mode": "name",
    "delta.columnMapping.maxColumnId": "6"
```

```
    },
    ...
    }
}
```

When we look at the data, we see all six rows, but all columns are set to null:

```
+--------------------+----------------------+--------------------+
|Rate_Code_Identifier|Rate_Code_Description|Rate_Code_Percentage|
+--------------------+----------------------+--------------------+
| null               | null                 | null               |
| null               | null                 | null               |
| null               | null                 | null               |
| null               | null                 | null               |
| null               | null                 | null               |
| null               | null                 | null               |
+--------------------+----------------------+--------------------+
```

The REPLACE COLUMNS operation sets all the column values to null because the new schema might have different data types or a different order of columns than the old schema. As a result, the existing data in the table may not fit the new schema. Therefore, Delta Lake sets the value of all columns to null to ensure that the new schema is applied consistently to all records in the table.

 It's important to note that the REPLACE COLUMNS operation can be a destructive operation, as it replaces the entire schema of the Delta table and rewrites the data in the new schema. Therefore, you should use it with caution and make sure to back up your data before applying this operation.

Dropping a Column

Delta Lake now supports dropping a column as a metadata-only operation without rewriting any data files. Note that column mapping must be enabled for this operation.

It is important to note that dropping a column from metadata does not delete the underlying data for the column in the files. To purge the dropped column data, you can use REORG TABLE to rewrite the files. You can then use the VACUUM command to physically delete the files that contain the dropped column data.

Let's start with the standard schema in the taxidb.TaxiRateCode table:

```
root
 |-- RateCodeId: integer (nullable = true)
 |-- RateCodeDesc: string (nullable = true)
```

Let's assume that we want to drop the `RateCodeDesc` column. We can use the `ALTER TABLE` with the `DROP COLUMN` SQL command to do this:

```
%sql
-- Use the ALTER TABLE... DROP COLUMN command
-- to drop the RateCodeDesc column
ALTER TABLE taxidb.TaxiRateCode DROP COLUMN RateCodeDesc
```

When we use the `DESCRIBE` command to view the schema, we see that we only have the `RateCodeId` column left:

```
+----------+---------+---------+
|col_name  |data_type|  comment|
+----------+---------+---------+
|RateCodeId|int      |  null   |
+----------+---------+---------+
```

When we check the table, we see that our data is still there, minus the dropped columns:

```
%sql
-- Select the remaining columns
SELECT * FROM taxidb.TaxiRateCode
```

```
+----------+
|RateCodeId|
+----------+
|    1     |
|    2     |
|    3     |
|    4     |
|    5     |
|    6     |
+----------+
```

We see the following sections in the corresponding transaction log entry:

- A `commitInfo` action that specifies the `DROP COLUMNS` operation:

```
{
        "commitInfo": {
        ...
            "operation": "DROP COLUMNS",
            "operationParameters": {
                "columns": "[\"RateCodeDesc\"]"
            },
        ...
        }
}
```

- A `metaData` action that specifies the new schema, including the column mapping in the metadata section:

```
{
         "metaData": {
         ...
         "schemaString": "{\"type\":\"struct\",\"fields\":
         [{\"name\":\"RateCodeId\",\"type\":\"integer\",
                 \"nullable\":true,
                 \"metadata\":{\"delta.columnMapping.id\":1,
                 \"delta.columnMapping.physicalName\":
                 \"RateCodeId\"}}]}",
         ...
         "configuration": {
           "delta.columnMapping.mode": "name",
          "delta.columnMapping.maxColumnId": "2"
         },
         ...
         }
}
```

Note that the `RateCodeDesc` column has only been "soft deleted." When we looked at the transaction log entry earlier, what was most remarkable was not what was there, but what was not there. There were no remove and add actions for a data file, so no part files were rewritten, and the old part file is still there with both the `RateCodeId` and the `RateCodeDesc` columns.

When we look at the part files, we see our one part file:

```
%sh
# Display the data file(s)
# You can see you only have our one part file, which was not
# touched at all
ls -al /dbfs/mnt/datalake/book/chapter07/TaxiRateCode.delta

drwxrwxrwx 2 root root 4096 Apr  6 00:00 _delta_log
-rwxrwxrwx 1 root root  980 Apr  6 00:00 part-00000-...-c000.snappy.parquet
```

When you download and view the file with a Parquet viewer,[1] you can see that both columns are still there (see Table 7-1).

_____

1 For example, Parquet Viewer (*https://oreil.ly/dldNb*)

Table 7-1. Viewing the Parquet file after DROP COLUMN

RateCodeId	RateCodeDesc
1	Standard rate
2	JFK
3	Newark
4	Nassau or Westchester
5	Negotiated fare
6	Group ride

DROP COLUMN only updates the metadata—it does not add or remove any part files. When working with large files, having this "soft-deleted" data around can result in the small file problem. Therefore, in the next section, we will use the REORG TABLE command to reclaim the space for the deleted column.

The REORG TABLE Command

The REORG TABLE command reorganizes a Delta Lake table by rewriting files to purge soft-deleted data, which we created in the previous section, where we dropped a column with the ALTER TABLE DROP COLUMN command.

To reclaim the space occupied by the RateCodeDesc column that we dropped, we can issue the following command:

```
%sql
-- Reorganize the table by removing the part file which included
-- the RateCodeDesc column and adding a new part file with just the
-- RateCodeId column
REORG TABLE taxidb.TaxiRateCode APPLY (PURGE)
```

After running this command, Delta Lake will display the path it used to execute the command, which in this case is *dbfs:/mnt/datalake/book/chapter07/TaxiRate-Code.delta*. It will also display the metrics, which contain the number of files added and removed:

```
{
    "numFilesAdded": 1,
    "numFilesRemoved": 1,
    "filesAdded": {
        "min": 665,
        "max": 665,
        "avg": 665,
        "totalFiles": 1,
        "totalSize": 665
    },
    "filesRemoved": {
        "min": 980,
        "max": 980,
        "avg": 980,
        "totalFiles": 1,
        "totalSize": 980
    },
    "partitionsOptimized": 0,
    ...
}
```

One file was removed (the part file with both columns) and another was added (the part file with just the `RateCodeId` column).

When we look at the corresponding transaction log entry, we see the following `add` and `remove` actions:

```
{
    "remove": {
        "path": "part-00000-....-c000.snappy.parquet",
        ...
    }
}
{
    "add": {
        "path": "9g/part-00000-....-c000.snappy.parquet",
        "partitionValues": {},
        ...
        "stats": "{\"numRecords\":6,\"minValues\":{\"RateCodeId\":1},
        \"maxValues\":{\"RateCodeId\":6},\"nullCount\":{\"RateCodeId\":0}}",
        ...
    }
}
```

In the `remove` action, we remove the original Parquet file containing both columns and add a file in a subdirectory. When we look at that location, we see the Parquet file:

```
%sh
# This is the new part file, which contains just the RateCodeId column
ls -al /dbfs/mnt/datalake/book/chapter07/TaxiRateCode.delta/9g

-rwxrwxrwx 1 root root  665 Apr  6 01:45 part-00000-....snappy.parquet
```

When you download this file and view it, you can see that only the `RateCodeId` column is present, as shown in Table 7-2.

Table 7-2. The newly added part file after the REORG TABLE *command*

RateCodeId
1
2
3
4
5
6

Changing Column Data Type or Name

We can change a column's data type or name or drop a column by manually rewriting the table. To do this, we can use the `overwriteSchema` option. Let's start with the standard schema:

```
root
 |-- RateCodeId: integer (nullable = true)
 |-- RateCodeDesc: string (nullable = true)
```

Next, change the data type of the `RateCodeId` column from integer to short. We can rewrite the table. First, we read the table, use the `.withColumn` PySpark function to change the data type of the `RateCodeId` column, and then write the table back with the `overwriteSchema` option set to `True`:

```
#
# Rewrite the table with the overwriteSchema setting
# Use .withColumn to change the data type of the RateCodeId column
#
spark.read.table('taxidb.TaxiRateCode')                                 \
        .withColumn("RateCodeId", col("RateCodeId").cast("short"))  \
        .write                                                       \
        .mode("overwrite")                                           \
        .option("overwriteSchema", "true")                           \
        .saveAsTable('taxidb.TaxiRateCode')
```

If we check the schema of the table with `DESCRIBE`, we see the data type change for the `RateCodeId` table:

```
%sql
DESCRIBE taxidb.TaxiRateCode

+-------------+---------+---------+
|col_name     |data_type| comment |
+-------------+---------+---------+
|RateCodeId   |smallint |null     |
|RateCodeDesc |string   |null     |
+-------------+---------+---------+
```

When we check the transaction log entry for this operation, we see four entries:

1. The `commitInfo` with the `CREATE OR REPLACE TABLE AS SELECT` operation:

   ```
   {
   "commitInfo": {...
       "operation": "CREATE OR REPLACE TABLE AS SELECT",
           ...
   }
   }
   ```

2. The `metaData` action with the `schemaString`:

   ```
   {
           "metaData": {
             ....
               "schemaString": "{\"type\":\"struct\",\"fields\":[
           {\"name\":\"RateCodeId\",\"type\":\"short\",\"nullable\":
           true,\"metadata\":{}},
             {\"name\":\"RateCodeDesc\",\"type\":\"string\",\"nullable\":
           true,\"metadata\":{}}]}",
                 ...
           }
       }
   ```

3. A `remove` action that removes the old part file from the table:

   ```
   {
             "remove": {
         "path": "part-00000-....snappy.parquet",
           ...
   }
   }
   ```

4. The `add` action that adds a part file with our six records:

   ```
   {
             "add": {
         "path": "part-00000-....snappy.parquet",
         "partitionValues": {},
           ...
         "stats": "{\"numRecords\":6,\"minValues\":{\"RateCodeId
         \":1,\"RateCodeDesc\":\"Group ride\"},
   ```

```
                    \"maxValues\":{\"RateCodeId\":6,\"RateCodeDesc
                    \":\"Standard Rate\"},
                    \"nullCount\":{\"RateCodeId\":0,\"RateCodeDesc
                    \":0}}",
       ...
             }
        }
```

Here we have demonstrated that we can use PySpark to change the data type of a column, albeit at the cost of completely rewriting the Delta table. The same approach can be used to drop columns or change column names.

Conclusion

Modern data platforms leveraging ETL for analytics will always be consumers of data as they ingest data from various data sources. And as organizations continue to collect, process, and analyze data from a growing number of data sources, the ability to swiftly handle schema evolution and data validation is a critical aspect of any data platform. In this chapter you have seen how Delta Lake gives you flexibility to evolve a table's schema through dynamic and explicit schema updates, while also enforcing schema validation.

Using transaction log entries, Delta Lake stores a Delta table's schema in the `metaData` action. This schema, which contains column names and data types, is used to support schema validation and report schema mismatches on attempted operations. This schema validation is atomic in nature for operations on Delta tables, which can be illustrated in transaction log entries, or rather the omission of transaction log entries for schema violations.

And while you learned that Delta Lake supports schema validation, you also learned that it supports dynamic schema evolution to add, remove, or modify columns in existing Delta tables. You can evolve a table's schema using the `mergeSchema` option, or you can explicitly update a schema to add, remove, or rename columns or data types, while also adding comments or changing the column order (which is important for data skipping) using SQL or DataFrame syntax. All of these types of schema operations, including supported conversions for data types, are demonstrated throughout the chapter along with their corresponding commands (e.g., `REPLACE COLUMNS`) and transaction log entries to play these actions out and illustrate these behaviors.

While schema evolution focuses primarily on changes in batch data operations, the following chapter will explore the requirements and operations needed for streaming data using Spark Structured Streaming.

Operations on Streaming Data

Spark Structured Streaming was first introduced in Apache Spark 2.0. The main goal of Structured Streaming was to build near-real-time streaming applications on Spark. Structured Streaming replaced an older, lower-level API called DStreams (Discretized Streams), which was based upon the old Spark RDD model. Since then, Structured Streaming has added many optimizations and connectors, including integration with Delta Lake.

Delta Lake is integrated with Spark Structured Streaming through its two major operators: `readStream` and `writeStream`. Delta tables can be used as both streaming sources and streaming sinks. Delta Lake overcomes many limitations typically associated with streaming systems, including:

- Coalescing small files produced by low-latency ingestion
- Maintaining "exactly-once" processing with more than one stream (or concurrent batch jobs)
- Leveraging the Delta transaction log for efficient discovery of which files are new when using files for a source stream

We will start this chapter with a quick review of Spark Structured Streaming, followed by an initial overview of Delta Lake streaming and its unique capabilities. Next, we will walk through a small "Hello Streaming World!" Delta Lake streaming example. While limited in scope, this example will provide an opportunity to understand the details of the Delta Lake streaming programming model in a very simple context.

Incremental processing of data has become a popular ETL model. The `AvailableNow` stream triggering mode enables developers to build incremental pipelines without needing to maintain their own state variables, resulting in simpler and more robust pipelines.

You can enable a Change Data Feed (CDF) on a Delta table. Clients can consume this CDF feed with SQL queries, or they can stream these changes into their application, enabling use cases such as creating audit trials, streaming analytics, compliance analysis, etc.

Streaming Overview

Although this chapter is specific to the Delta Lake streaming model, let's briefly review the basics of Spark Structured Streaming before delving into the unique capabilities of Delta Lake Structured Streaming.

Spark Structured Streaming

Spark Structured Streaming is a near-real-time stream processing engine built on top of Apache Spark. It enables scalable, fault-tolerant, and low-latency processing of continuous data streams. Spark Streaming provides a high-level API, allowing you to build end-to-end streaming applications that can read and write data from and to a variety of sources, such as Kafka, Azure Event Hubs, Amazon S3, Google Cloud Platform's Pub/Sub, the Hadoop Distributed File System, and many more.

The core idea behind Structured Streaming is that it allows you to treat a data stream as a boundless table-like structure that you can query and manipulate by using SQL-like operations, making it easy to analyze and manipulate the data. One of the many benefits of Spark Structured Streaming is its ease of use and simplicity. The API is built on top of the familiar Spark SQL syntax, so you can leverage your existing knowledge of SQL and DataFrame operations to build streaming applications without learning a new set of complex APIs.

Additionally, Structured Streaming provides fault-tolerance and reliability by leveraging Spark's processing engine, which can recover from failures and ensure that each data point is processed exactly once. This type of fault tolerance makes it ideal for building mission-critical applications that require low-latency and high-throughput data processing.

Delta Lake and Structured Streaming

When you leverage Delta Lake with Structured Streaming, you get both the transactional guarantees of Delta Lake and the powerful programming model of Apache Spark Structured Streaming. With Delta Lake, you can now use Delta tables as both streaming sources and sinks, enabling a *continuous processing model* that processes your data through the Raw, Bronze, Silver, and Gold data lake layers in a streaming fashion, eliminating the need for batch jobs, resulting in a simplified solution architecture. In a later part of this chapter, we'll present an example of such a continuous processing architecture.

In Chapter 7 we discussed schema enforcement and schema evolution. Streaming into Delta Lake offers schema enforcement, which ensures that incoming data streams are validated against the predefined schema, preventing data anomalies from entering the data lake. However, when changing business requirements introduce the need to capture additional information, you can leverage Delta Lake's schema evolution capabilities to allow the schema to change over time.

Streaming Examples

We will start this section by reviewing a very simple "Hello Streaming World!" example illustrating the basics of streaming from and to a Delta table.

Hello Streaming World

In this section we will create a simple Delta table streaming scenario and set up a streaming query that:

- Reads all changes from a source Delta table into a streaming DataFrame. In the case of Delta Lake tables, "reading the changes" equates to "reading the transaction log entries," since they contain the details of all changes to the table.
- Performs some simple processing on the streaming DataFrame.
- Writes the streaming DataFrame to a target Delta table.

The combination of reading a stream from a source and writing the stream to a target is often referred to as a *streaming query*, as illustrated in Figure 8-1.

Once we have the streaming query up and running, we will perform a number of small batch updates on the source table, allowing the data to flow through the streaming query to the target. During the execution of the query, we will query the query process log, and study the contents of the checkpoint files, which maintain the state of our streaming query.

This simple example will allow you to fully understand the basics of the Delta Lake streaming model before moving on to more complex examples. First, execute the "Chapter Initialization" notebook for Chapter 8[1] to create the required Delta tables. Next, open the "01 - Simple Streaming" notebook.

---

1 GitHub repo location: */chapter08/00 - Chapter Initialization*

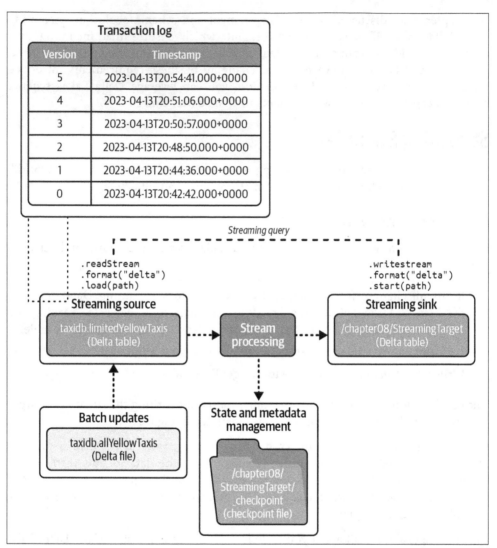

Transaction log	
Version	Timestamp
5	2023-04-13T20:54:41.000+0000
4	2023-04-13T20:51:06.000+0000
3	2023-04-13T20:50:57.000+0000
2	2023-04-13T20:48:50.000+0000
1	2023-04-13T20:44:36.000+0000
0	2023-04-13T20:42:42.000+0000

Streaming query

```
.readStream
.format("delta")
.load(path)
```

```
.writestream
.format("delta")
.start(path)
```

Streaming source

taxidb.limitedYellowTaxis
(Delta table)

Stream processing

Streaming sink

/chapter08/StreamingTarget
(Delta table)

Batch updates

taxidb.allYellowTaxis
(Delta file)

State and metadata management

/chapter08/
StreamingTarget/
_checkpoint
(checkpoint file)

Figure 8-1. Basic streaming example

Here we have a Delta table that contains 10 records of yellow taxi data, all contained in a single Parquet file:

```
%sh
ls -al /dbfs/mnt/datalake/book/chapter08/LimitedRecords.delta

drwxrwxrwx 2 root root 4096 Apr 11 19:40 _delta_log
-rwxrwxrwx 1 root root 6198 Apr 12 00:04 part-00000-....snappy.parquet

%sql
SELECT * from delta.`/mnt/datalake/book/chapter08/LimitedRecords.delta`
```

Output (only showing relevant portions):

```
+------+--------+----------------------------+----------------------------+
|RideId|VendorId|   PickupTime               |   DropTime                 |
+------+--------+----------------------------+----------------------------+
|1     |    1   |2022-03-01T00:00:00.000+0000|2022-03-01T00:15:34.000+0000|
|2     |    1   |2022-03-01T00:00:00.000+0000|2022-03-01T00:10:56.000+0000|
|3     |    1   |2022-03-01T00:00:00.000+0000|2022-03-01T00:11:20.000+0000|
|4     |    2   |2022-03-01T00:00:00.000+0000|2022-03-01T00:20:01.000+0000|
|5     |    2   |2022-03-01T00:00:00.000+0000|2022-03-01T00:00:00.000+0000|
|6     |    2   |2022-03-01T00:00:00.000+0000|2022-03-01T00:00:00.000+0000|
|7     |    2   |2022-03-01T00:00:00.000+0000|2022-03-01T00:00:00.000+0000|
|8     |    2   |2022-03-01T00:00:00.000+0000|2022-03-01T00:00:00.000+0000|
|9     |    2   |2022-03-01T00:00:00.000+0000|2022-03-01T00:00:00.000+0000|
|10    |    2   |2022-03-01T00:00:01.000+0000|2022-03-01T00:11:15.000+0000|
+------+--------+----------------------------+----------------------------+
```

Creating the streaming query

First, we are going to create our first simple streaming query. We start by reading a stream from the source table, as follows:

```
# Start streaming from our source "LimitedRecords" table
# Notice that instead of a "read", we now use a "readStream",
# for the rest our statement is just like any other spark Delta read
stream_df =                 \
        spark               \
        .readStream         \
        .format("delta")    \
        .load("/mnt/datalake/book/chapter08/LimitedRecords.delta")
```

The readStream is just like any other standard Delta table read except for the Stream suffix. We get back a streaming DataFrame in stream_df.

> A streaming DataFrame is very similar to a standard Spark Data-Frame, so you can use the Spark API with all the methods you already know. However, there are a few differences that you need to be aware of. First, a streaming DataFrame is a continuous, unbounded sequence of data where each piece of data is treated as a new row in the DataFrame. Since a streaming DataFrame is unbounded, you cannot perform a count() or a sort() operation on it.

Next, we perform some manipulations on our DataFrame. We add a timestamp, so we know when we read each record from our source table. We also don't need all columns in the source DataFrame, so we select the columns that we need:

```
# Add a "RecordStreamTime" column with the timestamp at which we read the
# record from stream
stream_df = stream_df.withColumn("RecordStreamTime", current_timestamp())
```

```python
# This is the list of columns that we want from our streaming
# DataFrame
select_columns = [
    'RideId', 'VendorId', 'PickupTime', 'DropTime',
    'PickupLocationId', 'DropLocationId', 'PassengerCount',
    'TripDistance', 'TotalAmount', 'RecordStreamTime'
]

# Select the columns we need. Note that we can manipulate our stream
# just like any other DataStream, although some operations like
# count() are NOT supported, since this is an unbounded DataFrame
stream_df = stream_df.select(select_columns)
```

Finally, we write the DataFrame to an output table:

```python
# Define the output location and the checkpoint location
target_location = "/mnt/datalake/book/chapter08/StreamingTarget"
target_checkpoint_location = f"{target_location}/_checkpoint"

# Write the stream to the output location, maintain
# state in the checkpoint location
streamQuery =                                                        \
        stream_df                                                    \
            .writeStream                                             \
            .format("delta")                                        \
            .option("checkpointLocation", target_checkpoint_location) \
            .start(target_location)
```

First, we define a target, or output location, where we want to write the stream. In the option, we define a *checkpoint file* location. This checkpoint file will maintain the metadata and state of the streaming query. The checkpoint file is necessary to ensure fault tolerance and enable the query's recovery in case of failure. Among many other pieces of information, it will maintain which transaction log entries of the streaming source were already processed, so it can identify the new entries that have not yet been processed.

Finally, we invoke the `start` method with the target location. Notice that we are using the same base directory for both the output and the checkpoint file. We just append the underscore (`_checkpoint`) for the checkpoint subdirectory.

Since we have not specified a trigger, the streaming query will continue to run, so it will execute, check for new records, process them, and then immediately check for the next set of records. In the following sections, you will see that you can change this behavior with a trigger.

The query process log

When we start the streaming query we see the stream initializing, and a *query progress log* (QPL) is displayed. The QPL is a JSON log generated by every single micro-batch, and provides execution details on the micro-batch. It is used to display a small streaming dashboard in the notebook cell. The dashboard provides various metrics, statistics, and insights about the stream application's performance, throughput, and latency. When you expand the stream display, you see a dashboard with two tabs (Figure 8-2).

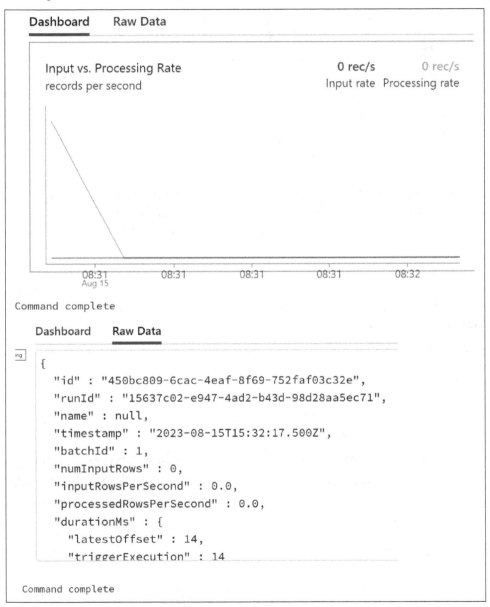

Figure 8-2. The query progress log display

The first tab contains the dashboard, where some of the key metrics from the QPL are displayed graphically. The raw metrics are displayed in the Raw Data tab.

A portion of the raw data of the query process log is shown here:

```
{
  "id" : "c5eaca75-cf4d-410f-b34c-9a2128ee1944",
  "runId" : "508283a5-9758-4cf9-8ab5-3ee71a465b67",
  "name" : null,
  "timestamp" : "2023-05-30T16:31:48.500Z",
  "batchId" : 1,
  "numInputRows" : 0,
  "inputRowsPerSecond" : 0.0,
  "processedRowsPerSecond" : 0.0,
  "durationMs" : {
    "latestOffset" : 14,
    "triggerExecution" : 15
  },
```

A key metric in the QPL is the stream unique id, the first entry in the log. This ID uniquely identifies the stream and maps back to the checkpoint directory, as you will see later. The stream unique id is also displayed above the streaming dashboard header.

The query log also contains the batchId, which is the micro-batch ID. For every stream, this ID will start with zero and increment by one for every processed micro-batch. The numInputRows field represents the number of rows that were ingested in the current micro-batch.

The next set of important metrics in the QPL are the Delta source and sink metrics:

- The sources startOffset and endOffset indicate where each batch started and ended. These include the following subfields:
  - The reservoirVersion is the version of the Delta table on which the current micro-batch is operating.
  - The index is used to keep track of which part file to start processing from.
  - The isStartingVersion boolean field is set to true if the reservoirVersion is set to the version of the Delta table at which the current stream was started.
- The sink field contains the location of the streaming sink.

When we look at the source and sink metrics for micro-batch 1, we see the following:

```
"sources" : [ {
    "description" : "DeltaSource[dbfs:/mnt/.../LimitedRecords.delta]",
    "startOffset" : {
      "sourceVersion" : 1,
      "reservoirId" : "6c25c8cd-88c1-4b74-9c96-a61c1727c3a2",
      "reservoirVersion" : 0,
```

```
      "index" : 0,
      "isStartingVersion" : true
    },
    "endOffset" : {
      "sourceVersion" : 1,
      "reservoirId" : "6c25c8cd-88c1-4b74-9c96-a61c1727c3a2",
      "reservoirVersion" : 0,
      "index" : 0,
      "isStartingVersion" : true
    },
    "latestOffset" : null,
    "numInputRows" : 0,
    "inputRowsPerSecond" : 0.0,
    "processedRowsPerSecond" : 0.0,
    "metrics" : {
      "numBytesOutstanding" : "0",
      "numFilesOutstanding" : "0"
    }
  } ],
  "sink" : {
    "description" : "DeltaSink[/mnt/datalake/book/chapter08/StreamingTarget]",
    "numOutputRows" : -1
  }
```

Notice numInputRows is 0. This might look a bit surprising, since we know that our source table had 10 rows in it. However, when we started the .writeStream, the streaming query started running and immediately processed the first 10 rows as part of batch 0. We can also see that our batchId is currently 1, and since batchIds start with 0, the first batch was already processed.

We can also see that the reservoirVersion is still 0 since this batch has not yet run, as no new records were processed. So, we are still at version 0 of our source table. We also see that the index is at 0, which means that we are processing the first data file, and we are indeed at the start version. We can verify this by displaying the version of the source table:

```
%sql
DESCRIBE HISTORY delta.`/mnt/datalake/book/chapter08/LimitedRecords.delta`
```

Output (only showing relevant portions):

```
+-------+---------------------------+
|version|                  timestamp|
+-------+---------------------------+
|0      |2023-05-30T16:25:23.000+0000|
+-------+---------------------------+
```

Here you can see that we are indeed at version 0 at this time. We can also verify this by querying our output streaming table:

```
%sql
SELECT count(*) FROM delta.`/mnt/datalake/book/chapter08/StreamingTarget`
```

We can see that we indeed have 10 rows:

```
+--------+
|count(1)|
+--------+
| 10     |
+--------+
```

Because we started the `writeStream` with `.start`, and without any indication of how often the query should run, it is running constantly. When the `writeStream` completes, it performs the next `readStream`, and so on. However, since no new rows are being produced in the source table, nothing really happens, and our output record count remains at 10. The `batchId` will not change until it picks up rows from the stream, so it remains at 1.

Next, we execute the following SQL statement that inserts 10 new records in the source table:

```sql
%sql
-- Use this query to insert 10 random records from the
-- allYellowTaxis table into the limitedYellowTaxis table
INSERT INTO
  taxidb.limitedYellowTaxis
SELECT
  *
FROM
  taxidb.allYellowTaxis
ORDER BY rand()
LIMIT 10
```

If we uncomment and run this query, the `batchId` is now set at 1, and we see the 10 new rows:

```
{
    "id" : "c5eaca75-cf4d-410f-b34c-9a2128ee1944",
    "runId" : "508283a5-9758-4cf9-8ab5-3ee71a465b67",
    "name" : null,
    "timestamp" : "2023-05-30T16:46:08.500Z",
    "batchId" : 1,
    "numInputRows" : 10,
    "inputRowsPerSecond" : 20.04008016032064,
```

Once this `batchId` is processed, the record count for `batchId` 2 will be back to 0, since no new rows are arriving from the stream.

Remember, the streaming query will keep running forever, looking for new transaction entries in the source table and writing the corresponding rows to the streaming target. Typically, Spark Structured Streaming is running as a micro-batch–based streaming service. It will read a batch of records from the source, process the records and write them to the target, and immediately afterward it will start the next batch looking for new records (or, in the case of Delta Lake, looking for new transaction entries).

This model, where we are doing batch updates to the source table, would not be economical in a real-world application. The source table is only periodically updated, but since our streaming query runs constantly, we have to keep its cluster running all the time, which runs up costs. Later in this chapter we will modify the streaming query to better fit our use case, but first, let's take a brief look at the checkpoint file.

The checkpoint file

Earlier, we saw that the checkpoint file will maintain the metadata and state of our streaming query. The checkpoint file is in the *_checkpoint* subdirectory:

```
%sh
ls -al /dbfs/mnt/datalake/book/chapter08/StreamingTarget/_checkpoint/

drwxrwxrwx 2 root root 4096 May  1 23:37 __tmp_path_dir
drwxrwxrwx 2 root root 4096 May  1 23:37 commits
-rwxrwxrwx 1 root root   45 May  2 15:48 metadata
drwxrwxrwx 2 root root 4096 May  1 23:37 offsets
```

We have one file (*metadata*), and two directories (*offsets* and *commits*). Let's take a look at each one. The *metadata* file simply contains the stream identifier in JSON format:

```
%sh
head /dbfs/mnt/datalake/book/chapter08/StreamingTarget/_checkpoint/metadata
{"id":"c5eaca75-cf4d-410f-b34c-9a2128ee1944"}
```

When we look at the *offsets* directory, you see two files, one for each `batchId`:

```
%sh
ls -al /dbfs/mnt/datalake/book/chapter08/StreamingTarget/_checkpoint/offsets

-rwxrwxrwx 1 root root 769 May 30 16:28 0
-rwxrwxrwx 1 root root 771 May 30 16:46 1
```

When we look at the contents of file 0, we see the following:

```
v1
{
    "batchWatermarkMs": 0,
    "batchTimestampMs": 1685464087937,
    "conf": {
        "spark.sql.streaming.stateStore.providerClass":
        "org.apache.spark.sql.execution.streaming
        .state.HDFSBackedStateStoreProvider",
        …..
    }
}
{
```

```
    "sourceVersion": 1,
    "reservoirId": "6c25c8cd-88c1-4b74-9c96-a61c1727c3a2",
    "reservoirVersion": 0,
    "index": 0,
    "isStartingVersion": true
}
```

The first section contains the Spark streaming configuration variables. The second section contains the same `reservoirVersion`, `index`, and `isStartingVersion` we saw in the QPL earlier. What is logged here is the state before the batch was executed, so we are at version zero, the file index is zero, and the `isStartingVersion` variable indicates that we are at the starting version.

When we look at file 1, we see the following:

```
v1
{
    "batchWatermarkMs": 0,
    "batchTimestampMs": 1685465168696,
    "conf": {
        "spark.sql.streaming.stateStore.providerClass":
        "org.apache.spark.sql.execution.streaming.state.
        HDFSBackedStateStoreProvider",
        …
    }
}
{
    "sourceVersion": 1,
    "reservoirId": "6c25c8cd-88c1-4b74-9c96-a61c1727c3a2",
    "reservoirVersion": 2,
    "index": -1,
    "isStartingVersion": false
}
```

In this batch, the 10 additional records were processed, and the next possible version that will be processed is 2, which is reflected in the `reservoirVersion`. Also, notice that the index is set to -1, which indicates that there are no additional files to be processed for the current version.

The *commits* folder contains one file per micro-batch. In our case, we will have two commits, one for each batch:

```
drwxrwxrw
-rwxrwxrwx 1 root root 29 Jun 9 15:55 0
-rwxrwxrwx 1 root root 29 Jun 9 16:15 1
```

Each file represents the successful completion of the micro-batch. It simply contains a watermark:

```
%sh
head /dbfs/mnt/datalake/book/chapter08/StreamingTarget/_checkpoint/commits/0
```

This produces:

```
v1 {"nextBatchWatermarkMs":0}
```

In this section, we had our first look at Delta streaming. We looked at a simple example, with a Delta table as both the source and the sink of the streaming query. In the following sections, we will look at how we can leverage Delta streaming in an incremental processing model.

AvailableNow Streaming

Spark Structured Streaming provides a number of possible trigger modes. The AvailableNow trigger option consumes all available records as an incremental batch with the ability to configure batch sizes with options such as maxBytesPerTrigger.

First, we need to cancel our currently running streaming query in the "02 - Simple Streaming" notebook by navigating to the streaming dashboard and clicking the cancel link. We can then confirm the cancellation and stop the streaming query.

Since the source table is only periodically updated, we don't want the streaming query to run continuously. Instead, we want to start the query, pick up the new transaction entries, process the corresponding records, write to the sink, and then stop. This is what the following trigger will allow us to do. If we add the code .trigger(availableNow=True) to the streaming query, the query will run once and then stop, as shown in notebook "02 - AvailableNow Streaming":

```
# Write the stream to the output location, maintain
# state in the checkpoint location
streamQuery =                                                    \
        stream_df                                               \
            .writeStream                                        \
            .format("delta")                                    \
            .option("checkpointLocation", target_checkpoint_location) \
            .trigger(availableNow=True)                         \
            .start(target_location)
```

When we run this notebook, the streaming query will run until no new records are found, but since no new records have been added to the source table, no records are found, and no records are written to the target table. We can verify this by looking at the raw data of the writeStream:

```
{
    "id" : "c5eaca75-cf4d-410f-b34c-9a2128ee1944",
    ...
    "numInputRows" : 0,
```

If we now run the SQL query below the writeStream in the notebook, we will add 10 records to the source table. If we then rerun the streaming query, we will again see the 10 new rows:

```
{
    "id" : "c5eaca75-cf4d-410f-b34c-9a2128ee1944",
    "runId" : "36a31550-c2c1-48b0-9a6f-ce112572f59d",
    "name" : null,
    "timestamp" : "2023-05-30T17:48:12.079Z",
    "batchId" : 2,
    "numInputRows" : 10,

    "sources" : [ {
        "description" : "DeltaSource[dbfs:/mnt/.../LimitedRecords.delta]",
        "startOffset" : {
          "sourceVersion" : 1,
          "reservoirId" : "6c25c8cd-88c1-4b74-9c96-a61c1727c3a2",
          "reservoirVersion" : 3,
          "index" : -1,
          "isStartingVersion" : false
```

In the output, we also see the sources section, with the reservoirVersion variable,
which is currently set to 3. Remember that the reservoirVersion represents the next
possible version ID in this case. If we do a DESCRIBE HISTORY of our table, we can see
that we are at version 2, so the next version would be 3:

```sql
%sql
describe history delta.`/mnt/datalake/book/chapter08/LimitedRecords.delta`
```

Output (only version column shown):

```
+-------+
|version|
+-------+
|   2   |
|   1   |
|   0   |
+-------+
```

In the next query, we add 20 more records to the source table. If we then rerun our
streaming query and look at the raw data, we see the 20 new records, and also see that
the reservoirVersion of the startOffset is now set at 3:

```
{
    "id" : "d89a5c02-052b-436c-a372-2445fb8d88d6",
    ..
    "numInputRows" : 20,
    ...
    "sources" : [ {
      "description" : "DeltaSource[dbfs:/mnt/.../LimitedRecords.delta]",
      "startOffset" : {
        "sourceVersion" : 1,
        "reservoirId" : "31611029-07d1-4bcc-8ee3-cad0d4fa8bc4",
        "reservoirVersion" : 3,
          ...
      },
```

This `AvailableNow` model means that we could now run the streaming query as shown in the "02 - AvailableNow Streaming" notebook just once a day, or once an hour, or in whatever time interval the use case demands. Delta Lake will always pick up all changes that happened to the source table since the last run, thanks to the state saved in the checkpoint file.

 With legacy solutions, this type of incremental processing was very complex. As an ETL developer, you had to maintain the date of the last run and then query from a dedicated date of the source data to discover the new rows, etc. `AvailableNow` streaming greatly simplifies this programming model, since it abstracts out all of this complex logic.

In addition to the `AvailableNow` trigger, there is also a `RunOnce` trigger, which behaves very similarly. Both triggers will process all available data. However, the `RunOnce` trigger will consume all records in a single batch, while the `AvailableNow` trigger will process the data in multiple batches when appropriate, typically resulting in better scalability.

 When you want to consume all available data with a streaming query, use the `AvailableNow` trigger, since it provides better scalability by executing multiple batches when needed.

Updating the Source Records

Next, let's take a look at what happens when we run an update like the following statement:

```
%sql
-- Update query to demonstrate streaming update
-- behavior
UPDATE
    taxidb.limitedyellowtaxis
SET
  PickupLocationId = 100
WHERE
  VendorId = 2
```

When we look at the `commitInfo` action for the corresponding transaction log entry, we see the following:

```
"commitInfo": {
    ...
    "operation": "UPDATE",
    ..
```

```
        },
        "notebook": {
            "notebookId": "3478336043398159"
        },
        …
        "operationMetrics": {
            …
            "numCopiedRows": "23",
            …
            "numUpdatedRows": "27",
            …
        },
        …
    }
```

We can see that 23 rows were copied to new data files and 27 rows were updated, for a total of 50 rows.

So, if we run our query again, we should see exactly 50 rows in our batch. When we run the "02 - AvailableNow Streaming" notebook again, we will see 50 rows:

```
{
    ...
    "batchId" : 4,
    "numInputRows" : 50,
```

If we go back and run the streaming query again, we will notice the following error:

```
Stream stopped...
com.databricks.sql.transaction.tahoe.DeltaUnsupportedOperationException:
Detected a data update (for example part-00000-....snappy.parquet) in the source
table at version 3. This is currently not supported. If you'd like to ignore
updates, set the option 'ignoreChanges' to 'true'. If you would like the data
update to be reflected, please restart this query with a fresh checkpoint
directory. The source table can be found at path
dbfs:/mnt/.../LimitedRecords.delta.
```

Here, Delta Lake is informing us that data updates in the stream are not currently supported. If we know that we really only want new records, and not changes, we can add the .option("ignoreChanges", "True") option to the readStream:

```
# Start streaming from our source "LimitedRecords" table
# Notice that instead of a "read", we now use a "readStream",
# for the rest our statement is just like any other spark Delta read

# Uncomment the ignoreChanges option when you want to receive only
# new records, and no updated records
stream_df =                                  \
        spark                                \
        .readStream                          \
        .option("ignoreChanges", True)       \
        .format("delta")                     \
        .load("/mnt/datalake/book/chapter08/LimitedRecords.delta")
```

If we now rerun the streaming query, it will succeed. However, when we look at the raw data, we still see all 50 input rows, which looks wrong:

```
{
    "id" : "d89a5c02-052b-436c-a372-2445fb8d88d6",
    "runId" : "b1304246-4083-4275-8637-1f99768b8e03",
    "name" : null,
    "timestamp" : "2023-04-13T17:28:31.380Z",
    "batchId" : 3,
    "numInputRows" : 50,
    "inputRowsPerSecond" : 0.0
```

This behavior is normal. The `ignoreChanges` option will still emit all rewritten files in the Delta table to the stream. This is typically the superset of all changed records. However, only the inserted records will actually be processed.

The StreamingQuery class

Let's look at the type of the `streamQuery` variable:

```
# Let's take a look at the type
# of the streamQuery variable
print(type(streamQuery))
```

Output:

```
<class 'pyspark.sql.streaming.query.StreamingQuery'>
```

We can see that the type is `StreamingQuery`. If we invoke the status property of our `streamQuery`, we get the following:

```
# Print out the status of the last StreamingQuery
print(streamQuery.status)
```

Output:

```
{'message': 'Stopped', 'isDataAvailable': False, 'isTriggerActive': False}
```

The query is currently stopped and there is no data available. No trigger is active. Another interesting property is `recentProgress`, which will print out the same output as the raw data section from our streaming output in the notebook. For example, if we want to see the number of input rows, we can print the following:

```
print(streamQuery.recentProgress[0]["numInputRows"])
```

Output:

```
50
```

This object also has some interesting methods. For example, if we want to wait until the stream terminates, we can use the `awaitTermination()` method.

Reprocessing all or part of the source records

As we have been processing a number of batches from the source table, the checkpoint file has systematically been building up all of these changes. If we delete the checkpoint file and run the streaming query again, it will start from the very beginning of the source table and bring in all records:

```sh
%sh
# Uncomment this line if you want to reset the checkpoint
rm -r /dbfs/mnt/datalake/book/chapter08/StreamingTarget/_checkpoint
```

Output of the streaming query:

```
{
    ...
    "numInputRows" : 50,
    ,..
    "stateOperators" : [ ],
    "sources" : [ {
      "description" : "DeltaSource[dbfs:/mnt/.../LimitedRecords.delta]",
      "startOffset" : null,
      "endOffset" : {
        ...
        "reservoirVersion" : 5,
        ...
      },
      "latestOffset" : null,
      "numInputRows" : 50,
```

We read all rows in the source table. We started at offset null and ended at `reservoir Version 5`.

We can also just stream in part of the changes. To do this, we can specify a `starting Version` in the `readStream` after we clear out the checkpoint again:

```
stream_df =                                 \
        spark                               \
        .readStream                         \
        .option("ignoreChanges", True)      \
        .option("startingVersion", 3)       \
        .format("delta")                    \
        .load("/mnt/datalake/book/chapter08/LimitedRecords.delta")
```

When we look at the raw data, we get the following result:

```
{
    ...
    "batchId" : 0,
    "numInputRows" : 70,
    "inputRowAnd" : 0.0,
    ...
    "stateOperators" : [ ],
    "sources" : [ {
```

```
...
"startOffset" : null,
"endOffset" : {
  "sourceVersion" : 1,
  "reservoirId" : "32c71d93-ca81-4d6e-9928-c1a095183016",
  "reservoirVersion" : 6,
  "index" : -1,
  "isStartingVersion" : false
},
```

We get 70 rows. That is incorrect because we started from version 3. Let's take a look at Table 8-1, which summarizes the versions and operations we've worked with so far.

Table 8-1. Record counts for each version

Version	Number of rows affected	From operation
5	50	Update
4	10	Insert
3	10	Insert
Total	70	

This validates the total number of input rows for the streaming query. Setting the `startingVersion` gives us many options when we combine it with the `DESCRIBE HISTORY` command. We can look at the history and decide from what point in time we would like to load the data.

Reading a Stream from the Change Data Feed

In Chapter 6, you read about how Delta Lake records "change events" for all the data written into the table via the CDF. These changes can be transmitted to downstream consumers. These downstream consumers can read the change events captured and transmitted in the CDF using streaming queries with `.readStream()`.

To get the changes from the CDF while reading a table with CDF enabled, set the option `readChangeFeed` to `true`. Setting `readChangeFeed` to `true` in conjunction with `.readStream()` will allow us to efficiently stream changes from a source table to a downstream target table. We can also use `startingVersion` or `startingTimestamp` to specify the starting point of the Delta table streaming source without processing the entire table:

```
# Read CDF stream with readChangeFeed since version 5
spark.readStream                              \
        .format("delta")                      \
        .option("readChangeFeed", "true")   \
        .option("startingVersion", 5)        \
        .table("<delta_table_name>")

# Read CDF stream since starting timestamp 2023-01-01 00:00:00
```

```
spark.readStream                                    \
        .format("delta")                            \
        .option("readChangeFeed", "true")  \
        .option("startingTimestamp", "2023-01-01 00:00:00")        \
        .table("<delta_table_name>")
```

Using .option("readChangeFeed", "true") will return table changes with the CDF schema that provides the _change_type, _commit_timestamp, and _commit_version that the readStream will consume. Here is an example of the CDF data (this is from Chapter 6):

VendorId	PassengerCount	FareAmount	_change_type	_commit_version
1	1000	2000	update_preimage	2
1	1000	2500	update_postimage	2
3	7000	10000	delete	3
4	500	1000	insert	4

The previous code snippets for reading the change feed specified the startingVersion or startingTimestamp. It's important to note that these methods are optional, and if not provided, the stream fetches the latest snapshot of the table at the time of streaming as an INSERT and future changes as change data.

 While initiating the streaming source from a specified version or timestamp is possible, the schema associated with the streaming source reflects the *most recent schema* of the Delta table. It's important to ensure there are no incompatible schema changes to the Delta table following the specified version or timestamp. Failing to do so could result in inaccurate outcomes when the streaming source retrieves data with a schema that doesn't match.

When reading change data, there are other options that we can specify, specifically around data changes and rate limits (how much data is processed in each microbatch). Table 8-2 highlights additional, important options for use in streaming queries when using Delta tables as a stream source.

Table 8-2. Additional streaming options

Option	Definition
maxFilesPer Trigger	Controls how many new files are considered in every micro-batch. The default is 1,000.
maxBytesPer Trigger	Controls how much data gets processed in each micro-batch. If you use `Trigger.Once`, this option is ignored. This option is not set by default.
ignoreDeletes	Ignores transactions that delete data at partition boundaries.
ignoreChanges	Reprocesses updates if files had to be rewritten in the source table due to a data changing operation such as UPDATE, MERGE INTO, DELETE (within partitions), or OVERWRITE. `ignoreChanges` also incorporates `ignoreDeletes`.

Rate limit options can be useful for better control of overall resource management and utilization. For example, we may want to avoid potentially overloading processing resources (e.g., our cluster) when there is an influx of new data files or a large volume of data to process. Controlling rate limits can help achieve a more balanced processing experience by controlling micro-batch size. If we want to effectively control rate limits, while also ignoring deletes to avoid disrupting the existing streaming query, we can specify these options in the streaming query:

```
# Read CDF stream with readChangeFeed and don't specify the
# starting timestamp or version. Specify rate limits and ignore deletes.
spark.readStream                                          \
        .format("delta")                                  \
   .option("maxFilesPerTrigger", 50)            \
   .option("maxBytesPerTrigger", "10MB")       \
   .option("ignoreDeletes", "true")            \
        .option("readChangeFeed", "true")          \
        .table("delta_table_name")
```

In this example, we are setting rate limit options, ignoring deletes, and omitting the starting timestamp and version options. This will read the latest version of the table (since no version or timestamp is specified) and give us better control over the size of micro-batches and processing resources to reduce potential interruptions to the streaming query.

Conclusion

One of Delta Lake's key features is the unification of batch and streaming data into a single table. This chapter dove into the particulars and examples of how Delta Lake is fully integrated with Structured Streaming, and how Delta tables support scalable, fault-tolerant, and low-latency processing of continuous data streams.

Integrated with Structured Streaming through `readStream` and `writeStream`, Delta tables can be used as both streaming sources and targets, and leverage streaming DataFrames. The examples in this chapter walked through reading changes into these streaming DataFrames and how to perform simple processing to write streams to a target. Then we explored checkpoint files and metadata, the query process log, and the streaming class to better understand how streaming works and keeps track of information under the hood. And finally, you learned how to leverage the CDF with `readStream` to transmit and read row-level changes in streaming queries.

Having unified both batch and streaming data into a single Delta table, Chapter 9 will dive into how to securely share this data with other organizations.

Delta Sharing

The data-centric nature of today's economy necessitates extensive data exchange among organizations and their customers, suppliers, and partners. While efficiency and immediate accessibility are crucial, they often clash with security concerns. Organizations require an open and secure approach to data sharing to thrive in the digital economy.

Often data sharing is required internally within an organization. Organizations have geographically dispersed locations with local cloud solutions. These companies often seek to implement a data mesh architecture, where ownership is decentralized and data management is distributed and federated. Efficient and secure data sharing is a critical enabler to efficiently share data products across the organization.

The different business groups across an enterprise need access to data to make critical business decisions. Data teams want to integrate their solutions to create a comprehensive enterprise view of the business.

Conventional Methods of Data Sharing

In the past, sharing data across various platforms, companies, and clouds has always presented a complex challenge. Organizations were reluctant to share data due to concerns about security risks, competition, and the considerable costs associated with implementing data-sharing solutions.

Conventional data-sharing technologies face difficulties in meeting the demands of modern requirements, such as compatibility with multiple cloud environments, and support for open formats, while still delivering the required performance. Many data-sharing solutions are tied to a specific vendor, creating problems for data providers and consumers operating on incompatible platforms.

Data-sharing solutions have been developed in three formats: legacy and homegrown (custom-built) solutions, modern cloud object storage, and proprietary commercial solutions. Each of these approaches has its pros and cons.

Legacy and Homegrown Solutions

Organizations have built homegrown systems to implement data-sharing solutions based on legacy technology like email, SFTP, or custom APIs, as shown in Figure 9-1.

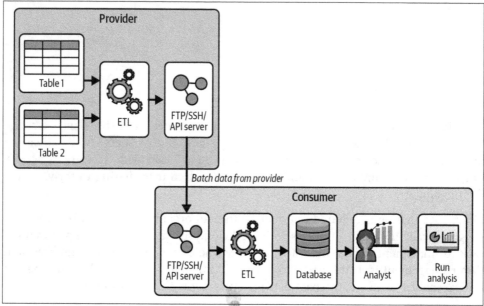

Figure 9-1. Homegrown solutions to data sharing

Advantages of these solutions:

Vendor agnostic
FTP, email, and APIs are well-documented protocols, enabling data consumers to utilize a variety of clients to access the data provided to them.

Flexibility
Many custom-built solutions are based on open source technologies, allowing them to function both on premises and in cloud environments.

Disadvantages of these solutions:

Data movement
> Extracting data from cloud storage, transforming it, and hosting it on an FTP server for different recipients requires significant effort. This approach also leads to data duplication, hindering organizations from instantly accessing real-time data.

Complexity of data sharing
> Custom-built solutions often involve complex architectures due to replication and provisioning. This complexity adds substantial time to data-sharing activities and can result in outdated data for end consumers.

Operational overhead for data recipients
> Data recipients need to perform data extraction, transformation, and loading (ETL) for their specific use cases, further delaying the time to gain insights. Whenever providers update the data, consumers must rerun the ETL pipelines repeatedly.

Security and governance
> As modern data requirements become more stringent, securing and governing homegrown and legacy technologies becomes increasingly challenging.

Scalability
> Managing and maintaining such solutions is costly, and they lack the scalability to accommodate large datasets.

Proprietary Vendor Solutions

Commercial data-sharing solutions are widely chosen by companies seeking alternatives to building in-house solutions. These solutions provide a balance between not wanting to allocate extensive time and resources to developing a proprietary solution, and desiring greater control than what cloud object storage can provide, as shown in Figure 9-2.

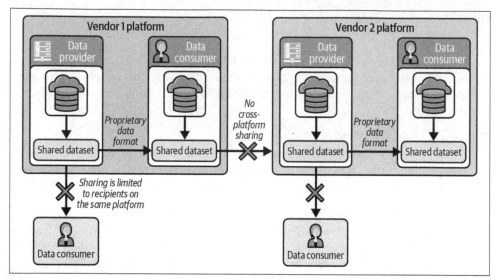

Figure 9-2. Proprietary vendor data-sharing solutions

Advantages of this solution:

Simplicity
> Commercial solutions offer an easy way for users to share data with others on the same platform.

Disadvantages of this solution:

Vendor lock-in
> Commercial solutions often lack interoperability with other platforms, making it difficult to share data with users of competing solutions. This limitation reduces the accessibility of data and results in vendor lock-in. Additionally, platform disparities between data providers and recipients introduce complexities in data sharing.

Data movement
> Data needs to be loaded onto a specific platform, which involves additional steps, such as ETL and creating copies of the data.

Scalability
> Commercial data-sharing solutions may have limitations on scaling imposed by the vendors.

Cost
> The aforementioned challenges contribute to additional costs for sharing data with potential customers, as data providers need to replicate data for different recipients across various cloud platforms.

Cloud Object Storage

Object storage is highly regarded as a well-suited solution for cloud environments due to its elastic nature and seamless scalability, allowing it to handle vast amounts of data and effortlessly accommodate unlimited growth. Leading cloud providers, such as Amazon S3, Azure Data Lake Storage (ADLS), and Google Cloud Storage (GCS), offer cost-effective object storage services and deliver exceptional scalability and reliability.

One noteworthy feature of cloud object storage is the capability to generate signed URLs. These URLs provide time-limited permissions for downloading specific objects. By sharing a pre-signed URL, anyone possessing it can conveniently access the designated objects, facilitating efficient data sharing.

Advantages of this solution:

Sharing data in place
Object storage can be shared in place, allowing consumers access to the latest available data.

Scalability
Cloud object storage profits from availability and durability guarantees that typically cannot be achieved on premises. Data consumers retrieve data directly from the cloud providers, saving bandwidth for the providers.

Disadvantages of this solution:

Limited to a single cloud provider
Recipients have to be on the same cloud to access the objects.

Cumbersome security and governance
There is complexity associated with assigning permissions and managing access. Custom application logic is needed to generate signed URLs.

Complexity
Personas managing data sharing (database administrators, analysts) find it difficult to understand identity and access management policies and how data is mapped to underlying files. For companies with large volumes of data, sharing via cloud storage is time-consuming, cumbersome, and nearly impossible to scale.

Operational overhead for data recipients
The data recipients must ETL pipelines on the raw files before consuming them for their end use cases.

The lack of a comprehensive solution creates a struggle for data providers and consumers to share data easily. Cumbersome and incomplete data sharing also constrains the development of business opportunities from shared data.

Open Source Delta Sharing

Unlike proprietary solutions, open source data sharing is not associated with a vendor-specific technology that introduces unnecessary limitations and financial burdens. Open source Delta Sharing is readily available to anyone who needs to share data at scale.

Delta Sharing Goals

Delta Sharing is an open source protocol designed with the following objectives:

Open cross-platform data sharing
> Delta Sharing provides an open source, cross-platform solution that avoids vendor lock-in. It allows data sharing in Delta Lake and Apache Parquet formats with any platform, whether on premises or another cloud.

Share live data without data movement
> Data recipients can directly connect to Delta Sharing without replicating the data. This feature enables the easy and real-time sharing of existing data without unnecessary data duplication or movement.

Support a wide range of clients
> Delta Sharing supports a diverse range of clients, including popular tools like Power BI, Tableau, Apache Spark, pandas, and Java. It offers flexibility for consuming data using the tools of choice for various use cases, such as business intelligence, machine learning, and AI. Implementing a Delta Sharing connector is quick and straightforward.

Centralized governance
> Delta Sharing provides robust security, auditing, and governance capabilities. Data providers have granular control over data access, allowing them to share an entire table or specific versions or partitions of a table. Access to shared data is managed and audited from a single enforcement point, ensuring centralized control and compliance.

Scalability for massive datasets
> Delta Sharing is designed to handle massive structured datasets, and supports sharing unstructured data and future data derivatives such as machine learning models, dashboards, notebooks, and tabular data. Delta Sharing enables the economical and reliable sharing of large-scale datasets by leveraging the cost-effectiveness and scalability of cloud storage systems.

Delta Sharing Under the Hood

Delta Sharing is an open protocol that defines REST API endpoints that enable secure access to specific portions of a cloud dataset. It leverages the capabilities of modern cloud storage systems like Amazon S3, ADLS, or GCS to ensure the reliable transfer of large datasets. The process involves two key parties: data providers and recipients, as depicted in Figure 9-3.

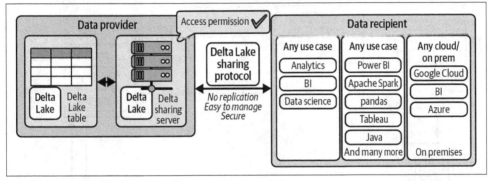

Figure 9-3. Overview of the Delta Sharing protocol

Data Providers and Recipients

As the data provider, Delta Sharing lets you share existing tables or parts thereof (e.g., specific table versions of partitions) stored on your cloud data lake in Delta Lake format. The data provider decides what data they want to share and runs a sharing server in front of it that implements the Delta Sharing protocol and manages access for recipients. Open source Delta Lake includes a reference sharing server, and Databricks provides one for its platform; other vendors are expected to soon follow.

As a data recipient, you only need one of the many Delta Sharing clients supporting the protocol. Open source Delta Lake has released open source connectors for pandas, Apache Spark, Rust, and Python, and is working with partners on more clients.

The actual exchange is carefully designed to be efficient by leveraging the functionality of cloud storage systems and Delta Lake. The Delta Sharing protocol works as follows (see Figure 9-4):

1. The recipient's client authenticates to the sharing server (via a bearer token or other method) and asks to query a specific table. The client can also provide filters on the data (e.g., "country = US") as a hint to read just a subset of the data.

2. The server verifies whether the client is allowed to access the data, logs the request, and then determines which data to send back. This will be a subset of the data objects in ALDS (on Azure), S3 (on AWS), or GCS (on GCP) that make up the table.

3. To transfer the data, the server generates short-lived pre-signed URLs that allow the client to read these Parquet files directly from the cloud provider, so that the transfer can happen in parallel with massive bandwidth, without streaming through the sharing server. This powerful feature available in all the major clouds makes it fast, cheap, and reliable to share very large datasets.

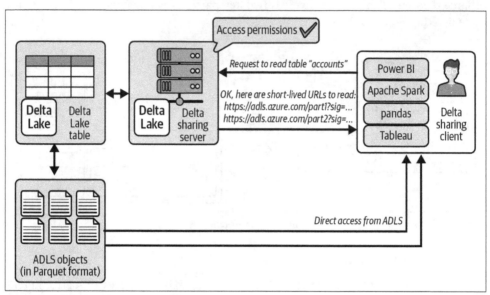

Figure 9-4. Delta Sharing protocol details

Benefits of the Design

The Delta Sharing design provides many benefits for both providers and consumers:

- Data providers can easily share an entire table, or just a version of a partition of the table, because clients are only given access to a specific subset of the objects in it.

- Data providers can update data reliably in real time using the ACID transactions on Delta Lake, and recipients will always see a consistent view.

- Data recipients don't need to be on the same platform as the provider, or even in the cloud at all, sharing works across clouds and even from cloud to on-premise users.

- The Delta Sharing protocol is simple for clients to implement if they already leverage Parquet.

- Data transfer using the underlying cloud system is fast, cheap, reliable, and parallelizable.

The delta-sharing Repository

You can find the `delta-sharing` GitHub repository online (*https://oreil.ly/GOO7V*). It contains the following components:

- The *Delta Sharing protocol* specification (*https://oreil.ly/vLlgG*).
- The *Python connector*. This is a Python library that implements the Delta Sharing protocol to read shared tables as pandas or PySpark DataFrames.
- An *Apache Spark connector*. This connector implements the Delta Sharing protocol to read shared tables from a Delta Sharing Server. You can then use SQL, Python, Scala, Java, or R to access the tables.
- A reference implementation (*https://oreil.ly/lB3vm*) of the *Delta Sharing Protocol* in a *Delta Sharing Server*. Users can deploy this server to share existing tables in Delta Lake and Parquet format on Azure, AWS, or GCP storage systems.

Next, let's use the Python connector to access Delta tables in an example Delta Sharing Server, hosted by delto-io (*https://oreil.ly/TWX9h*).

Step 1: Installing the Python Connector

The Python connector is offered as a PyPi library named `delta-sharing`, so we just need to add this library to our cluster, as shown in Figure 9-5.

	Status	Name ⇌↑	Type
☐	⊘	delta-sharing	PyPI

Figure 9-5. Installing the `delta-sharing` PyPi library on our cluster

Step 2: Installing the Profile File

The Python connector accesses shared tables based on profile files. You can download the profile file (*https://oreil.ly/pSVri*) for the example Delta Sharing Server by following the link. This file will download as a file named *open-datasets.share*. This is a simple JSON file with the credentials for the server (the bearer token in this example is obfuscated):

```
{
  "shareCredentialsVersion": 1,
  "endpoint": "https://sharing.delta.io/delta-sharing/",
  "bearerToken": "faaiexxxxxxxxxxxxxxxxxxxxxxxxxxxxxxxxxxx"
}
```

Upload the share file to a *dbfs:/* location in the Databricks filesystem using the dbfs cp command:

```
C:\Users\bhael\Downloads>dbfs cp open-datasets.share dbfs:/mnt/.../delta-sharing/

C:\Users\bhael\Downloads>dbfs ls dbfs:/mnt/datalake/book/delta-sharing
open-datasets.share

C:\Users\bhael\Downloads>
```

Step 3: Reading a Shared Table

In the "01 - Sharing Example" notebook we can then reference the file:

```
# Point to the profile file. It can be a file on the local
# file system or remote file system. In this case, we have
# uploaded the file to dbfs
profile_path = "/dbfs/mnt/datalake/book/delta-sharing/open-datasets.share"
```

 Depending on how you will access a shared table, you will have to use a different path syntax. The profile_path specified here will work when you access the table as a pandas DataFrame. If you want to access the table with Spark, you will have to use the dbfs:/ syntax instead of the /dbfs/ port.

Next, we can create a SharingClient, passing it the profile path, and list all shared Delta tables:

```
# Create a SharingClient and list all shared tables
client = delta_sharing.SharingClient(profile_path)
client.list_all_tables()
```

This produces the following output:

```
Out[22]: [Table(name='COVID_19_NYT', share='delta_sharing',
schema='default'), Table(name='boston-housing', share='delta_sharing',
schema='default'), Table(name='flight-asa_2008', share='delta_sharing',
schema='default'), Table(name='lending_club', share='delta_sharing',
schema='default'), Table(name='nyctaxi_2019', share='delta_sharing',
schema='default'), Table(name='nyctaxi_2019_part', share='delta_sharing',
schema='default'), Table(name='owid-covid-data', share='delta_sharing',
schema='default')]
```

To create a URL to a shared table, we use the following syntax:

```
<profile file base name>#<share-name>.<schema-name>.<table-name>
```

We can now build the URL and read the contents of the shared Delta table as a pandas DataFrame:

```
# Create a URL to access a shared table
# A table path is the profile path following with
# ('<share-name>.<schema_name>.<table_name>)
# Here, we are loading the table as a pandas DataFrame
table_url = profile_path + "#delta_sharing.default.boston-housing"
df = delta_sharing.load_as_pandas(table_url, limit=10)
df.head()
```

Output (only showing relevant portions):

```
+--+-------+----+-----+----+-----+-----+
|ID|crim   |zn  |indus| chas| nox | rm  |
+--+-------+----+-----+----+-----+-----+
|1 |0.00632|18  | 2.31|  0 |0.538|6.575|
|2 |0.02731| 0  | 7.0 |  0 |0.469|6.421|
|4 |0.03237| 0  | 2.18|  0 |0.458|6.998|
|5 |0.06905| 0  | 2.18|  0 |0.458|7.147|
|7 |0.08829|12.5| 7.87|  0 |0.524|6.012|
+--+-------+----+-----+----+-----+-----+
```

If we want to load the table as a standard PySpark DataFrame, we can use the load_as_spark() method:

```
# We can also access the shared table with Spark. Note that we have to use the
# dbfs:/ path prefix here
profile_path_spark = "dbfs:/mnt/datalake/book/delta-sharing/open-datasets.share"
table_url_spark = profile_path_spark + "#delta_sharing.default.boston-housing"

df_spark = delta_sharing.load_as_spark(table_url_spark)
display(df_spark.limit(5))
```

Notice the slight change in the URL, as discussed earlier. This will produce the same output as the pandas example.

Conclusion

Enabling data exchange using open source technology opens up many benefits for both internal and external use. First, it offers significant flexibility, allowing the team to tailor the data exchange process to meet specific business use cases and requirements. Support from the active open source community ensures continuous improvements, bug fixes, and access to a vast amount of knowledge, further empowering the team and business users to stay at the forefront of data sharing practices.

Among the key benefits of using Delta Sharing for data providers and data recipients, the following are the most important:

- Scalability is critical for data teams working with ever-growing datasets and high-demand use cases.
- Interoperability is another significant benefit. Delta Sharing, as an open source technology, is designed to work in harmony with other components of the data ecosystem, facilitating seamless integration.
- In addition, transparency and security are improved compared to the proprietary solutions, as the Delta Sharing source code is available for review, which allows for stronger security measures and the ability to respond to and proactively address identified vulnerabilities.

By using Delta Sharing, teams avoid vendor lock-in by having the freedom to switch between tools or vendors with no investment needed in adapting to the new architecture. The rapid pace of innovation in the open source community allows teams to embrace cutting-edge features and quickly adapt to new trends in data management and analytics.

The ability to share data using Delta Sharing allows for a more agile, cost-effective, and innovative data ecosystem by delivering better data-driven solutions and insights for organizational success in an ever-changing environment and data landscape.

Building on the foundational components you have learned about to this point, in Chapter 10 you will dive into the details of how to build a complete data lakehouse.

Building a Lakehouse on Delta Lake

Chapter 1 introduced the concept of a data lakehouse, which combines the best elements of a traditional data warehouse and a data lake. Throughout this book you have learned about the five key capabilities that help enable the lakehouse architecture: the storage layer, data management, SQL analytics, data science and machine learning, and the medallion architecture.

Before diving into building a lakehouse on Delta Lake, let's quickly review the industry's data management and analytics evolution:

Data warehouse

From the 1970s through the early 2000s, data warehouses were designed to collect and consolidate data into a business context, providing support for business intelligence and analytics. As data volumes grew, velocity, variety, and veracity also increased. Data warehouses had challenges with addressing these requirements in a flexible, unified, and cost-effective manner.

Data lake

In the early 2000s, increased volumes of data drove the development of data lakes (initially on premises with Hadoop and later with the cloud), a cost-effective central repository to store any format of data at any scale. But again, even with added benefits there were additional challenges. Data lakes had no transactional support, were not designed for business intelligence, offered limited data governance support, and still required other technologies (e.g., data warehouses) to fully support the data ecosystem. This led to overly complex environments with a patchwork of different tools, systems, technologies, and multiple copies of the data.

The emergence of a coexisting data lake and data warehouse still leaves much to be desired. The incomplete support for use cases and incompatible security and governance models has led to increased complexity from disjointed and duplicative data silos that contain subsets of data across different tools and technologies.

Lakehouse
In the late 2010s, the concept of the lakehouse emerged. This introduced a modernized version of a data warehouse that provides all of the benefits and features without compromising the flexibility of a data lake. The lakehouse leverages a low-cost, flexible cloud storage layer, a data lake, combined with data reliability and consistency guarantees through technologies that feature open-table formats with support for ACID transactions. This flexibility helps support diverse workloads such as streaming, analytics, and machine learning under a single unified platform, which ultimately enables a single security and governance approach for all data assets. With the advent of Delta Lake and the lakehouse, the paradigm of end-to-end data platforms has begun to shift due to the key features enabled by this architectural pattern.

By combining the capabilities of the lakehouse with what you have learned in this book, you will learn how to enable the key features offered by a lakehouse architecture and be fully up and running with Delta Lake.

Storage Layer

The first step, or layer, in any well-designed architecture is deciding where to store your data. In a world with increasing volumes of data coming in different forms and shapes from multiple heterogeneous data sources, it is essential to have a system that allows for storing massive amounts of data in a flexible, cost-effective, and scalable manner. And that is why a cloud object store like a data lake is the foundational storage layer for a lakehouse.

What Is a Data Lake?

Previously defined in Chapter 1, a data lake is a cost-effective central repository to store structured, semi-structured, or unstructured data at any scale, in the form of files and blobs. This is possible in a data lake because it does not impose a schema when writing data, so data can be saved as is. A data lake uses a flat architecture and object storage to store data, unlike a data warehouse, which typically stores data in a hierarchical structure with directories and files while imposing a schema. Every object is tagged with metadata and a unique identifier so that applications can use it for easy access and retrieval.

Types of Data

One of the key elements of a data lake is that a cloud object store provides limitless scalability to store any type of data. These different types of data have been covered in this book, but it is best to define the three classifications of data to demonstrate how they are structured and where they originate:

Structured data
- What is it? In structured data all the data has a predefined structure, or schema. This is most commonly relational data coming from a database in the form of tables with rows and columns.
- What produces it? Data like this is typically produced by traditional relational databases and is often used in enterprise resource planning (ERP), customer relationship management (CRM), or inventory management systems.

Semi-structured data
- What is it? Semi-structured data does not conform to a typical relational format like structured data. Rather it is loosely structured with patterns or tags that separate elements of the data, such as key/value pairs. Examples of semi-structured data are Parquet, JSON, XML, CSV files, and even emails or social feeds.
- What produces it? Common data sources for this type of data can include nonrelational or NoSQL databases, IoT devices, apps, and web services.

Unstructured data
- What is it? Unstructured data does not contain an organized structure; it is not arranged in any type of schema or pattern. It is often delivered as media files, such as photo (e.g., JPEG) or video files (e.g., MP4). The underlying video files might have an overall structure to them, but the data that forms the video itself is unstructured.
- What produces it? A vast majority of an organization's data comes in the form of unstructured data, and is produced from things like media files (e.g., audio, video, photos), Word documents, log files, and other forms of rich text.

Unstructured and semi-structured data are often critical for AI and machine learning use cases, whereas structured and semi-structured data are critical for BI use cases. Because it natively supports all three types of data classifications, you can create a unified system that supports these diverse workloads in a data lake. These workloads can complement each other in a well-designed processing architecture, which you will learn about further on in this chapter. A data lake helps solve many of the challenges related to data volumes, types, and cost, and while Delta Lake runs on top of a data lake, it is optimized to run best on a *cloud* data lake.

Key Benefits of a Cloud Data Lake

We've discussed how a data lake helps address some of the shortcomings of a data warehouse. A cloud data lake, as opposed to an on-premises data lake or a data warehouse, best supports a lakehouse architecture as the storage layer for a number of reasons:

Single storage layer

One of the most important features of a lakehouse is unifying platforms, and a cloud data lake helps eliminate and consolidate data silos and different types of data into a single object store. The cloud data lake allows you to process all data on a single system, which prevents creating additional copies of your data moving back and forth between different systems. Decreased movement of data across different systems also results in fewer integration points, which means fewer places for errors to occur. A single storage layer reduces the need for multiple security policies that cover different systems and helps resolve difficulties with collaboration across systems. It also offers data consumers a single place to look for all sources of data.

Flexible, on-demand storage layer

Whether it is velocity (streaming versus batch), volume, or variety (structured versus unstructured), cloud data lakes allow for the ultimate flexibility to store data. According to Rukmani Gopalan in his recently published book, *The Cloud Data Lake*,[1] "these systems are designed to work with data that enters the data lake at any speed: real-time data emitted continuously as well as volumes of data ingested in batches on a scheduled basis." Not only is there flexibility with the data, but there is flexibility with the infrastructure as well. Cloud providers allow you to provision infrastructure on demand, and quickly scale up or down elastically. Because of this level of flexibility, the organization can have a single storage layer that provides unlimited scalability.

Decoupled storage and compute

Traditional data warehouses and on-premises data lakes have traditionally had tightly coupled storage and compute. Storage is generally inexpensive, whereas compute is not. The cloud data lake allows you to decouple this and independently scale your storage and store vast amounts of data at very little cost.

Technology integration

Data lakes offer simple integration through standardized APIs so organizations and users with completely different skills, tools, and programming languages (e.g., SQL, Python, Scala, etc.) can perform different analytics tasks all at once.

Replication

Cloud providers offer easy to set up replication to different geographical locations for your data lake. The ease of enabling replication can make it useful in meeting compliance requirements, failover for business-critical operations, disaster recovery, and minimizing latency by storing the objects closer to different locations.

---

1 Gopalan, Rukmani (2022). *The Cloud Data Lake*, 1st ed. Sebastopol, CA: O'Reilly.

Availability

Most cloud systems offer different types of data availability for cloud data lakes. This means that for data that is infrequently accessed, or archived, compared to "hot" data that is accessed frequently, you can set up lifecycle policies. These lifecycle policies allow you to move data across different storage availability classes (with lower costs for infrequently accessed data) for compliance, business needs, and cost optimization.

Availability can also be defined through service-level agreements (SLAs). In the cloud, this is the cloud provider's guarantee of the resources' minimal level of service. Most cloud providers guarantee greater than 99.99% uptime for these business-critical resources.

Cost

With cloud data lakes you typically pay for what you use, so your costs always align with your data volumes. Since there is only a single storage layer, less data movement across different systems, availability settings, and decoupled storage versus compute, you have isolated and minimized costs for just data storage. For greater cost allocation, most cloud data lakes offer buckets, or containers (filesystems, not to be confused with application containers), to store different layers of the data (e.g., raw versus transformed data). These containers allow you to have finer-grained cost allocation for different areas of your organization. Since data sources and volumes are growing exponentially, it is extremely important to allocate and optimize costs without limiting the volume or variety of data that can be stored.

Figure 10-1 illustrates the different types of popular cloud-based data lakes at the time of writing, along with the different types of data that are stored in them.

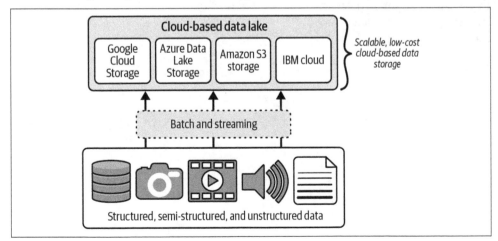

Figure 10-1. Example of cloud-based data lakes and the types of data they support

Overall, the storage layer is a critical component of a lakehouse architecture, as it enables organizations to store and manage massive amounts of data in a cost-effective and scalable manner. Now that you have a defined place to store your data, you also need to appropriately manage it.

Data Management

Although a cloud data lake allows you to elastically store data at scale in its native format, among other benefits, the next piece of the lakehouse foundation is facilitating data management. According to Gartner, data management (DM) consists of the practices, architectural techniques, and tools for achieving consistent access to and delivery of data across the spectrum of data subject areas and data structure types in the enterprise, to meet the data consumption requirements of all applications and business processes.[2]

Data management is a key function for any organization and greatly hinges on the tools and technologies used in the access and delivery of data. Traditionally, data lakes have managed data simply as a "bunch of files" in semi-structured formats (e.g., Parquet), which makes it challenging to enable some of the key features of data management, such as reliability, due to lack of support for ACID transactions, schema enforcement, audit trails, and data integration and interoperability.

Data management on a data lake begins with a structured transactional layer for reliability. This reliability comes from a transaction layer that supports ACID transactions, open-table formats, integration between batch and streaming data processing, and scalable metadata management. This is where Delta Lake is introduced as a core component of the lakehouse architecture that supports data management.

In Figure 10-2, you can see the different types of data types that a cloud-based data lake supports, with Delta Lake built on top of the data lake, acting as a structured transactional layer.

---

2 "Data Management (DM)." Gartner, Inc, Accessed April 24, 2023, *https://oreil.ly/xK4ws*.

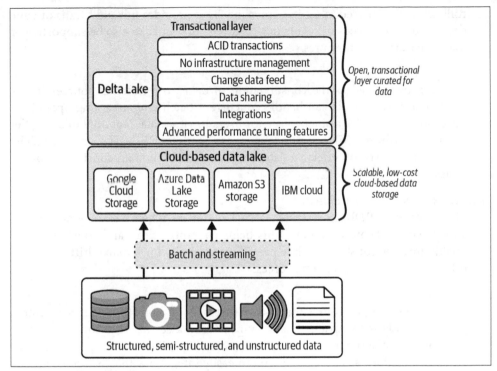

Figure 10-2. Delta Lake transactional layer

Delta Lake brings durability, reliability, and consistency to your data lake. There are several key elements of Delta Lake that help facilitate data management:

Metadata
At the core of Delta Lake is the metadata layer. This layer provides extensive and scalable metadata tracking that enables most of the core features of Delta Lake. It provides a level of abstraction to implement ACID transactions and a variety of other management features. These metadata layers are also a natural place to begin enabling governance features, such as access control and audit logging.

ACID transactions
Delta Lake will ensure that data is kept intact in case concurrency transactions are active on a single table. Support for ACID transactions brings consistency and reliability to your data lake, which is made possible through the transaction log. The transaction log keeps track of all commits, and uses an isolation level to guarantee consistency and accurate views of the data.

Versioning and audit history
Since Delta Lake stores information about which files are part of a table as a transaction log, it allows users to query old versions of data and perform

rollbacks, also referred to as time traveling. This provides full audit trails of your data for business needs or regulatory requirements, and can also be supportive of machine learning procedures.

Data integration

This can be defined as the consolidation of data from different sources into a single place. Delta Lake can handle concurrent batch and streaming operations on a table; it provides a single place for users to view data. Not only this, but the ability to perform DML operations such as INSERTs, UPDATEs, and DELETEs allows you to perform effective data integration and maintain consistency on all tables.

Schema enforcement and evolution

Like traditional RDBMS systems, Delta Lake offers schema enforcement along with flexible schema evolution. This helps guarantee clean and consistent data quality through constraints while providing flexibility for schema drift caused by other processes and upstream sources.

Data interoperability

Delta Lake is an open source framework that is cloud agnostic, and since it interacts seamlessly with Apache Spark by providing a set of APIs and extensions, there are a vast number of different integration capabilities across projects, other APIs, and platforms. This enables you to easily integrate with existing data management workflows and processes through different tools and frameworks. Delta UniForm offers format interoperability with Apache Iceberg, further expanding the set of systems and tools you can integrate with. Together with Delta Sharing, which makes it simple to securely share data across organizations, Delta Lake avoids vendor lock-in and enables *interoperability*.

Machine learning

Because machine learning (ML) systems often require processing large sets of data while using complex logic that isn't well suited for traditional SQL, they can now easily access and process data from Delta Lake using DataFrame APIs. These APIs allow ML workloads to directly benefit from the optimizations and features offered by Delta Lake. Data management across all different workloads can now all be consolidated to Delta Lake.

By adding a structured transactional layer better equipped to handle data management, the lakehouse simultaneously supports raw data, ETL/ELT processes that curate data for analytics, and ML workloads. The curation of data through ETL/ELT has traditionally been thought of and presented in the context of a data warehouse, but through the data management features offered by Delta Lake, you can bring those processes to a single place. That also allows ML systems to directly benefit from the features and optimizations offered by Delta Lake to complete the management and consolidation of data across different workloads. By combining all these efforts, you can bring greater reliability and consistency to your data lake and create a lakehouse that becomes the single source of truth across the enterprise for all types of data.

SQL Analytics

In the world of data analysis, business intelligence, and data warehousing, it is generally known that SQL is one of the most common and flexible languages. Part of the reason for this is not only because it offers an accessible learning curve with low barriers to entry, but because of the complex data analysis operations it can perform. While allowing users to interact with data quickly, SQL also allows users of all skill levels to write ad hoc queries, prepare data for BI tools, create reports and dashboards, and perform a wide array of data analysis functions. For reasons like this, SQL has become the language of choice for business intelligence and data warehousing by the likes of everyone from data engineers to business users. This is why it is necessary that the lakehouse architecture achieves great SQL performance with respect to scalability and performance, and enables SQL analytics.

Fortunately, a lakehouse architecture built around Delta Lake as the transactional layer for curated data has scalable metadata storage that is easily accessible through Apache Spark and Spark SQL.

SQL Analytics via Spark SQL

Spark SQL (*https://oreil.ly/a5HvG*) is Apache Spark's module, also referred to as a library, for working with structured data. It provides a programming interface to work with structured data using SQL and DataFrame APIs, all of which is underpinned by the Spark SQL engine. Similar to other SQL engines, the Spark SQL engine is responsible for generating efficient queries and compact code. This execution plan is adapted at runtime. The Apache Spark ecosystem consists of different libraries, where the Spark Core and Spark SQL engine are the substrate on which they are built (Figure 10-3).

Figure 10-3. Apache Spark ecosystem, including Spark SQL

The Spark SQL library supports ANSI SQL, which allows users to query and analyze data using SQL syntax that they are familiar with. As we have seen in previous chapters, Delta tables can easily be queried using Spark SQL and the `sql()` method in PySpark, for example:

```python
%python
spark.sql("SELECT count(*) FROM taxidb.tripData")
```

Or, similar to how most queries in this book have been written, you can use magic commands and `%sql` in notebooks or some IDEs to specify the language reference and just write Spark SQL directly in the cell:

```sql
%sql
SELECT count(*) as count FROM taxidb.tripData
```

And not only SQL, but the Spark SQL library also allows you to use the DataFrame API to interact with datasets and tables:

```python
%python
spark.table("taxidb.tripData").count()
```

Analysts, report builders, and other data consumers will typically interact with data through the SQL interface. This SQL interface means that users can leverage Spark SQL to perform their simple, or complex, queries and analysis on Delta tables, taking advantage of the performance and scalability that Delta tables offer, while also taking advantage of the Spark SQL engine, distributed processing, and optimizations. Since Delta Lake ensures serializability, there is full support for concurrent reads and writes. This means that all data consumers can confidently read the data even as data is updated through different ETL workloads. In short, the Spark SQL engine generates an execution plan that is used to optimize and execute queries on your Spark cluster to make queries as fast as possible.

Figure 10-4 illustrates that you can express SQL queries using the Spark SQL library, or you can use the DataFrame API to interact with datasets and leverage the Spark SQL engine and execution plan. Whether you are using Spark SQL or the DataFrame API, the Spark SQL engine will generate a query plan used to optimize and execute the command on the cluster.

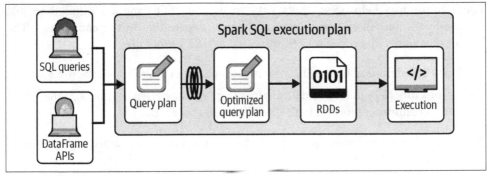

Figure 10-4. Spark SQL execution plan

In Figure 10-4, it is important to note that the Resilient Distributed Datasets (RDDs) in the execution plan are not referring to traditional user-defined RDDs that leverage low-level APIs. Rather, the RDDs mentioned in the figure are Spark SQL RDDs, also referred to as DataFrames or datasets, that do not add additional overhead, as they are optimized specifically to structured data.

Generally, it is recommended to use the DataFrame API for your ETL and data ingestion processes[3] or machine learning workloads, whereas most of the data consumers (e.g., analysts, report builders, etc.) will interact with your Delta tables using Spark SQL. You can also interact with the SQL interface over standard JDBC/ODBC database connectors or using the command line. The JDBC/ODBC connectors mean that Spark SQL also provides a bridge between external tools such as Power BI, Tableau, and other BI tools to interact with and consume tables for analytics.

SQL Analytics via Other Delta Lake Integrations

While Delta Lake provides powerful integration with Spark SQL and the rest of the Spark ecosystem, it can also be accessed by a number of other high-performance query engines. Supported query engines include:

- Apache Spark
- Apache Hive
- Presto
- Trino

---

3 Damji, Jules S, et al. (2020). *Learning Spark*, 2nd ed. Sebastopol, CA: O'Reilly.

These connectors help bring Delta Lake to big-data SQL engines other than just Apache Spark and allow you to read and write (depending on the connector). The Delta Lake connectors repository (*https://oreil.ly/cfKKY*) includes:

- Delta Standalone, a native library for reading and writing Delta Lake metadata
- Connectors to popular big-data engines (e.g., Apache Hive, Presto, Apache Flink) and to common reporting tools like Microsoft Power BI.

There are also several managed services that allow you to integrate and read data from Delta Lake, including:

- Amazon Athena and Redshift
- Azure Synapse and Stream Analytics
- Starburst
- Databricks

Please consult the Delta Lake website (*https://oreil.ly/TWX9h*) for a complete list of supported query engines and managed services.

When it comes to performing SQL analytics, it is important to leverage a high-performance query engine that can interpret SQL queries and execute them at scale against your Delta tables for data analysis. In Figure 10-5, you can see that the lakehouse is comprised of three different compounding layers, plus APIs that allow different layers to communicate with one another:

Storage layer
Data lake used for scalable, low-cost cloud data storage for structured, semi-structured, and unstructured data.

Transactional layer
ACID-compliant open-table format with scalable metadata made possible through Delta Lake.

APIs
SQL APIs enable users to access Delta Lake and perform read and write operations. Then metadata API help systems understand the Delta Lake transaction log to read data appropriately.

High-performance query engine
A query engine that interprets SQL so users can perform data analysis through Apache Spark SQL or another query engine that Delta Lake integrates with.

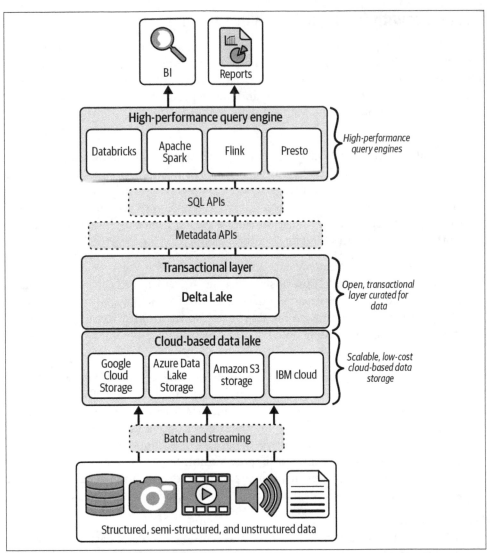

Figure 10-5. Example of the lakehouse layered architecture, with the high-performance query engine used for BI and reports

Data for Data Science and Machine Learning

Since Delta Lake helps provide reliable and simplified data management across your lakehouse, it helps bring a variety of benefits to data and data pipelines leveraged for data science activities and machine learning.

Challenges with Traditional Machine Learning

Generally speaking, *machine learning operations* (MLOps) are the set of practices and principles involved in the end-to-end machine learning lifecycle. In MLOps, there are a number of common challenges that a vast majority of organizations and data scientists face when attempting to build and finally productionalize machine learning models in their organization:

Data silos

Data silos often start to develop as the gap between data engineering activities and data science activities begins to grow. Data scientists frequently spend the majority of their time creating separate ETL and data pipelines that clean and transform data and prepare it into features for their models. These silos usually develop because the tools and technologies used for data engineering don't support the same activities for data scientists.

Consolidating batch and streaming data

Machine learning models use historical data to train models in order to make accurate predictions on streaming data. The problem is that traditional architectures don't support reliably combining both historical and streaming data, which creates challenges in feeding both types of data into machine learning models.

Data volumes

Machine learning systems often need to process large sets of data while using complex code that isn't necessarily well suited for SQL. And if data scientists wish to consume data via ODBC/JDBC interfaces from tables created through data engineering pipelines, these interfaces can create a very inefficient process. These inefficient processes are largely because these interfaces are designed to work with SQL and offer limited support for non-SQL code logic. This results in inefficient non-SQL queries that can be caused by data volume, data conversions, and complex data structures that non-SQL code logic can often include.

Reproducibility

MLOps best practices include the need to reproduce and validate every stage of the ML workflow. The ability to reproduce a model reduces the risk of errors, and ensures the correctness and robustness of the ML solution. Consistent data is the most difficult challenge faced in reproducibility, and an ML model will only reproduce the exact same result if the exact same data is used. And since data is constantly changing over time, this can introduce significant challenges to ML reproducibility and MLOps.

Nontabular data

While typically we think of data as being stored in tables, there are growing use cases for machine learning workloads to support large collections of nontabular data, such as text, image, audio, video, or PDF files. This nontabular data requires the same governance, sharing, storage, and data exploration capabilities that tabular data requires. Without having some type of feature to catalog these collections of directories and nontabular data, it is very challenging to provide the same governance and management features used with tabular data.

Due to the challenges that traditional architectures create for productionalizing machine learning models, machine learning often becomes a very complex and siloed process. These siloed complexities introduce even more challenges for data management.

Delta Lake Features That Support Machine Learning

Fortunately, Delta Lake helps negate these data management challenges traditionally introduced by machine learning activities, and bridges the gap between data and processes used for BI/reporting analytics and advanced analytics. There are several different features of Delta Lake that help support the machine learning lifecycle:

Optimizations and data volumes
> The benefits that Delta Lake offers all start with the fact that it is built on top of Apache Spark. Data science activities can access data directly from Delta Lake tables using DataFrame APIs via Spark SQL, which allows machine learning workloads to directly benefit from the optimization and performance enhancements offered by Delta Lake.

Consistency and reliability
> Delta Lake provides ACID transactions, which ensures consistent and reliable data. This is important for machine learning and data science workflows because model training and predictions require this level of reliability to avoid negative impacts from inaccurate or inconsistent data.

Consolidating batch and streaming data
> Delta Lake tables can seamlessly handle the continuous flow of data from both historical and streaming sources, made possible through Spark Streaming and Spark Structured Streaming. This means that you can simplify the data flow process for machine learning models since both types of data are consolidated into a single table.

Schema enforcement and evolution
> By default, Delta Lake tables have schema enforcement, which means that better data quality can be enforced, thus increasing the reliability of data used for machine learning inputs. But Delta Lake also supports schema evolution, which means data scientists can easily add new columns to their existing machine learning production tables without breaking existing data models.

Versioning

You have learned in previous chapters that Delta Lake lets you easily version your data and perform time travel via the transaction log. This versioning helps mitigate the challenges often seen with ML reproducibility because it allows you to easily re-create machine learning experiments and model outputs given a specific set of data at a specific point in time. This helps significantly reduce some of the challenges seen in the MLOps process since simplified versioning can provide greater traceability, reproducibility, auditing, and compliance for ML models.

Integrations

In Chapter 1, and in this chapter, you read about how Delta Lake can be accessed using the Spark SQL library in Apache Spark. You also read about Spark Streaming and Delta Lake's integration with that library in Chapter 8. An additional library in the Spark ecosystem is MLlib. MLlib gives you access to common learning algorithms, featurization, pipelines, persistence, and utilities. In fact, many machine learning libraries (e.g., TensorFlow, scikit-learn) can also leverage DataFrame APIs to access Delta Lake tables.

The Spark ecosystem consists of multiple libraries running on top of Spark Core to provide multifunctional support for all types of data and analytics use cases (Figure 10-6). Outside of the Spark standard libraries, Spark also has integrations with other platforms such as MLflow, a popular open source platform for managing the end-to-end machine learning lifecycle, which allows Spark MLlib models to be tracked, logged, and reproduced.

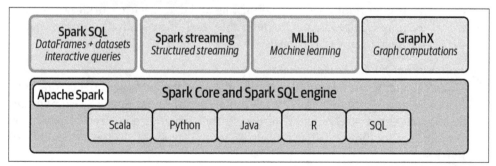

Figure 10-6. Apache Spark ecosystem showing the Spark SQL, Spark Streaming, and MLlib libraries

As previously mentioned, machine learning models are typically built using libraries such as TensorFlow, PyTorch, scikit-learn, etc. And while Delta Lake is not directly a technology for building models, it does focus on addressing and providing valuable, foundational support for many of the challenges that machine learning activities face. MLOps and models are reliant on the data quality and integrity, reproducibility, reliability, and unification of data that Delta Lake provides. The robust data management and integration features offered by Delta Lake simplify MLOps and make it easier for machine learning engineers and data scientists to access and work with the data used to train and deploy their models.

Putting It All Together

Through the features enabled by Delta Lake, it becomes much easier to unify both the machine learning and data engineering lifecycles. Delta Lake enables machine learning models to learn and predict from historical (batch) and streaming data, all sourced from a single place while natively leveraging Delta table optimizations. ACID transactions and schema enforcement help bring data quality, consistency, and reliability to the tables used for machine learning model inputs. And Delta Lake's schema evolution helps your machine learning outputs change over time without introducing breaking changes to existing processes. Time travel enables easy auditing or reproduction of your machine learning models, and the Spark ecosystem brings additional libraries and other machine learning lifecycle tools to further enable data scientists.

In Figure 10-7, you can see all of the resulting layers of a fully constructed lakehouse environment. All together, the features of Delta Lake help bridge the gap between data engineers and data scientists in an effort to reduce silos and unify workloads. Together with Delta Lake and a robust lakehouse architecture, organizations can start to build and manage machine learning models in a faster, more efficient way.

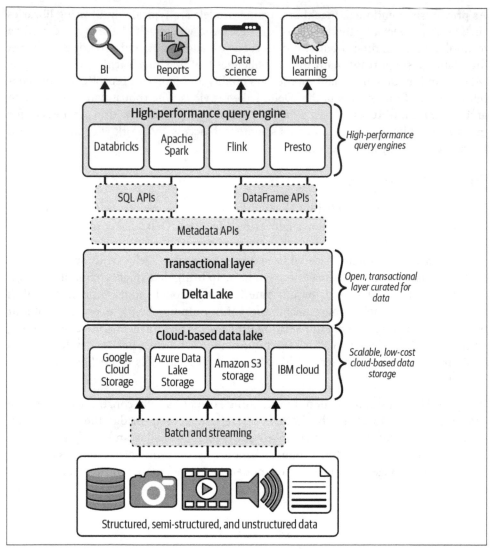

Figure 10-7. The lakehouse architecture with the addition of data science and machine learning workloads

Medallion Architecture

The lakehouse is centered around the idea of unification and combining the best elements of different technologies in a single place. This means it is also important that the data flow within the lakehouse itself supports this unification of data. In order to support all use cases, this data flow requires merging batch and streaming data into a single data flow to support scenarios across the entire data lifecycle.

Chapter 1 introduced the idea of the medallion architecture, a popular data design pattern with Bronze, Silver, and Gold layers that is ultimately enabled via Delta Lake. This popular pattern is used to organize data in a lakehouse in an iterative manner to improve the structure and quality of data across your data lake, with each layer having specific functions and purposes for analytics while unifying batch and streaming data flows. An example of the medallion architecture is provided in Figure 10-8.

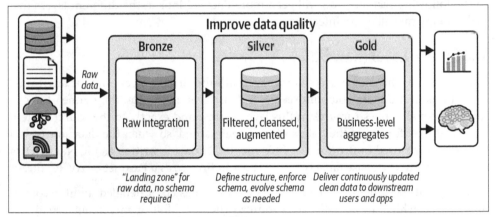

Figure 10-8. Data lakehouse solution architecture

The Bronze, Silver, and Gold layers shown in Figure 10-8 are summarized in Table 10-1. For each layer, you will see its business value, properties, and implementation details (such as "how it's done").

Table 10-1. Medallion architecture summary

	Bronze	Silver	Gold
Business value	• Audit on exactly what was received from the source • Ability to reprocess without going back to the source	• First layer that is useful to the business • Enables data discovery, self-service, ad hoc reporting, advanced analytics, and ML	• Data is in a format that is easy for business users to navigate • Highly performant
Properties	• No business rules or transformations of any kind • Should be fast and easy to get new data to this layer	• Prioritize speed to market and write performance—just enough transformations • Quality data expected	• Prioritize business use cases and user experience • Precalculated, business-specific transformations • Can have separate views of the data for different consumption use cases

	Bronze	Silver	Gold
How it's done	• Must include a copy of what was received • Typically, data is stored in folders based upon the date received	• Delta merge • Can include light modeling (3NF, vaulting) • Data quality checks should be included	• Prioritize denormalized, read-optimized data models • Fully transformed • Aggregated

In the following sections, you will get a more detailed look at the different layers that make up the medallion architecture.

The Bronze Layer (Raw Data)

Raw data from the data sources is ingested into the Bronze layer without any transformations or business rule enforcement. This layer is the "landing zone" for our raw data, so all table structures in this layer correspond exactly to the source system structure. The format of the data source is maintained, so when the data source is a CSV file, it is stored in Bronze as a CSV file, JSON data is written as JSON, etc. Data extracted from a database table typically lands in Bronze as a Parquet or AVRO file.

At this point, no schema is required. As data is ingested, a detailed audit record is maintained, which includes the data source, whether a full or incremental load was performed, and detailed watermarks to support the incremental loads where needed. The Bronze layer includes an archival mechanism, so that data can be retained for long periods of time. This archive, together with the detailed audit records, can be used to reprocess data in case of a failure somewhere downstream in the medallion architecture.

The ingested data lands in the Bronze layer "source system mirrored," maintaining the structure and data types of the source system format, although it is often augmented with additional metadata, such as the date and time of the load, and ETL process system identifiers. The goal of the ingestion process is to land the source data quickly and easily in the Bronze layer with just enough auditing and metadata to enable data lineage and reprocessing.

The Bronze layer is often used as a source for a Change Data Capture (CDC) process, allowing newly arriving data to be immediately processed downstream through the Silver and Gold layers.

The Silver Layer

In the Silver layer we first cleanse and normalize the data. We ensure that standard formats are used for constructs such as date and time, enforce the company's column naming standard, de-duplicate the data, and perform a series of additional data quality checks, dropping low-quality data rows when needed.

Next, related data is combined and merged. The Delta Lake MERGE capabilities work very well for this purpose. For example, customer data from various sources (sales, CRM, POS systems, etc.) is combined into a single entity. Conformed data, which are those data entities that are reused across different subject areas, is identified and normalized across the views. In our previous example, the combined customer entity would be an example of such conformed data.

At this point, the combined *enterprise view* of the data starts to emerge. Note that we apply a "just-enough" philosophy here, where we provide just enough detail with the least amount of effort possible, making sure that we maintain our agile approach to building our medallion architecture.

At this point, we start enforcing schema, and allow the schema to evolve downstream. The Silver layer is also where we can apply GDPR and/or PII/PHI enforcement rules.

Because this is the first layer where data quality is enforced, and the enterprise view is created, it serves as a useful data source for the business, especially for purposes such as self-service analytics and ad hoc reporting. The Silver layer proves to be a great data source for machine learning and AI use cases. Indeed, these types of algorithms work best with the "less polished" data in the Silver layer instead of the consumption formats in the Gold layer.

The Gold Layer

In the Gold layer, we create business-level aggregates. This can be done through a standard Kimball star schema, an Inmon snowflake schema dimensional model, or any other modeling technique that fits the consumer business use case. The final layer of data transformations and data quality rules is applied here, resulting in high-quality, reliable data that can serve as the *single source of truth* in the organization.

The Gold layer continuously delivers business value by offering high-quality, clean data to downstream users and applications. The data model in the Gold layer often includes many different perspectives or views of the data, depending on the consumption use cases. The Gold layer will implement several Delta Lake optimization techniques, such as partitioning, data skipping, and Z-ordering, to ensure that we deliver quality data in a performant way.

Curated for optimal consumption by BI tools, reporting, applications, and business users, this becomes the primary layer where data is read using a high-performance query engine.

The Complete Lakehouse

Once you have implemented the medallion architecture as part of your Delta Lake–based architecture, you can start seeing the full benefits and extensibility of the lakehouse. While building the lakehouse throughout this chapter, you have seen how the different layers complement each other in order to unify your entire data platform.

Figure 10-9 illustrates the entire lakehouse, including how it looks with the medallion architecture. While the medallion architecture is certainly not the only design pattern for data flows in a lakehouse, it is one of the most popular, and for good reason. Ultimately, the medallion architecture, through features enabled by Delta Lake, supports the unification of data in a single data flow to support batch and streaming workload, machine learning, business-level aggregates, and analytics as a whole for all personas.

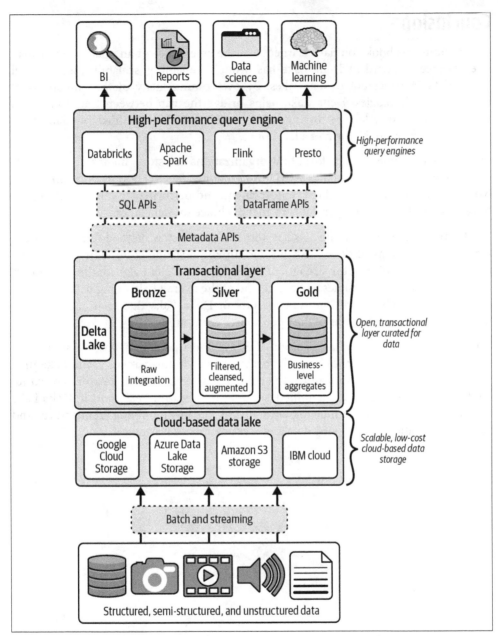

Figure 10-9. The complete end-to-end lakehouse architecture

Conclusion

Throughout this book you have learned how the emergence of an open-table format, open source standard in Delta Lake has brought reliability, scalability, and overall better data management to data lakes. By overcoming many of the limitations of traditional technologies, Delta Lake helps bridge the gap between traditional data warehouses and data lakes, bringing to organizations a single unified, big data management platform in the form of a lakehouse.

Delta Lake continues to transform how organizations can store, manage, and process data. Its robust features, such as ACID transactions, data versioning, streaming and batch transaction support, schema enforcement, and performance tuning techniques, have made it the de facto open-table format of choice for data lakes.

At the time of writing, Delta Lake is the world's most widely adopted lakehouse format with millions of downloads per month and a strong community of growing contributors. As contributor strength and adoption of Delta Lake continues to grow, the Delta ecosystem continues to expand, and as the overall field of big data continues to evolve, naturally so will the functionality of Delta Lake due to its open source format and the contributions of the open source community.

The continued rise of Delta Lake and the lakehouse paradigm poses a significant milestone in the evolution of data platforms and data management. Delta Lake provides the functionality and features to succeed at scale in today's data-driven world, while the lakehouse provides a unified, scalable architecture to support it. Delta Lake and the lakehouse will continue to play a critical role in simplifying architectures and driving innovation in a growing data and technologies ecosystem.

Index

A

ACID (atomicity, consistency, isolation, durability), 2, 223
  lakehouses and, 17
ADLS (Azure Data Lake Storage Gen 2), 11, 209
ALTER COLUMN command, 168-169
ALTER TABLE command, 121, 168-169
ALTER TABLE REPLACE COLUMNS command, 172-174
ALTER TABLE...ADD COLUMN command, 166-167
Amazon Simple Storage Service (S3), 11
Apache Hadoop, 11
Apache Spark (see Spark)
architecture
  data warehouses, 3-6
  lakehouse, Delta-based, 19
  medallion, 21-22
  monolithic, 5
archiving data, time travel and, 137
atomicity, 2
  transaction log and, 36
audit history, 223
auditing, time travel and, 125
AvailableNow option, Structured Streaming, 195-197
AWS S3, 209
Azure Data Lake Storage Gen 2 (ADLS), 11, 209

B

BI (Business Intelligence), 9
big data, 9-10

Bronze layer, medallion architecture, 236

C

CDF (Change Data Feed), 143
  audit trail table, 144
  downstream consumers, 144
  enabling, 144-146, 184
  ETL operations, 143
  reading streams from, 201-203
  records, modifying, 145
  viewing, 146-149
  warnings and considerations, 149-150
checkpoint file, 193-195
cloud object storage, data sharing and, 209-210
CLUSTER BY command, 121
clustered columns
  changing, 121
  removing, 122
  viewing, 121
clusters
  data on write, 120
  liquid clustering, 118
    enabling, 119-120
    partitions, 118
    warnings and considerations, 122-123
  schema evolution and, 157
compact files, 109
  compaction, 109
    OPTIMIZE command, 110-113
    size removed versus added, 112
compaction, 109
compute power, 12
consistency, 2
consumers

About the Author

Bennie Haelen is a principal architect with Insight Digital Innovation, a Microsoft and Databricks partner. As principal architect with Insight, Bennie's primary focus areas are modern data warehousing, machine learning, AI, and IoT on various commercial cloud platforms. Bennie has overseen many data+AI projects in different application domains such as health care, the public sector, oil and gas, and financial applications. Bennie has architected and delivered real-time streaming data lakehouse applications with Databricks, Spark Structured Streaming, Delta Lake, and Microsoft Power BI for various application domains. Bennie brings a wealth of practical experience in implementing secure, enterprise-scale data lakehouse-based solutions to support business intelligence, data science, and machine learning. Bennie has also been a frequent speaker at Databricks events at Microsoft Technology Centers around the country, and was a speaker at the Data+AI 2021 summit.

Dan Davis is a cloud data architect with a decade of experience delivering analytic insights and business value from data. Using modern tools and technologies, Dan specializes in designing and delivering data platforms, frameworks, and processes to support data integration and analytics for on-premises, hybrid, and cloud environments on an enterprise scale.

Colophon

The animal on the cover of *Delta Lake: Up and Running* is an Indian hare (*Lepus nigricollis*). They are also called black-naped hares because of the black patch of fur that grows along the nape of their neck.

Aside from the black hairs on their neck, Indian hares also have black tails. Their neck and back are mostly brown with a smattering of black hairs and their underparts are white. Like other hares, they have long ears and long, fur-covered hind feet. They can grow between 16 and 28 inches long and weigh 3 to 15 pounds. Females are often larger than males.

Indian hares are native to the Indian subcontinent and Java. They can be found in India, Bangladesh, Indonesia, Nepal, Sri Lanka, and Pakistan, where they live in tropical forests, grasslands, scrublands, and deserts. During the rainy season, they predominantly eat a variety of grasses, and during the dry season they will eat flowering plants. They are also found in agricultural land, where they eat crops and germinate seeds.

Indian hares are abundant and considered a species of least concern on endangered species lists. The main threats to their existence are hunting and habitat loss due to agricultural expansion. Many of the animals on O'Reilly covers are endangered; all of them are important to the world.

The cover illustration is by Karen Montgomery, based on an antique line engraving from *Histoire Naturelle*. The cover fonts are Gilroy Semibold and Guardian Sans. The text font is Adobe Minion Pro; the heading font is Adobe Myriad Condensed; and the code font is Dalton Maag's Ubuntu Mono.

Printed in the USA
CPSIA information can be obtained
at www.ICGtesting.com
JSHW052032231023
50693JS00006B/72

9 781098 139728